Making Music in the Arab World
The Culture and Artistry of *Ṭarab*

A. J. Racy is well known as a scholar of ethnomusicology and as a distinguished performer and composer. In this pioneering study on music in the Arab world, he provides an intimate portrayal of the Arab musical experience and offers insights into how music generally affects us all. The focus is *ṭarab*, a multifaceted concept that has no exact equivalent in English and refers to both the indigenous music and the ecstatic feeling associated with it. Richly documented, the book examines various aspects of the musical craft, including the basic learning processes, how musicians become inspired, the love lyrics as tools of ecstasy, the relationship between performers and listeners, and the influence of technological mediation and globalization. Racy also probes a variety of world musical and ecstatic contexts and analyses theoretical paradigms from other related disciplines. Written in a lucid style, *Making Music in the Arab World* will engage the general reader as well as the specialist.

A. J. Racy is Professor of Ethnomusicology at the University of California, Los Angeles, and one of the leading experts on music in the Arab world. He is a performer and composer in his own right.

Celebrated Egyptian singer Umm Kulthūm (ca. 1904–1975) performing.
Photo courtesy of Dār al-Ṣayyād.

Cambridge Middle East Studies has been established to publish books on the nineteenth- and twentieth-century Middle East and North Africa. The aim of the series is to provide new and original interpretations of aspects of Middle Eastern societies and their histories. To achieve disciplinary diversity, books will be solicited from authors writing in a wide range of fields including history, sociology, anthropology, political science and political economy. The emphasis will be on producing books offering an original approach along theoretical and empirical lines. The series is intended for students and academics, but the more accessible and wide-ranging studies will also appeal to the interested general reader.

A list of books in the series can be found after the index

Making Music in the Arab World
The Culture and Artistry of *Ṭarab*

A. J. Racy
University of California, Los Angeles

CAMBRIDGE
UNIVERSITY PRESS

PUBLISHED BY THE PRESS SYNDICATE OF THE UNIVERSITY OF CAMBRIDGE
The Pitt Building, Trumpington Street, Cambridge, United Kingdom

CAMBRIDGE UNIVERSITY PRESS
The Edinburgh Building, Cambridge CB2 2RU, UK
40 West 20th Street, New York NY 10011–4211, USA
477 Williamstown Road, Port Melbourne, VIC 3207, Australia
Ruiz de Alarcón 13, 28014 Madrid, Spain
Dock House, The Waterfront, Cape Town 8001, South Africa

http://www.cambridge.org

First published 2003
First paperback edition 2004

Typeface Times (*Adobe*) 10/12 pt. *System* QuarkXPress® [PH]

A catalogue record for this book is available from the British Library

National Library of Australia Cataloguing in Publication data

Racy, A. J.
Making music in the Arab world : the culture and artistry
of tarab.

Bibliography.
Includes index.
ISBN 0 521 30414 8 hardback

1. Arabs – Music. 2. Music – Arab countries. I. Title.
(Series : Cambridge Middle East studies; 17).

780.953

ISBN 0 521 30414 8 hardback
ISBN 0 521 31685 5 paperback

To my family,
And all the *sammīʿah*

Contents

List of Illustrations

Preface

Why does music move us so profoundly? What makes it special as a human expression? How does it really affect us? Music is said to inspire and elate the listeners and to transform them mentally, physically, and emotionally. And similarly, musicians are thought to possess an extraordinary ability to impress and engage through an aural medium that on the surface seems rather innocuous and beyond obvious utility. These and other related questions have preoccupied philosophers, religious leaders, politicians, scientists, music critics, and musicians throughout human history. This book represents the persistent and seemingly universal quest for understanding music and its unmistakable appeal. More directly, however, it is about a specific musical tradition, one that establishes strong links between music and emotional transformation. I write as a native performer in that tradition, but one whose perspectives are those of a historically minded ethnomusicologist. Although the overall orientation is cross-cultural and cross-disciplinary, the core component is an in-depth study of Arab music and its emotional dimension. My work does not aim at advancing a single "grand theory," one that explains musical affect globally, nor does it make exclusive allegiance to one such theory. Rather, it offers numerous theoretical constructs and conclusions whose implications extend beyond the immediate subject matter. It is my hope that by developing better theoretical comprehension of how the Arab musical experience is culturally sustained, contextually produced, and personally processed, this research will provide insights into comparable experiences in other world contexts. This and similar endeavors can make us more cognizant, as well as more appreciative of how as humans we think, behave, and feel musically.

This research could not have been done without the assistance of many individuals and institutions. I am particularly grateful to the late Professor Albert Hourani of Oxford University for encouraging me to write this book and for offering his characteristically gracious and enthusiastic support over the years. I also extend my gratitude to Dr. George Sawa, ethnomusicologist, medievalist, and fellow musician, who read the original manuscript and inserted his own remarks, which were extremely helpful and at times delightfully humorous. My appreciation also goes to Dr. Dwight F. Reynolds, Professor of Arabic Language and Literature at the University of

California at Santa Barbara for his most useful input into various literary and historical matters. I am also indebted to those who provided assistance during the various stages of my research, including Dr. Deanna McMahon, Dr. Virginia Danielson at Harvard University, and Dr. Robert Moser at Brown University. Similarly, I wish to thank the Lebanese music scholar Dr. Victor Saḥḥāb for his valuable help, especially in facilitating my contacts with Dār al-Ṣayyād in Lebanon in 1997–1998. I am deeply touched by Dār al-Ṣayyād's staff, especially Dr. Antoine Buṭrus, director of the research division and Sharbal Farḥāt, the supervising archivist, for giving me access to their archival material and granting me permission to include some of their archival photos in this book.

I also express my gratitude to the numerous singers, instrumentalists, composers, music thinkers, and listening connoisseurs with whom I have conversed and in many cases performed music both in the United States and in the Arab world. Although many are individually recognized through the ensuing discussions, I am particularly thankful to the late Muḥammad al-ʿAqqād, Ṣabaḥ Fakhrī, Wadīʿ al-Ṣāfī, the late Sayyid Makkāwī, ʿAbd al-Ḥamīd al-Tannārī, Simon Shaheen, the late Mūnīr Bashīr, Dr. Ḥasan al-Bazzāz, Maḥmūd Kāmil, Buthaynah Farīd, Maʾmūn al-Shinnāwī (Jr.), and the late ʿAlī Reda. These and many others have shared with me their artistic knowledge, and in some cases helped me establish key contacts in the field.

I would also like to mention the encouragement of my students and colleagues at the University of California at Los Angeles (UCLA), where some of my classes and seminars have addressed topics related to this work. I am similarly appreciative of those who assisted in the preparation of the manuscript, especially Jay Keister, Heidi Feldman, Tonya Culley, Leigh Creighton, Kathleen Hood, Sami Asmar, and Antoine Harb. Also to be recognized are my friends and neighbors in a small coastal town in central Maine, where I did most of the writing. Many of these folks expressed genuine interest in my subject matter, and often spoke to me about their own ecstatic musical experiences.

Last but not least, my gratitude goes to my family, including my parents Salam and Emily Racy and my brothers Khaled and Ramzi, all of whom have shown tremendous enthusiasm about my work. I give my deepest appreciation to my wife Dr. Barbara Racy, for her boundless support. Barbara has made valuable editorial and photographic contributions to my research, and particularly through her specialty as a clinical psychologist and her expertise in dance ethnology and dance movement therapy, has offered truly insightful suggestions.

Technical Note

In this book, I provide my own English translations of the quotes from various Arabic sources. For the Arabic transliterations, I basically follow the conventional system used by the Library of Congress and the standard Near-Eastern studies journals. However, I represent one of the Arabic consonants differently, namely the one usually indicated by the symbol "*ẓ*". As specifically applied in the above system, this symbol is inconsistent with the manner in which other dotted letters relate phonetically to the same letters without dots, for example, the "*ṣ*" and the "*s*", and the "*ṭ*" and the "*t*". Furthermore, the sound suggested by the symbol "*ẓ*" disagrees with the proper classical pronunciation of the Arabic consonant being represented. Therefore, to be consistent with both correct Arabic phonology and the transliteration system itself, I use the symbol "*ḍḥ*," which is pronounced roughly as the "th" in the English words, "thus" and "brother," and appears in such Arabic words as *ḍḥālim*, *naḍḥīf*, and Maḥfūḍḥ.

For the various commonly used expressions, I tend to adhere to the standard classical transliteration, particularly since the colloquial patterns of pronunciation can differ considerably from one Arab country to another. In this case, the consonant I represent with the letter "*j* " whether in a classical or colloquial expression, would be pronounced as a "*g*" (as for example in "game" or "go") by Egyptians. Also in the spoken idiom of Egypt, and the Levant region, the characteristic Arabic sound represented by the transliterated symbol "*q*" is usually changed into a glottal stop similar to the sound represented by the transliteration symbol " ʾ ". Deviations from the conventional system appear mostly in the spellings of some proper names and Arabized foreign words and in colloquial song lyrics and certain song titles. With respect to the plural constructions of Arabic nouns, I essentially follow the Arabic plural forms. For the sake of clarity I often list both the singular and the plural forms in the text.

Since two key terms in this study have a distinct tendency to be mispronounced by English speakers, a brief note on their proper pronunciation is presented here. In the word *ṭarab*, both vowelled syllables must be short, as in the English word "salad" (e.g., without artificially lengthening the second syllable) and furthermore, the accent must fall on the first syllable. In the word, *salṭanah*, all three vowels must maintain the "ah" sound, as in "salary" (e.g., without converting the first vowel into an "o" or a Latin "u"). Also, all three vowelled syllables must be short (e.g., without lengthening the second syllable), keeping in mind that the first syllable, "*sa*" is usually accentuated.

The dates, particularly of published works, include a few that originally follow the Islamic Hejira system and are listed in the text as such, with the symbol "AH" inserted before each date. Also, some key sources that are not explicitly or officially dated but incorporate clues to their approximate time of publication are listed accordingly (e.g., al-Khulaʿī ca. 1904). Sometimes two years appear side by side (e.g. 1929/1973) to indicate the dates of both the original publication and the reprinted version. Finally, the dates of birth and death for individual artists are elicited from a wide variety of biographical sources and oral reports. Thus, some may be tentative or approximate.

1 Introduction

At the end of the eighteenth century, Guillaume André Villoteau observed that Arab music evoked powerful emotions. Leading a musicological research team as part of Napoleon's scientific mission to Egypt (1798–1799), he described a typical performance that he and his team had attended. As he noted, when the religious singers prolonged certain syllables, rendered their melodic creations with lavish embellishments, and repeated some passages several times at the request of the ecstatic listeners, they provoked bursts of enthusiastic exclamations and highly impassioned gestures. Admitting his lack of appreciation for the music, and even his team's annoyance at what to them seemed a bizarre display of passion and unreasonably extravagant praise for the performers, Villoteau declared that the phenomenon he had witnessed was integral to the musical disposition of the Egyptians. He stated that such responses were difficult for outsiders to comprehend or appreciate, adding that "it is pointless to pass an absolute judgment against the taste of a whole nation" (1826: 209).[1]

Later, an Easterner had an opportunity to experience European music closely and to record his own impressions. Visiting the island of Malta in 1834, then London in 1854 and France in 1855, the celebrated Arab writer Aḥmad Fāris al-Shidyāq attempted to explain how music of the West compared with its Eastern counterpart.[2] Discussing the variety of ways in which the two musics differed, for example in the use of notation and harmony in the former as compared to the emphasis on modal variety and rhythmic flexibility in the latter, he took special notice of how each of the two musics affected the listener. As he explained, whereas Europe's music was ideally suited for representing images and concepts, music of the Arab Near-East specialized in the evocation of intense emotions. Accordingly, the latter, which was "concerned entirely with tenderness and love"

1 After his visit to Egypt, Guillaume André Villoteau (1759–1839) published a number of works on Egyptian music. Among them were two volumes of the collection *Description de l'Égypte*, which contained the various reports of the Napoleonic Expedition.

2 al-Shidyāq played the *ṭunbūr*, a long-necked string instrument for his own leisure. He also made frequent references to the music and dance practices of the time, particularly in Egypt (see al-Maṭwī 1989: 768–777 and al-Shidyāq 1966: 96–99).

(Cachia 1973: 45), generated an emotional state that was deeply felt by the Arab listeners.

As these two accounts show, first impressions can be quite telling. Through a mixture of spontaneity and scholarly acumen, Villoteau and al-Shidyāq shed some interesting light on each other's musical cultures. Keeping in mind that first reactions can be highly impressionistic and stereotypical, the two at least implicitly agree in their characterizations of European art music (as being "depictive," "cerebral," "emotionally reserved," and marked by discreet modes of listening) and of Arab music (as an art that emphasizes emotional extroversion, the evocation of powerful sensations, and direct interaction between performers and listeners). Such characterizations are significant in part because they are reflexive, in other words indicative of the musical attitudes of those who made them. Villoteau's sense of shock, as well as notable air of scholarly objectivity, clearly informs us on this European's musical upbringing and his intellectual background, which was rooted in the climate of the enlightenment that engulfed late eighteenth century Europe. Similarly, al-Shidyāq's encounter with European music, which left a deep impression upon him, highlighted his consciousness of his own music and illustrated the special aesthetic lens through which he interpreted the Western musical experience.

Moreover, the two impressions are noteworthy because they are consistent with those made by contemporaneous and succeeding Western and Arab musicians, critics, theorists, and musicologists. Since Villoteau, the apparently overwhelming emotional effect of Arab music and the highly ecstatic behavior marking Arab musical events continued to intrigue and fascinate Europeans. During the first half of the nineteenth century, the eminent British Orientalist Edward Lane observed the distinct state of rapture that Egyptians experienced during musical performances and commented on the listeners' frequent impassioned exclamations, which they addressed to the vocalists and instrumentalists.[3] Similarly, during the second half of the nineteenth century, George Moritz Ebers reported that a German lady who attended a performance by the Egyptian female celebrity Almaḍḥ was amazed at the singer's tremendous emotional impact upon her female audience. As "she sang a few verses at a time" (1879: 316), the listeners responded with highly animated expressions of approval. Also around that time, Francesco Salvador-Daniel, musicologist and Director of the Paris Conservatory, explained that in order for him to learn Arab music as a theoretical system and to appreciate it aesthetically he had to learn to feel its distinctive and powerful emotional effect.[4] Later, the modern French ethnomusicologist Gilbert Rouget, in a seminal work that investigates the

[3] Lane 1860/1973: 354.
[4] Salvador-Daniel 1915/1976: 44.

different styles emotional / intellectual

relationship between music and trance cross culturally, spoke in superlative terms of the Arab predisposition toward trance experiences. He stressed that of all world peoples, Arabs make the strongest association between music and trance and that such association applied to both sacred and secular practices.[5]

In the Arab world, the comparative image painted by al-Shidyāq was echoed by later theorists, critics, and listening connoisseurs. Indeed, "East-versus-West" characterizations became quite prevalent. Since the late nineteenth century the Easterners' attempts to define themselves musically have been accompanied by a strong desire to emulate Europe as a "superior," or "culturally advanced" model of civilization, but at times also by an urge to defend the indigenous music and to recognize it on its own aesthetic terms. At the Congress of Arab Music held in Cairo in 1932, an event that brought together renowned composers, theorists, educators and musicologists from Europe and the Near East, one Egyptian participant, Muḥammad Fatḥī, pleaded that the mostly-European Congress Committee on Musical Instruments fully condone the introduction of European instruments into Arab music, because such instruments possessed tremendously varied expressive means and depictive powers. He added that the "Oriental" instruments were suited for nothing except the expressing of love and infatuation.[6] By comparison, the mid-twentieth century theorist and violinist Tawfīq al-Ṣabbāgh of Syria chided those who, as he put it, give up Near-Eastern music in favor of Western music, considering them not only culturally biased but also ignorant of the emotional essence of their own musical heritage. Al-Ṣabbāgh argued that unlike European music, which he contended placed the highest premium on technical perfection, Near Eastern, or "Oriental," music was first and foremost an emotive expression.[7]

Despite the differences in the sentiments expressed, the above statements are similar in that they both allude to an essential affective component within Arab music. In various degrees, such declarations are polemical and political, as well as Western inspired and referenced. Even the concept of "Orient," as Edward Said writes, was a European invention embracing what Westerners deemed to be "exotic," or dramatically opposed to their own culture.[8] Nonetheless, intercultural encounters often prompt informative self-analyses. Like those of Villoteau and of al-Shidyāq, who wrote through "an ear attuned to Arab melodies and an eye dazzled by European technical achievements" (Cachia 1973: 42), the above constructs are revealing

5 Rouget 1985: 255.

6 *Kitāb Mu'tamar al-Mūsīqá al-ʿArabiyyah* 1933: 427. See also Racy 1991a. For more information on the nationalist and intellectual climate of this period refer to Hourani 1991: 333–349.

7 al-Ṣabbāgh 1950: 15.

8 Said 1978: 1–2.

technique vs. emotive expression

because they are both projective and self-reflective. Certainly, it can be argued that Western music, or for that matter all music, is in one way or another emotive and affective. However, specifically in the case of the Arab world, one is struck by the centrality of emotional evocation both as a musical aesthetic and a topic of concern.

Throughout history, Near Easterners in general have associated music with extraordinary powers. In antiquity, Babylonians and Egyptians linked musical sound to the cosmological fabric of the universe and in certain Semitic cultures musical modes were connected to various celestial and terrestrial entities. In ancient Biblical traditions, we encounter ample testimony to the efficacies of music and musical instruments. Also, in pre-Islamic Arabia, music embraced magical associations and similarly, musical sound conjured powerful spirits and was thought to exert tremendous influence upon humans and other living beings. Throughout Islamic history, religious chanting, which is not considered "music" as such, has evoked profound spiritual feelings within members of the religious community. Similarly, secular music has been recognized for its unmistakable transformative powers and at times feared and condemned for its sensuous connotations and its potential for generating emotional excesses and disagreeable behaviors. In medieval Islamic courts, singers and instrumentalists are known to have cast an overwhelming emotional effect upon their audiences. Medieval Arabic treatises on the science of music sometimes spoke of an organic connection between music and other aspects of the broader cosmos. Like their ancient Greek counterparts, the medieval authors often discussed the phenomenon of *ethos*, or in Arabic, *ta'thīr*, namely music's moral, cosmic, and therapeutic influence. Music appealed directly to the spiritually connotative sense of hearing and had fundamental affinities with the human soul, which in turn was endowed with supreme otherworldly properties and distinct susceptibility to musical sound. Similarly, in Islamic Sufi traditions, music assumed a special position as a medium of spiritual transcendence. For almost a thousand years, numerous mystical practices have incorporated music and dance as catalysts for experiencing *wajd*, or religious ecstasy. [9]

Today, the direct association between music and emotional transformation pervades the performers' and listeners' world. Modern Arab musicians and musical connoisseurs stress that above all, Arab music must engage the listener emotionally. Frequently heard are statements such as *al-fann iḥsās*, which means "art [namely music], is feeling." After a performance that took place in Los Angeles, I heard a young Arab man explain to his Western companion: "This music is different; it really forces one to become immensely involved both emotionally and physically." In a small gathering,

[9] For further historical information, see Henry George Farmer 1929/1973 and 1943.

after hearing an improvisation I performed on the *nāy* (reed-flute), one middle-aged Arab woman said: "The music makes me cry, the sound of the instrument is overpowering." In the same gathering, an Arab university professor described his profound emotional reactions somewhat philosophically: "There is something powerful, almost sinful about this instrument." Similarly, members of the musical public utilize various emotion-based criteria for judging the performances of the traditional vocalists and instrumentalists. Listeners often describe their own musical sensations through such metaphors as becoming intoxicated and losing the sense of time. Comparably, musicians speak about a haunting state of inspiration they sometimes experience before and while performing.

The emotive orientation of Arab music is also "played out" during the traditional performance events. Unlike the formal Western classical concert, the Arab performance tends to be highly interactive and emotionally charged.[10] The listeners' reactions to the music are quite demonstrable and often appear involuntary and virtually uninhibited. Furthermore, the music elicits a distinct variety of vocal exclamations, typically voiced by the listening connoisseurs, gestures that remind us of the performances that were held at the opulent courts of Baghdad during the ʿAbbāsid era.[11]

Certainly, modern technology and Western cultural and artistic values have made deep inroads into Arab life. During the early twentieth century, Arab music witnessed the growing influence of European music theory, the use of Western notation, and the assimilation of various Western instruments, compositional techniques, and methods of musical instruction. By World War II, many indigenous musical genres and performance mannerisms had gradually disappeared or had been drastically transformed. In some cases, comments such as "music is feeling" are intended to bemoan, and indirectly attest to the erosion of the traditional musical aesthetic. Today, some may argue that the emotive emphasis of Arab music is something of the past, or that such emphasis becomes more obvious the further we go back in time. However, despite the recent climate of change, the affective dimension continues to dominate certain performance repertoires and to have a strong influence upon music related outlooks and behaviors.

In Arab culture, the merger between music and emotional transformation is epitomized by the Arabic concept of *ṭarab*, which may not have an exact equivalent in Western languages. Widely encountered in medieval writings on music and musicians, it is still current today and denotes a number of closely related phenomena. First, the word is used generically as a reference to the indigenous, essentially secular music of Near-Eastern Arab cities. In

[10] For this reason I have found it preferable not to use the word "concert" in reference to traditional Arab performances.
[11] See Sawa 1981: 73–86, and 1989: 159–164.

other words, it denotes the theoretically based, modally structured, and professionally oriented tradition of music making, a domain that Western scholars sometimes refer to as "art music." The term ṭarab is similar in meaning to the word *fann*, which literally means "art," or "craft," and has been used in reference to the local urban music.[12] Quite prevalent is the expression *fann al-ṭarab*, which means "the art of ṭarab" and similarly denotes the music as an artistic domain. In a more specific sense however, the word "ṭarab" refers to an older repertoire, which is rooted in the pre-World-War I musical practice of Egypt and the East-Mediterranean Arab world and is directly associated with emotional evocation.

The term "ṭarab" also describes the musical affect *per se*, or more specifically, the extraordinary emotional state evoked by the music. In this sense, the term has been frequently used in medieval and modern writings on music and musicians. Similarly, the word *muṭrib* (female, *muṭribah*) is a standard designation for the ṭarab singer, or the provider of ṭarab ecstasy. Comparably *ālāt al-ṭarab*, which means "tools of ṭarab music" or "instruments of ṭarab evocation," refers to musical instruments, especially those associated with ṭarab music.

In familiar terms, ṭarab can be described as a musically induced state of ecstasy, or as "enchantment" (Danielson 1997: 11–12), "aesthetic emotion" (Lagrange 1996: 17) and "the feeling roused by music" (Shiloah 1995: 16). In this book the familiar term "ecstasy" is used because it appears relatively flexible and capable of being redefined to fit the musical phenomenon being studied. In fact, the word "ecstasy" has been included in some English–Arabic dictionaries as one of the equivalents of ṭarab.[13] Furthermore, the basic nuances and connotations of the word "ṭarab" as commonly used today are consistent with the concept of "ecstasy" as explained in standard English sources. Accordingly, ecstasy, like ṭarab, implies experiences of emotional excitement, pain or other similarly intense emotions, exaltation, a sense of yearning or absorption, feeling of timelessness, elation or rapturous delight.[14] Moreover, the term "ecstasy" tends to fit the various conditions associated with ṭarab as a transformative state, for example those connected with intoxication, empowerment, inspiration, and creativity.[15] The term has also been commonly used by modern ethnomusicologists to indicate states of consciousness that are musically based, and in some cases also mystically oriented.[16]

[12] For more information on ṭarab as an urban mainstream and on other stylistic domains in Cairo largely prior to the mid 1980s see Racy 1981.

[13] See for example Doniach ed. 1982: 115.

[14] See James 1902/1929: 370–375; Sharma 1978: 11; Furguson 1976: 51; and *Webster's Third New International Dictionary* 1966: 720–721.

[15] See for example the section on "Ecstasy and Rapture" in Underhill 1955/1974: 358–379 and the discussions in Waugh 1989: 132 and Ghose 1982: 788.

[16] See for example Becker 1983: 75 and During 1988.

This book explores ṭarab as a multifaceted domain within which the music and its ecstatic influence are conceptually and experientially interlinked. The setting is the East-Mediterranean or Near-Eastern Arab world.[17] Although many of the observations and conclusions apply to urban Arab music in general, or to a variety of regional idioms in North Africa, the Arabian Peninsula, and West Asia, the center of attention is the secular practice in such cities as Cairo, Alexandria, Jerusalem, Beirut, Damascus, Aleppo, and to some extent Baghdad.[18] The work primarily addresses the modern period, roughly from the late nineteenth century to the present. Envisaged as a moving target rather than a phenomenon fixed in time, ṭarab music of the Near-Eastern Arab world is studied as an art of creating ecstatic sensations. A basic premise is that emotive considerations, although by no means the sole motive for making music, have shaped the form and content of the indigenous music. Given its thematic focus, my research aims at developing a qualitative understanding of traditional Arab music, and therefore would complement other more general works on music of the Arab world or the Near East at large.

My overall presentation embraces a distinct experiential component. A Lebanese-born performer of Arab music and a trained ethnomusicologist, I tend to view this book as a self-reflexive statement. To a large extent, the underlying insights have developed since my early formative years, through such processes as learning to play the *buzuq* (long-necked fretted lute), the *ʿūd* (short-necked lute), and the nāy, and learning to *feel* the music and to correlate musical feeling with certain behaviors and verbal responses. At the same time, this book speaks about a broader cultural milieu, as it draws together the opinions and individual experiences of a vast number of ṭarab makers and audience members from such diverse places as Beirut, Cairo, New York, and Los Angeles. In my narratives, I attempt to create a balance between speaking from the inside and communicating from the outside. In other words, I seek "a productive distanciation" (Rice 1994: 6) from my own object of study without abandoning my intuitions as an insider. Furthermore, I present the various interpretations in the form of a theoretically unified "polyphony" with a few conspicuous "leading voices," namely those of key artists and experts on the topic.

In the process of eliciting information on ṭarab as a musical experience,

[17] The concept of "Near-East," or for that matter "Orient" is obviously Eurocentric, or Western conceived. Essentially, I use such familiar and rather convenient concepts as "Eastern," or "Near-Eastern" Arab world to differentiate this area from other Arab areas, particularly in North Africa.

[18] The indigenous Iraqi tradition centers around a distinct repertoire and theoretical legacy known as *maqām ʿIrāqī*. This tradition and some of the instruments associated with it, for example the *sanṭūr* (hammer-dulcimer) and *jawzah* (spike-fiddle), have counterparts in the musics of Iran and Central Asia. However, the urban music of Iraq shares many significant practices and outlooks with the East-Mediterranean, Arab musical mainstream.

I came to realize that the duality of my position as an investigator and as a member of the community being investigated, as a music researcher and as a practicing musician, can create certain methodological complications. Our rootedness in the musical cultures we study usually gives us valuable access to the data and grants us a special air of credibility. At times, however, playing the double role of performer and investigator, or alternating between the participatory and the observational postures, tends to place the scholar-insider in an unnatural position vis-à-vis other insiders. Furthermore, the researcher's duality of roles tends to impose a comparable duality upon the "others," both as fellow musicians or fellow listeners and as subjects of questioning. Our "academically" conceived, formulated, and presented modes of inquiry can produce certain distancing and repositioning. Also, because as native performers we are expected to understand or intuit the music, our inquiries may strike those whom we are presumably studying as being contrived, and the issues we raise as being nonissues.

My research is further challenged by the nature of the subject matter. In Arab culture, the phenomenon of musical ecstasy is essentially experiential and seldom isolated and discussed in direct or clearly articulated terms. In many cases, neither I nor the individuals I interviewed seemed to possess a standard vocabulary for communicating about musical sensations as such. What ṭarab listeners feel can be compared to the mystical state, which American philosopher, psychologist, and writer on religion William James (1842–1910) described as being inherently ineffable.[19] Although ṭarab as an artistic commodity has been socially consumed, informally discussed, and widely written about in books and popular magazines, ṭarab as musical emotion tends to operate within the realm of practice, through a somewhat autonomous path of creation and recreation comparable to what Pierre Bourdieu describes as "an acquired system of generative schemes" (1990: 55). For that reason, ṭarab related sensations are most often expressed through metaphors, similes, and familiar analogies, as well as implied in performance related conversations, musical analyses, and observable physical and emotional responses to the music.

Furthermore, I came to realize that musical emotions are not only transient and conceptually elusive, but also private and context-bound. As an ecstatic experience, ṭarab tends to occur in relatively distinct social venues, in specialized contexts that are separate from the flow of ordinary daily life. With physical and emotional manifestations that can be quite noticeable, ṭarab ecstasy is usually approached with an air of discreetness. When it becomes excessive or when publicly displayed, the musical emotion can provoke social ridicule, if not moral and religious criticism. Thus, direct questioning about personal ecstatic experiences may seem out of context,

[19] James 1902/1929: 371

after the fact, and hypothetically conceived. More importantly, it may strike a note of impropriety or appear to intrude into the individual's private psychological "space." Particularly when related to socially suspect activities, for instance the use of drugs, such questioning may make those questioned too self-conscious and uncomfortable, if not distrustful of the questioner and his or her motives. Similarly, awareness of being observed and analyzed, or at times photographed, during a ṭarab event may adversely interfere with the natural or spontaneous modalities of performing and reacting to music.

With these various considerations in mind, my data was by and large assembled informally and through extended exposure. Although in certain cases focused probes were conducted, my role as a researcher looking for causalities, correlations, and concrete proofs often yielded to a dialectical mode of intercommunication with others who "felt" the music. I often found myself collaborating with fellow musicians and listeners in an effort to find the most feasible frameworks for explaining music as affect, as well as discovering together how enigmatic the entire phenomenon of musical ecstasy can be. On many levels, my informants, or as I prefer to call them "communicators," were musical analysts in their own right. On various occasions I was able to share with them my own knowledge and perspectives, particularly as someone who is academically trained and who had done extensive research on the music of early twentieth century Cairo. I remember one such occasion in New York City in the early 1980s, when I played the nāy in a small ensemble that included the late qānūn player Muḥammad al-ʿAqqād of Egypt, then in his seventies. During intermission, as the musicians conversed about earlier Egyptian artists, al-ʿAqqād was so moved by my knowledge about his grandfather, who incidentally was one of the highly celebrated qānūn players of Egypt in the late nineteenth and early twentieth centuries, that he pointed at me and said to the rest of the group: "This man is a hundred years old!" In turn, al-ʿAqqād became one of my major sources of information.[20]

Such communications provided valuable insights into the performance practice, but also revealed the extent to which music and its ecstatic sensations appear to influence the musicians' self-image, professional attitudes, opinions about creativity, and performance strategies. As a whole, the field research provided a panoramic vision of ṭarab, as a complex that embraces an aesthetic-experiential core, but also intertwines with a thick network of

[20] In this book I refer to both this artist and his grandfather, who carried the same name, but later was given the title "al-Kabīr," namely "Senior" to differentiate him from his grandson. Unless obvious in the text, I usually distinguish between them by adding the designations Jr. and Sr. to their names. Born sometime before 1915 the younger al-ʿAqqād died around 1992. During the last several decades of his life he lived and worked in the United States, primarily New York City.

cultural values, economic relationships, and social hierarchies. The preparatory work also furnished a framework for interpreting related sources of information, not only local musical biographies, critiques, and textbooks, but also theoretical writings and cross-cultural studies on music as an emotive experience.

The task of establishing meaningful and mutually informative links between the ṭarab phenomenon and a relevant body of knowledge that seems overwhelmingly extensive and diversified calls for a pertinent methodology that is both practical and broadly conceived. In this work, the ṭarab complex is treated as a research design. Accordingly, I envision and subsequently pursue four complementary lines of inquiry, namely: 1) a contextual base of some sort, be it a broader physical or geographical setting, or a certain expressive orientation similar to what Villoteau had described as "the taste of a whole nation," or a specific milieu directly linked to music making; 2) a performative dimension, in other words the process of making music and by extension the physical and temporal "space" within which the music is usually presented; 3) a musical substance, which includes sung poetry and is directed toward the evocation of musical ecstasy; and 4) the ecstatic sensation itself. Thus, the ṭarab design resembles a prism through which light is refracted into separately identifiable colors. The overall conglomerate can also be compared to a group of concentric circles that narrow down gradually, first the broader setting, then the performative process, then ultimately the experiential core. In turn, this core may be subdivided into the music followed by its ecstatic effect, if we envision ecstasy as the end result of music making, or into the ecstatic effect followed by the music, if we recognize music as the quintessential ingredient of the ṭarab experience. Although I address other related domains, such as musical composition and text writing, this four-part design provides both an analytical base for investigating the ṭarab phenomenon and a vantage point for interpreting related theories and world models.

In the following chapters, the *contextual base* is studied largely in terms of what Kwabena Nketia (1981) has described as "musical culture," as compared to culture in general.[21] In other words, I paint an overall picture of ṭarab as a milieu, or musically specialized subculture. Essentially, such realms as professional jargon, musical training, and music related codes of

[21] Others have defined "context" in various ways. For example, such transformative experiences as spirit possession and shamanism, and by extension the ecstatic subcultures that embrace them, have been explained in terms of natural habitat (Goodman 1988); evolutionary-neurophysiological factors (Laughlin et al. 1979: 1–116 and Lex 1979); social and religious institutions and tensions between the sexes (Lewis 1971/1989); and value systems in different world communities (Bourguignon 1976). Meanwhile, Lomax (1968), who viewed singing as a prime emotive expression, has correlated specific singing styles with individual techno-environmental culture types throughout the world.

behavior are examined in order to demonstrate how in its totality, the ṭarab culture feeds into, as well as socializes and streamlines the ecstatic musical experience.

From a wider perspective, I examine the relationship between this cultural domain and Arab culture in general. Specifically addressed is the extent to which the former can be considered an extension to, or a reflection of its surrounding societal landscape, or conversely, how it may differ from other Arab or Near-Eastern cultural domains. In theoretical terms, do such transformative states as ecstasy, or trance, which are emotionally distinct, as well as culturally relevant, or which embrace "feeling," as well as "meaning" (Geertz 1973: 134–135), grant the cultural practices that uphold them a sense of individuality and power, although at times also render them socially or morally threatening?[22] Are such practices empowered to modify or reverse conventional relationships and hierarchies? Also historically, has the culture of ṭarab provided an emotional alternative to other more formal, verbal or intellectual facets of Arab life, as the late French sociologist Jacques Berque has suggested?[23]

With respect to *performance*, I investigate the primary settings and processes of music making; when and where performing takes place and what characterizes the typical ṭarab musical event. More specifically, the discussions address the performance structure; the usual human and physical ambiance; the role of extra-musical sensory modes of stimulation, including the consumption of food and alcohol; the listeners' characteristic behaviors; and the dynamics of interaction between the performers and the audience. Similarly, explored are such significant departures as playing for one's own ecstatic gratification, without the physical presence of an audience; the role of sound recording in creating new modalities of listening to ṭarab music; and the channeling of ṭarab feeling through the technological media. Of special interest throughout the various inquiries are the ways in which the performance event both propagates and shapes the ecstatic message.

More broadly, the ṭarab performance is viewed vis-à-vis its cultural backdrop. Indeed, the concept of performance is complex and multidimensional; probing it closely, like using a camera zoom can reveal numerous thematic subcategories each with its theoretical nuances and implications. In a sense, the musical event is an interface between sound and society, a set of recognizable behaviors that link music to various broadening social and expressive spheres. With this in mind, I study the ṭarab performance both in context and as context. Basically, I use ritual, or secular ritual, as a

22 The distinct efficacy of ecstatic or artistic systems of expression has been recognized by ethnomusicologists. See Herndon and McLeod 1979: 120–124, Blacking 1980: 64–87, and Becker 1983: 65–76.

23 Berque 1964: 211–236.

referential model, particularly since ritual and performance, as concepts and processes are closely interlinked.[24] Thus, I ask if the ṭarab event reflects broader societal patterns and worldviews as well as stands out as being distinct or special.[25] In the latter sense, does it, for example, utilize specific symbols or emulate the separation-transition-incorporation progression generally associated with rites of passage?[26] Does it embody "efficacy," which has been associated with ritual, as compared to "entertainment," which has been attributed to theater (Schechner 1976: 196–222)? I also consider the elements of flexibility, spontaneity, and improvisation, which are widely encountered in world rituals.[27] Ultimately, my probe takes into account the aesthetic content of the ṭarab event, more specifically the ways in which the underlying ecstatic dimension of the performance contributes to both its cultural connectedness and its individuality as a social process.

The realm of *ecstasy* is investigated along a number of related paths. First, I look into the basic characteristics of the ṭarab experience, for example the physical, emotional, and musical conditions that lead to its fruition; who feels it; how it is expressed or exteriorized by the various listeners; and the role played by audience–performer interactions throughout the ecstatic process. The discussions are referenced by commonly held notions about ecstasy, for example that: it is found pleasurable or desirable by those who seek it; it has physiological as well as psychological components; it can lead to heightened mental or creative abilities; it is often difficult to isolate or distinguish from other "ordinary" states; and its manifestations, meanings, and functions may differ cross-culturally.[28]

Also, given the focal position of ecstasy in both secular and sacred traditions, the state of ṭarab is viewed in relation to its counterparts in the world of religious mysticism. Mystical states are known to vary considerably in their durations and, as William James (1902/1929) has explained, are transient, noetic (in other words leading to some form of higher knowledge), and passive, as well as ineffable. They may be metaphorically or directly linked to intoxication, or mind-altering substances, and may render those who experience them particularly susceptible to various creeds or agendas, a phenomenon that Arnold Ludwig has referred to as "hypersuggestibility"

24 Interpretations of ritual in terms of performance are outlined in Bell 1997: 72–76, whereas studies of performance from the perspective of ritual are discussed in Carlson 1996: 13, 20–21.

25 For information about the relationship between ritual and culture see Moore and Meyerhoff eds. 1977, and Herndon and McLeod 1979: 27.

26 See Van Gennep 1960: 11–13 and Turner 1969: 94–203.

27 The informality of certain rituals is discussed in Rosaldo 1984: 184–193 and furthermore, the flexible nature of verbal performance is addressed in Bauman 1986: 4.

28 Such traits of ecstasy are discussed, sometimes under the concept of trance, in Tart 1969: 2, Rouget 1985: 326, Herndon and McLeod 1979: 120, and others.

(1969: 19–20). Mystical states are also associated with artistic creativity and genius, sometimes in the form of divine inspiration.[29]

Furthermore, I explore the emotional basis of ṭarab and by extension, *salṭanah*, an ecstatic state that enables the performers to produce highly affective musical renditions. I investigate the listeners' and performers' views on ṭarab as feeling and look critically into other emotion-related interpretations. Although fundamentally agreeing with Rouget's direct linkage between the ṭarab condition and the musical-aesthetic stimulus, I question his profiling of ṭarab as "trance," or for that matter his strict dichotomy between "trance" and "ecstasy" and the models he uses for representing Arab "trances." Thus, I modify or differ with some of Rouget's constructs and provide my own alternative perspectives and analyses. Similarly examined are theories that explain the causes of ecstatic or trance-related transitions, for example, theories of sensory deprivation and sensory overload.[30] In the same vein, I revisit the common emotion-based terminology and reassess its applicability to the study of ṭarab.

Also addressed are issues of representation, specifically the relationship between ecstasy and its broader contextual base. Notably, ṭarab has been attributed to a variety of local agents that presumably make it characteristically Arab. Whereas Rouget has linked the Arabs' exceptional proclivity toward trancing to indigenous sociocultural factors,[31] William Kay Archer (1964: 20, 23, 28) has spoken of "Arabitude," as a quintessential Arab trait directly linked to the notion of ta'thīr, or "musical influence." Comparably, a European by the name Muhammad Asad (1954) has explained the profound ecstatic nature of Arab music in terms of the indigenous peoples' inner psyche, their Islamic spiritual ethos, and their desert, or nomadic-based unitary transcendentalism.[32] In this book, I provide my own outlook on such culture-specific interpretations, or profile theories.

The *music* is analyzed qualitatively, in terms of how the various musical

29 These and other attributes of the mystical state have been presented in Sharma 1978: 16, Huxley 1954, Winkelman 1986, and Myerhoff 1975, as well as in James 1902/1929. Furthermore, the relationship between mystical ecstasy and artistic creativity has been expounded in Underhill 1955/1974, Khan 1988, Nasr 1987, and the various excerpts in Godwin ed. 1987.

30 Theories of sensory deprivation and sensory overload have been widely discussed and applied. See for example Tart 1969, Ludwig 1969, Crapanzano 1973, and Besmer 1983, as well as Rouget, who associates trance with overload and ecstasy with deprivation (1985: 3–12). Rouget, however (1985: 315–326) rightfully cautions against assuming direct or predictable causalities between music and possession trance, for example those established by Neher 1962 and Needham 1967/1979. Similar caution is expressed in Blacking 1968 and 1980, Erlmann 1982, and DjeDje 1984.

31 Rouget 1985: 298.

32 Asad, whose original name was Leopold Weiss, was born into a Jewish family in Galicia, now in Poland. A convert to Islam, he was a noted scholar and writer who traveled extensively in the Arab world and at one time was a correspondent for *Die Frankfurter Zeitung*, see "The Legacy of Muhammad Asad," n.d.: 18–19.

elements, techniques, and maneuvers operate ecstatically. Accordingly, I investigate such individual realms as texture, ornaments, text–music relationships, cadential patterns, improvisation, modality, microtonal subtleties, and rhythmic applications. Also studied are the ways in which the various musical components operate on the level of composition and in the context of actual music performance. Comparably, I provide an extended treatment of the lyrics. Incorporating numerous textual illustrations, the discussions introduce the essential poetical genres, the typical literary styles, and the basic thematic motifs. Most importantly, the study offers explanations of how the lyrics as sung love poems contribute to the overall ecstatic experience.

Meanwhile, I examine a number of theories that deal with music and emotion. Here, the underlying themes include a) how and why music affects us,[33] b) the connection between music's affect and its abstract, or nonrepresentational tendencies,[34] and c) the role of musical syntax in emotional arousal.[35] Similarly investigated are the correlations made between specific musical styles or compositional designs and ecstatic evocation.[36] In this regard, I do not agree with Rouget's assumption that semantics, or verbal meaning, is an absolute prerequisite for trance-related experiences among the Arabs and argue instead for a more flexible and multidimensional relationship between music and emotional transformation.

Finally, this book reintegrates the various components of the ṭarab complex and places them in a broader world setting. I allude to the connections between ṭarab and comparable phenomena outside the Arab Near-East, as well as between ṭarab music and local musical styles that emerged and became influential during the last few decades. Demonstrating the impact of recent intercultural contacts and patterns of globalization upon Arab music in general, I present an encompassing view of ṭarab as a world culture and aesthetic experience.

33 For explanations of how or why music affects us emotionally, see for example Langer 1953: 125–132, Storr 1992: 64, and Tame 1984.

34 Music's abstract nature and its unique ability to transcend literal representations or depictions of standard emotions was particularly expounded by Susanne Langer (1942/1979: 219) and similarly argued for in Scruton 1974, Newcomb 1984, Budd 1985: 175, Kivy 1989: 258, and Davies 1994. The notion that music defies semantic representation was advanced by ethnomusicologist and music thinker Charles Seeger (1961: 77–80).

35 Discussion on musical syntax and emotional arousal appear in Meyer, 1956.

36 Along these lines Rouget observes that trance-related musics are generally part of the local cultures' prevalent or mainstream musical language, but also display such typical features as abrupt rhythmic changes or breaks, gradual acceleration in tempo, and *crescendo*, namely gradual increase in volume (1985: 94–104 and 81, 91). Meanwhile, "Redundancy through time" has been discussed in Herndon and McLeod 1979: 113–114. As far as compositional processes are concerned, Robert Jourdain speaks of the necessity of achieving a balance between stability and consistency on the one hand, and deviation and variation on the other (1997: 312).

2 Culture

Ṭarab can be viewed as a specialized cultural domain. Sometimes referred to as *ʿālam al-ṭarab*, "the world of ṭarab," this domain encompasses artists, repertoires, and music related ideologies, attitudes, and behaviors, including ways of listening and reacting to music. The ṭarab culture is also associated with a craft-based jargon pertaining to social, technical, and professional aspects of music making and with certain musical values and outlooks. Public ambivalence toward the ṭarab profession is deeply rooted, but often yields to, or coexists with full recognition of the established ṭarab artist. Although members of the ṭarab community tend to come from relatively low economic and social ranks, successful male or female artists, especially singers, may rank among the wealthy and influential members of Arab society.

As a group, *ahl al-ṭarab*, "the people of ṭarab," incorporate an indigenous professional milieu of vocalists, instrumentalists, composers, and text writers. This category may also be extended to peripheral specializations, for example makers of ṭarab instruments such as the ʿūd, qānūn, and nāy. Also somewhat tangentially, it includes Arab-music academicians and conservatory staff-members. Although the concept of ṭarab has strong professional overtones, the ṭarab world tends to overlap with the domain of the accomplished ṭarab amateurs, who perform for their own gratification. Indirectly attached to this world are the local music critics, journalists, and biographers and even recording engineers. Meanwhile, the intellectual endeavors of the music theorists essentially remain distinct from the world of the hard-core musical entertainer. Theorists, whose published works usually take the form of editions or commentaries on medieval treatises, or convey abstract and systematized melodic and rhythmic theories, belong to a community basically separate from that of the radio-station composer, nightclub instrumentalist, and the like. Totally extraneous to this domain are Western and Arab performers and composers of European music. Finally, the world of ṭarab embraces the *jumhūr*, or "audience," particularly the listening connoisseurs. The performers and their public are interconnected economically, socially, and emotionally.

Essentially, ṭarab is an urban phenomenon native to cities such as Cairo,

Beirut, and Damascus. Ṭarab artists are either born in these cities or have lived a good portion of their lives in, or were amply exposed to, urban centers where ṭarab had been established as a craft. After World War II, with the growth of urbanization, the popularization of ṭarab music through the modern mass media, and the emulation of Cairo's musical model in neighboring urban communities, the practice and appeal of East-Mediterranean ṭarab music has been widely expanded.

Gender roles

At least outwardly, ṭarab projects a strong male orientation. In the medieval courts, many women excelled in singing and playing the ʿūd, some even amassing considerable fame and prestige. However, throughout history the position of female entertainers has been directly challenged by conservative attitudes. Commenting on the status of female professional musicians in Tunisia, L. JaFran Jones wrote:

> Perhaps never adequately isolated within a blurred gamut of "pleasures" – divine and profane – music has always been a controversial legal and social issue in orthodox Islam. While its attraction for peoples under the domination of Islam has been irresistible, the compulsion on the part of pious guardians of public probity to condemn it has been equally inevitable. (1987: 69)

In traditional Arab society, women are expected to demonstrate the virtue of *ḥasham*, or "propriety as a voluntary gesture that earns them respect and raises their position in a male dominated society" (Abu-Lughod 1986: 103–117). It is generally believed that for women, pursuing music professionally is incompatible with private family life and with the established norms of social decorum, as the life of the ṭarab singer Almaḍḥ (1860–1896) illustrates. When her male singing competitor ʿAbduh al-Ḥāmūlī (1841–1901) married her, he felt compelled to prevent her from pursuing the singing profession altogether, although he himself continued to lead an active career as a singer and composer.[1] A comparable attempt to uphold the common standards of decency was made by Umm Kulthūm (ca. 1904–1975) and her family at the very beginning of this singer's performance career. When she saw her picture at the center of an advertisement announcing her performances, she reportedly cried of embarrassment. Her father, Shaykh Ibrāhīm, who permitted her to sing only a religious repertoire consisting mostly of *qaṣāʾid* and *tawāshīḥ*, refused to allow her performances to take place until

[1] Al-Khulaʿī ca. 1904: 144.

the performance manager had removed her picture from the advertisement.[2] In her earliest public performances, while singing with her father and brother as vocal accompanists, she appeared garbed in traditional male attire, thus projecting a modest demeanor or perhaps toning down her image as a woman artist. For several years she sang while wearing the *ʿabāyah* (male gown) and the *kūfiyyah* and *ʿuqāl* (male head-dress).[3]

However, several factors account for the special appeal of women as ṭarab artists. To begin with, female singing is recognized as an effective conveyor of musical ecstasy. In various historical epochs, male audiences have marveled at women who sing, partly because the ecstasy conveyed by their voices was supposedly reinforced by their physical appearance. In a book on ṭarab in the Mameluk period, we read that:

> the princes used to prefer the female singer over the male singer and so did the upper class and the common people . . . Undoubtedly, the *jawārī* (female slave-singers) had an attribute that made them rise above the male singers, that is if they enjoyed a suitable and beautiful voice, and certainly if they were attractive. It is [physical] beauty, added to the beauty of the voice, that gave them distinction above the male singers and made them preferable. In the case of the former [the females], the listener is undoubtedly captivated by two things, whereas in the case of the latter [the males] he is captivated by one thing, namely the beauty of the voice and nothing else . . . Indeed, Plato was not far off when he said that the singing of beautiful females evokes desire and ecstasy (ṭarab). (al-Baqlī 1984: 65–66)

Female singing retained its mystique during and after the nineteenth century. It seems ironic that al-Ḥāmūlī, who barred his wife from entertaining in public, had married her reportedly because he was deeply enamored by her singing. Even those who criticized the female singers on musical bases sometimes admitted that these singers' sexual identity was a factor in their popularity. In the early twentieth century, Kāmil al-Khulaʿī (1880–1938), an Egyptian composer, theorist, and musical thinker, wrote an encompassing treatise in which he attempted to familiarize his generation with the rudiments of Near-Eastern music and to reform the musical culture in light of the modern scientific and cultural accomplishments of the West. In it, al-Khulaʿī remarked with characteristic pessimism that, "as typical everywhere and at all times," the female singers are pathetically ignorant of their art and that in the eyes of many "nothing redeems them except that they are women" (ca. 1904: 91).

Since the early twentieth century, the status and visibility of female singers has improved significantly. Many achieving fame as recording artists

2 See Buṭrus 1967: 127.

3 See Fernea and Bezirgan eds. 1976: 145. For further information about the professional dilemmas of female singers and dancers in Egypt, see Nieuwkerk 1995.

and film stars, modern female artists have been working closely with male accompanists, composers, and lyricists. Some teach at public and private academies and occupy powerful positions in various music related pedagogical and government bureaucracies.[4] Above all, countless women have excelled as ṭarab artists. Notwithstanding the historical centrality of the male perspective and the tensions that have surrounded female artistry, the ṭarab culture grants women qualitative importance in an area considered quintessential to affective ṭarab making, namely singing.

Learning Ṭarab

Ṭarab performers tend to share certain learning experiences. The long process of becoming a ṭarab artist usually consists of five different phases: 1) the appearance of talent, usually during childhood; 2) musical obsession, accompanied by struggle against family and cultural barriers; 3) family and societal recognition of budding talent, and in some cases reluctant acquiescence to the novice's musical desires; 4) training of some sort; and 5) the undertaking of a performance career. These general phases do not always follow a strict linear order and may overlap or coincide with one another.

Talent

In the ṭarab culture, music making is believed to have a quintessential prerequisite, namely talent, or *mawhibah*, literally, "gift" or "endowment." Musical talent may also be referred to as *mayl*, literally, "inclination" or *raghbah* literally, "desire." Showing musical talent constitutes the earliest sign of a person's potential as an artist. Talent is generally considered innate and predetermined. Individuals are simply born with it, and thus they either have it or do not have it.[5]

Belief in the innate nature of talent is expressed in various ways. In his early twentieth century treatise Kāmil al-Khulaʿī presented an old anecdote that explains musical talent and, as it turns out, sheds significant light upon the general ideology of ṭarab. After referring to ancient philosophical arguments in favor of the auditory sense, al-Khulaʿī told the anecdote as

4 See Danielson 1991a.

5 This traditional notion of talent may differ from certain modern Western views that project a more liberal or egalitarian attitude toward musical ability. One such view is expressed in John Blacking's ethnomusicological writings (e.g. Blacking 1973).

follows: During a meeting in his royal court, one king claimed that humans learn to listen to music (*samā*ʿ) by developing the habit of attending musical assemblies (*majālis al-ṭarab*). A sage in the group disagreed and said that humans appreciate music "due to a certain disposition, they are born with" (ca. 1904: 11). Dissatisfied, the king asked if the sage could substantiate his claim. The sage responded positively and asked that the court bring in one hundred babies ten months and younger from parents of different backgrounds, including ministers, scientists, writers, farmers, slaves, and others. The sage ordered that their nursing mothers stay away from them for half a day so that they become very hungry. Subsequently, he ordered that the babies be returned to their mothers and while they were busy feeding, the sage gave orders to have musical instruments (*ālāt al-ṭarab*) play at once. Consequently, some babies stopped nursing and focused their attention toward the sound as they moved their bodies and laughed. Others abandoned nursing but remained quiet and motionless, whereas some began to alternate between feeding for a short while and looking toward the source of the sound. Others began to move their feet and hands to the music without forsaking feeding, but there also were those who put all their energy into feeding and ignored everything else. As the story went, it was then that the king became convinced that musical disposition was inborn. Ending with the standard phrase "and God creates whatever He wills" (ca. 1904:11), al-Khulaʿī not only provided an explanation of talent, but also called our attention to important corollaries such as the different levels of musicality among humans and the variety of ways in which listeners respond to music, ways that, as the anecdote implied, are also predetermined. The anecdote also alluded to various visceral and emotional responses to music, which the author referred to categorically as ṭarab. As presented in this tale, the indicators of talent are manifestly psycho-physiological.

Talent is often linked to heredity. A musician is thought to acquire his or her talent from a gifted parent or a relative, typically, a maternal uncle. Often used to describe the hereditary nature of talent are folk proverbs such as *farkh al-baṭṭ ʿawwām*, roughly, "a fledgling duck floats like a duck." Also sometimes, talent is seen as a correlate to ethnicity, for example Gypsies are presumably endowed with exceptional musical ability. When music aficionados speak about the virtuosity of the late buzuq players, Muḥammad ʿAbd al-Karīm (1905–1989) of Syria or Maṭar Muḥammad (d. 1995) of Lebanon, they usually hasten to point out that these artists are of Gypsy origins and to remark that musical virtuosity, and the buzuq itself, are "native" to Gypsy culture. Furthermore, musicianship may be associated with specific nationalities or geographical areas. For example, numerous musical connoisseurs stress that the Syrian city of Aleppo is *umm al-ṭarab*, literally, "the mother of ṭarab." It is also said that Egyptian performers have a natural affinity for ṭarab, as well as a good sense of rhythm and ensemble coordination. "They have these things in their blood," or as one amateur female singer from Lebanon put it, "ṭarab was born in Egypt."

Attitudes toward talent tend to be ambivalent. Talent may be viewed as a natural inclination toward the craft practiced by one's own family and as such may be appreciated as an emblem of familial or ethnic continuity. Similarly, musical talent may be tolerated and even encouraged if the talented person intends to become a mere amateur, namely a *hāwī*, literally, "one who is enamored," or *ghāwī*, "one who is infatuated," or "obsessed." However, if the family is particularly sensitive to the negative stigma of professional music making, then musical talent may be considered threatening and basically undesirable. Yet even then, despite its long-term social and moral implications, genuine musical talent may be recognized as being mystically or metaphysically special. Actually, some musicians attribute talent to a force outside themselves, and similarly see their musicality as an endowment they are responsible for maintaining. As one elderly violinist from Aleppo reverently explained to me, music is an *amānah*, namely a "trust" or "consignment" that someone else (God) has left with us and entrusted us to care for. It is our moral duty to live up to that trust.[6]

Obsession and struggle

Musical talent usually manifests itself as a burning passion. A child destined to become a musician shows predilection toward singing or playing an instrument. Actually, his or her musical urge may verge on the bizarre or mischievous, as illustrated by the musicians' typical reports about their own experiences. In his memoirs, the renowned Egyptian singer and composer Muḥammad ʿAbd al-Wahhāb (ca. 1901–1991) recounted that as a child he often missed school because he frequently gathered the neighborhood children and sang for them. To justify his truancies, he repeatedly gave the schoolmaster one single excuse, namely that his aunt had died, until his ploy was discovered after the school master investigated the matter with Muḥammad's father. As a result, the boy received a spanking from his father, but that did not dissuade him from following his musical urges, as demonstrated by one specific incident. One time, the famous singer Shaykh Sayyid al-Ṣafṭī (1875–1939) was invited to sing at a wedding in a *khaymah*, or performance tent, in Cairo. After walking into the tent in order to satisfy his musical curiosity, the young Muḥammad was soon discovered and chased out, "since children were not welcome at such events." However, in order to make his way back he offered to help an old waiter, who carried a food tray

[6] From a conversation with the artist, ʿAbd al-Ḥamīd al-Tannārī, in Los Angeles in 1990.

on his head, by carrying the tray for him. As the waiter accepted what he thought was an admirable gesture, the young Muḥammad was able to go in, but for fear of being expelled again he hid under the *dikkah*, the performance sofa, upon which al-Ṣafṭī sat while performing. He remained there all night listening to the performance.[7]

In a large number of cases, obsession is violently suppressed by the child's parents and dampened by social pressures. Consequently, the potential musician, especially the less obsessive (or the less talented), may relinquish music, at least as a serious concern, or perhaps maintain it as a hobby. However, in many cases talent affirms itself, thus leading to a general realization that a) the young person's obsession is too strong and attempts to stifle it are futile, and b) his or her talent is impressive enough to deserve recognition on the part of the parents, the family, and the community.

The following are three illustrative cases. The late qānūn player Muḥammad al-ʿAqqād told me that his father and grandfather, Muḥammad al-ʿAqqād (Sr.), although both were musicians, at first tried to prevent him from following the path of music.[8] Their attitude was prompted by conservatism and by a feeling on the grandfather's part that one may pursue a profession only if he were to excel in it, or as the grandfather put it, "a good shoemaker is better than a mediocre musician." Looking toward a "decent" future, the family insisted on sending Muḥammad to a private French school. However, despite going to school, Muḥammad remained musically obsessed. The young boy used to tell his aging grandfather after an evening performance: "Why don't you leave the qānūn with me and I will carry it for you and bring it to your house tomorrow morning?" At his parents' home, however, he used to open the case surreptitiously and "experiment" with the strings; trying simple melodies by Sayyid Darwīsh (1893–1923), an innovative composer of songs and dramatic works, and by others. It was not long before he was discovered and beaten by his father. According to Muḥammad, the grandfather hated to see others play his qānūn, "as musicians in general were very sensitive about others using or touching their instruments."

Gradually, the young Muḥammad proved himself a serious learner. A man close to the family, Muṣṭafá Bey Riḍā, convinced the grandfather that the boy should join the Cairo Academy of Arab Music and pursue serious study under the qānūn teacher there, who happened to be the grandfather himself. Riḍā, who also played the qānūn and worked as a music instructor and administrator at the Academy, had himself been a student of the older al-ʿAqqād. He told the grandfather, "Look how you helped me and helped your son become respectable musicians. Why can't you allow the grandson to take a path similar to ours?"

7 The artist's memoirs appeared in Rifʿat ed. n.d. See pages 18–20.
8 From a conversation that took place in Los Angeles in the summer of 1984.

Eventually, the full recognition of Muḥammad as a prospective qānūn player took place through a symbolic, yet very significant gesture. Toward the end of his life the grandfather (d. 1931) gave a well-attended performance at the Academy of Arab Music. At the end of the performance, the old man rose from his seat and placed his qānūn in the lap of the young Muḥammad. The gesture signaled the old musician's decision to retire but also his acceptance of his grandson as a musician and successor.[9]

Another illustration comes from a published interview with a Palestinian composer who worked for many years in Syria and Lebanon. Riyāḍ al-Bandak traced his artistic life back to elementary school in Bethlehem, particularly to the encouragement of his school principal, a violinist and music aficionado from Ramallah. When the principal wanted to form a choir of musically-gifted students, Riyāḍ was one of those chosen, although he was under eleven years of age. As al-Bandak explained, "I was the only one able to memorize any anthem that the principal taught us . . . That is why the principal had appointed me to sing for the students before they entered their classes every morning" (Munawwar 1989: 71).

Al-Bandak added that his love for music was a kind of a craze (*hawas*) and that he was able to learn immediately any song he would hear whether by Umm Kulthūm, Muḥammad ʿAbd al-Wahhāb, Shaykh Abū al-ʿUlā Muḥammad, or others. As he explained, "Arab musical classicism was in my blood since I was very young, but the great obstacle was my father, who at the time was the mayor of Bethlehem" (Ibid.). The father stated emphatically that education came first, and after that Riyāḍ could do whatever he wanted. However, becoming a young man, Riyāḍ chose to follow his own passion. He attempted to find an artistic outlet through the Palestinian Radio Station in Jerusalem, which was directed by Yaḥyá al-Lababīdī, a well-known composer and administrator at the time. After auditioning and gaining admission to the radio station and becoming highly appreciated by the radio staff, he composed and sang a song that was broadcast by the station. Discovering his young son's intentions, the shocked father contacted al-Lababīdī and complained angrily, insisting that his son never be allowed to pursue "the path of artistry" (*ṭarīq al-fann*). As al-Bandak vividly remembered, on the following day when he went to the station, the guard prevented him from entering, thus following the father's instructions. Upon returning to Bethlehem, he tried to satisfy his musical passion by performing at various local musical venues.

According to al-Bandak, a "miracle" brought him back to the radio station and eventually made him famous as a composer. In 1938 the British arrested

9 This ceremony was also described in the notes on an LP featuring qānūn performances by al-ʿAqqād, the grandson. The LP, issued in New York, is titled "El Salam; Mohammad El Akkad, the King of the Kanoon" (El Akkad Records, Stereo RC 412).

his father and exiled him to Greece, thus giving the young artist full freedom to pursue his art. After World War II, when his father was returned to Bethlehem and became head of the local National Committee in 1947, Riyāḍ refused the father's immediate orders to join the newly formed armed-resistance movement, which two of Riyāḍ's brothers had already joined. Instead, the young artist left for Damascus, where his already established name enabled him to work with the radio station there and to compose songs for renowned vocalists such as Mary Jibrān, "the Umm Kulthūm of Syria" at the time (Ibid.).[10]

Finally, Souhail Kaspar, an accomplished *ṭablah* (Arab hand-drum) player now living in Los Angeles, grew up in a climate that was musically conducive, although not devoid of family concerns.[11] Born in 1950 in a small town in Central Lebanon, Mr. Kaspar came from a very musical family: his mother sang and his father played the ʿūd. At age seven, he showed phenomenal rhythmic talent, clearly demonstrated when he tapped the meters on a table as his parents performed. Souhail's father, deeply taken by his son's talent, bought him a small clay drum to play on, but was also worried that music was distracting the son from schoolwork. As Souhail remembered, "My father tried to hide the drum from me, but every time he left the house I was able to find it and play on it." Realizing that the son's obsession was impossible to ignore and feeling that if music were to be pursued it had to be learned properly, he enrolled his son at age thirteen at a music academy in Aleppo. Living with his maternal aunt's family in the Syrian city, Souhail studied at the academy for approximately three years and earned a certificate in percussion playing. After returning to Lebanon he performed with numerous artists, including very well-known singers and instrumentalists, thereby establishing himself as a career percussionist.

Obviously, there are notable exceptions to the various adverse circumstances. Certain ṭarab artists speak of encouraging parents who wish for their children to learn the musical trade and to master it. In the 1950s, one very musical father from Beirut reportedly used the following metaphor to explain his philosophy to his talented sons: "a head without any music in it might as well be cut off." The sons grew up to be highly accomplished amateur performers on ṭarab instruments.

10 Mary Jibrān was one of the most accomplished singers of the Arab world. Born in Beirut, Lebanon in 1911, she traveled to and worked in Egypt, where she learned the older ṭarab repertoire from such master artists as Dāwūd Ḥusnī, and Zakariyyā Aḥmad. Later on, she lived and worked in Syria. See al-Jundī 1954: 279–280.

11 From an interview with Mr. Kaspar (Suhayl Kasbār) in Los Angeles on October 7, 1998.

Discovery and recognition

The stories presented above are typical in their depictions of obsession, struggle, and triumph, and in their portrayals of the processes through which potential artists are initiated into the path of artistry. More specifically, they allude to a very important phenomenon, namely the "discovery," or *iktishāf*, of the budding talent. Ṭarab performers generally cite at least one memorable incident marking their own early discovery by other performers. Similarly, elder musicians and musical connoisseurs often take pride in mentioning the names of established young artists whom they had discovered themselves. The discovery process usually constitutes a point of departure, marking a transition from troubling uncertainties to full confirmation of the authenticity and promise of the novice's talent. It may also put an end to personal and familial tribulations by ushering the budding artist into a road of specialization, although even then the artist may continue to be haunted by the prospects of professional struggle and social rejection. The discoverer, or as often is the case, numerous discoverers, is usually a senior musician who, after recognizing the talent, may take the talented person under his or her wing, and sometimes introduce him or her to the public.

Biographies of ṭarab artists, as well as the artists' own reports, are replete with discovery stories. Among the more famous of these stories is ʿAbduh al-Ḥāmūlī's vocal talent being discovered by Muʿallim Shaʿbān, a nineteenth-century teacher and reportedly a very selfish impresario.[12] Also well-known is the story of Umm Kulthūm's discovery by the famous singer Shaykh Abū al-ʿUlā Muḥammad (1878–1927). We are told that hearing the young girl sing his songs when he met her at one of her countryside performances, this senior artist was so touched that he had tears in his eyes and added his enthusiastic support to those insisting that Umm Kulthūm perform in Cairo. He reportedly told her father "Oh, Shaykh Ibrāhīm, it is a pity for the girl to remain here, she has real talent, she is a treasure" (Fu'ād 1976: 101–102). In the early life of Muḥammad ʿAbd al-Wahhāb there were a series of comparable encounters, the one with the celebrated poet Aḥmad Shawqī (1868–1932) in Alexandria around 1925 being a watershed in the young artist's career. Shawqī took ʿAbd al-Wahhāb as his protégé and introduced him to exclusive literary and political circles and to European, particularly French, culture. Writing modern lyrics for ʿAbd al-Wahhāb, the Egyptian poet encouraged the young artist to create new and innovative musical works.[13]

The artist's "discovery" usually paves the way for a certain training process. Natural talent, although quintessential to artistic ability, is consid-

[12] Kāmil 1971: 8–9.
[13] Rifʿat ed. n.d.: 64–94.

ered crude and in need of refinement. The craft-oriented word *khāmah*, which literally means "raw material" or "uncut stone" or "fabric," is widely applied to talent in its unrefined natural state. Promising artists whose talents have not received the proper attention yet are referred to collectively as *khāmāt*, or "raw talents." Such artists may for example appear on television talent shows, which have also been credited with discovering budding musical talent.[14] The concept may also apply to the voice when it is rough yet potentially good. A young, musically untrained singer may possess the right khāmah, namely a type of voice that has demonstrable artistic merit.

Like a raw piece of diamond a khāmah needs *ṣaql*, or "polishing." In other words, natural ability to sing or play an instrument needs refining, or as the musicians' jargon goes, *tanḍhīf*, literally, "cleaning up." What is implied here is that the material to be "cleaned" is of desirable quality to begin with. Another related need is recognized, namely, *tawjīh*, or professional "guidance." The tasks of "guiding," "polishing," or "cleaning" may be performed or at least initiated by the discoverer of the talent. However, in most cases they are part of a prolonged effort that involves a number of teachers and formal and informal modalities of learning.

The learning process

Traditionally, learning ṭarab music has been linked either directly or indirectly to religious contexts. Before World War I, a large number of Egyptian singers developed their vocal artistry through the performance of Sufi liturgies. Their Sufi training was usually reflected by the religious title "Shaykh," which preceeded their names. Similarly, in Aleppo, which was well-exposed to the music of Ottoman Turkey, many of the renowned composers and performers were affiliated with the city's Sufi orders, including the Mawlawiyyah (Mevlevis).[15] Also, famous singers such as ʿAbduh al-Ḥāmūlī and Shaykh Salāmah Ḥijāzī (1852–1917), a ṭarab singer, actor, and one of the pioneers of the dramatic movement in Egypt, trained their voices through performing the call to prayer from the top of the minarets. Prior to sound amplification, the *muʾadhdhin* (or caller-to-prayer) needed to

14 In the last twenty years or so, one example has been the weekly talent show *Studio al-Fann* on Lebanese television. In Lebanon, this show is known to have discovered and initiated a large number of amateur and professional musicians, especially singers.

15 We are told, for example, that toward the late nineteenth century, Aleppo had more than forty *takāyā*, or Sufi worship centers (from a report quoted in Bin Dhurayl 1969: 131). Among those who were directly influenced by Aleppo's Sufi music were composer ʿUmar al-Baṭsh (1885-1950), composer and theorist Shaykh ʿAlī al-Darwīsh (1872–1952) and nāy player ʿAbd al-Laṭīf al-Nabakī (b. 1875). The latter two had certain connections with the Mawlawī order (see al-Jundī 1954: 284–289, 326–327, and 328).

develop a powerful voice, which was a real asset in secular performance settings as well. A further traditional path toward vocal proficiency has been Qurʾanic chanting. The art of *tajwīd*, or the melodically elaborate recitation of the Qurʾān, entails mastering certain rules for proper enunciation and textual delivery, developing knowledge of the *maqāmāt* (or melodic modes), and cultivating effective improvisatory skills.[16] Similarly, in some communities, learning has been acquired through the mastering of other religious repertoires, for example certain church liturgies.

Ṭarab music has also been learned through essentially secular professional paths. During the Ottoman Period, members of various professions, including musicians belonged to individual professional guilds that in turn granted them protection and structured their learning and work patterns. This was the case in major Near-Eastern cities. Historical sources provide little information on how guild musicians learned their craft, for example how systematic the learning process was. However, it is generally shown that the mastery of the craft was assimilated gradually through an extended apprentice–master relationship, which led to an initiation ceremony that gave the learner formal access to professional work.[17]

In Egypt, apprenticeship centered around the *takht*, the small ensemble that was prevalent in Arab cities before World War I. Young and promising individuals treated the takht ensemble as a learning context and as a stepping stone toward becoming accomplished performers. As indicated by older musicians and earlier writings, male novices learned from male takht musicians, whereas females learned from members of the *ʿawālim*, or female performing, groups. Moreover an instrumentalist, for example a qānūn player, learned from an established professional instrumentalist, whereas a vocalist learned from an accomplished singer, typically someone who was Sufi trained. For example, toward the middle of the nineteenth century, the Egyptian singer and composer Muḥammad al-Muqaddam, who mastered the liturgy of the Laythī Sufi order, had taught a number of Cairo's singers at the time.[18]

During the twentieth century, apprenticeship as a traditional form of musical training gradually lost its appeal. As we learn from Philip Schuyler's research on Moroccan music, the decline of the apprentice system stemmed in part from the diminished mutual trust between masters and pupils, the waning of the older repertoires, the rise of conservatory teaching, and the fading interest in old and prolonged teaching methods.[19] Also to be considered is the appearance of the recorded disc, which served as a convenient teaching device, since the recorded content could be reproduced repeatedly and

16 See Nelson 1985.

17 For further information on Ottoman guilds, see Von Hammer ed. 1846/1968, Ḥāfiḍh 1971: 192, Racy 1983a: 159, and Baer 1964.

18 Kāmil 1971: 9.

19 Schuyler 1979: 25–27.

learned as such. To these factors may be added the eventual collapse of the guild system and the strong impact of Western cultural values and institutions.

After World War I, some musicians continued to learn their craft through prolonged exposure to teachers, or in some cases from performing parents or relatives. In this instance, learning would still have relied upon informal processes of emulation and coaching. However, the traditional modalities of apprenticeship generally moved closer to, and in many cases were replaced by, the modern practice of tutoring. Inspired by Western musical pedagogy, tutors have provided systematic instruction through private lessons and sometimes through printed textbooks that employ Western notation. Furthermore, tutoring on ṭarab instruments such as the ʿūd and the qānūn have coexisted in the same cities and even same city quarters, with tutoring in Western music by both native and Western teachers.

In one autobiographical novel, a modern Syrian writer (Mīnah 1978) described his own early efforts to become an instrument player, but also his lack of patience for learning how to play. Sometimes quite satirical, the narratives illustrate the salient musical attitudes in Damascus in the early 1940s. Furthermore, they depict the tensions between two methods of musical learning, a Western mode that was considered structured and serious, and a local rote approach that appeared informal and old-fashioned. The author mentioned his short lived attempts to learn the piano, the nāy, and the ʿūd. After beginning to take lessons on the violin with an Italian teacher who taught through Western notation, the author met an old barber who tried to win him as a student. The latter tried to dissuade him from studying with the European teacher, claiming that he himself taught "the genuine Eastern art," *al-fann al-Sharqī al-aṣīl*. Although probably fictitious, one account shows the traditional teacher's desperation, as well as caricatures the old ways of teaching and listening to Arab music:

> With the barber I learned some *duwālīb* [singular *dūlāb*, an instrumental genre], as he also used to accompany me on the *ṭablah* in order for the *bashraf* [an instrumental genre] to become well-established in my mind. Toward the end of the lesson he would teach me what he called *taḥmīlah* [an instrumental genre]. He used to shake his shoulders while playing. I asked him why. He said "the shaking of shoulders is for becoming [musically] involved (*insijām*) . . . Eastern music!; it is ṭarab, insijām, tunes that cause the body to shake." I said: "the Italian teacher confirmed to me that music is something from the spirit, from the brain." He then stopped playing and shouted: "what an animal! Why didn't he say from the belly too? How would you learn the *bashārif* [plural of bashraf] which are the foundation? Music is from the body . . . learn the shaking of the shoulders, but don't say this to others . . . I can teach you the rudiments of the craft (*uṣūl al-mihnah*) in its entirety." (23–24)

The twentieth century also witnessed the proliferation of modern conservatory training. By the early decades of the century, music academies began to appear in cities such as Cairo and Alexandria. Today in almost all large Arab cities there are music conservatories that are typically sponsored by the local governments. These institutions tend to share such features as: the existence of two sections, one for teaching "Occidental," or European music, the other for "Oriental," or Arab music; instruction on specific work days; a specialized administrative staff; and the teachers' reliance on government salaries, rather than on the students' usually nominal registration fees.

In some respects, conservatory training illustrates the traditional modalities of instruction. Many conservatory teachers are practicing musicians who had taught apprentices before. Despite the contractual and less personal nature of the student–teacher relationship, some instructors still expect a certain loyalty from the students and follow teaching methods that are reminiscent of the earlier apprenticeship practice. As bearers of the indigenous musical traditions, conservatories teach men and women to play ṭarab instruments such as the ʿūd, qānūn, violin, nāy, and riqq, and sometimes provide courses in the analysis of the maqāmāt, and the traditional compositional forms. They also instruct students in instrumental genres such as the dūlāb, bashraf, and samāʿī, and other vocal ones, particularly the muwashshaḥ, a preparation considered basic to the musical background of a traditional Arab performer.

Representing a balance between formal instruction and direct emulation was the conservatory experience of Souhail Kaspar. In Aleppo's official music and acting academy, which he entered as a ṭablah student in 1963, Kaspar studied with Muḥammad al-Qabbānī, a middle-aged teacher who played the *riqq* (small tambourine) and other percussion instruments. Percussion students studied on four week days, three of which were devoted to in-house individual and group instruction. The students were taught a large number of metric modes, which they were expected to perform and simultaneously to sing *muwashshaḥāt* (plural of *muwashshaḥ*, a vocal genre typical of the city of Aleppo) that employed these modes. However, on one of the four instruction days, the students were taken to a meeting place of one of the Sufi orders in the city in order to learn through musical participation. As Mr. Kaspar recounts, the *mashāyikh* (members of the Sufi sect) sat in a circle, played large frame-drums (*ṭārāt*, singular *ṭār*), and sang muwashshaḥāt as well as other genres that typically followed a call-and-response pattern. The conservatory students formed a circle around them and tried to emulate their performance, while similarly playing large frame-drums, which are characteristically used in Sufi performances. Accordingly, the religious men were averse to using such secular instruments, as the ṭablah and the riqq, whose percussive qualities they considered incompatible with the feeling of reverence associated with the mystical performance. The students were instructed to play whenever they felt musically comfortable, and were allowed to stop if they found a certain meter too complex or difficult to follow. Eventually, the conservatory student, who received structured and often extremely rigorous class instruction, was able to assimilate some of the musical skills that the dervishes themselves had mastered.[20]

At the same time, the modern conservatory establishment represents a significant departure from the traditional ways of musical learning. Inspired by the European pedagogical model, the conservatory format tends to formalize, as well as limit the contact between the student and the teacher, or teachers. Furthermore, using European notation as a basis of instruction, the Arab musical curriculum may incorporate Western theory, Arab and Western solfège, and in some cases, courses in keyboard technique, in polyphony, and in "the harmonization of the Arab maqāmāt."[21] Most important perhaps, conservatories essentially teach precomposed pieces rather than improvisatory skills, which are relegated to the area of modal practice. The music student whose interest lies totally in the performance of traditional ṭarab music often joins a conservatory after he has already begun to absorb the elements of ṭarab from mere musical exposure or from informal contact with musical role models.

Furthermore, some ṭarab artists do not go to conservatories altogether, thus relying on extended methods of musical assimilation. Others pursue both formal and informal modes of learning either simultaneously or at different times in their lives. The latter situation seems to apply to a large number of contemporary artists whose skills and abilities are developed through a combination of the following: informal contact with other musicians; listening to recordings and radio broadcasts; private tutoring on an instrument; joining a private music academy or a government conservatory; singing or playing with a semi-professional group; learning pieces from published notated anthologies; and listening to criticism or praise from peer musicians. Moreover, actual performing remains an important mode of learning. I am often told by musicians that the nightclub is the best place to learn the trade. One Lebanese nāy player and nightclub veteran usually tells novice performers "roughing it up (*daʿk*) for a few years in the cabaret is what makes you a good musician."[22]

Today's ṭarab artists also tend to be musically eclectic. Many are either quite familiar with, or even well-versed in Western music. In fact, some

[20] Regarding instruction at this academy, namely *Nādī Shabāb al-ʿUrūbah li-al-Funūn wa-al-Tamthīl*, Mr. Kaspar stresses the rigor of the instruction and alludes to students who make mistakes or who are lax being separated momentarily and compelled to drill vigorously on their instruments and even to repeat certain patterns for extended periods of time. Incidentally, Kaspar's descriptions did not specify the sect that the dervishes belonged to. The information is from the same 1998 interview with Mr. Kaspar.

[21] I found that to be the case in Cairo in the early 1970s. A topic of continued interest for Egyptian music educators, instruction in maqām harmonization has probably continued throughout the ensuing years.

[22] From a conversation I had with this artist in Beirut in the early 1980s.

highly accomplished ṭarab artists are bi-musical, an example being Simon Shaheen. A violin and ʿūd virtuoso, Simon assimilated the rudiments of Arab music from his father, Ḥikmat Shaheen, who directed an Arab musical ensemble in Haifa. Simon also received formal training in European art music. Now living in New York, where he leads an active teaching, composing, and performing career, he explains that the two sides of his musicality coexist without one detracting from the other. "In the same recital I may switch from one idiom to the other. When I reset my violin strings from the Western to the Arab tuning, my mind makes the shift accordingly."[23]

My own musical learning is typical at least of those who grew up in post-World War II, pre-civil war, cosmopolitan Lebanon. As the following glimpse illustrates, my own experience with ṭarab was to a large degree informal and multi-tracked. The technical, social, and emotional facets of the ṭarab culture were assimilated gradually and through prolonged and unstructured ways. During my formative years, essentially from the late 1940s through the mid-1960s, I was exposed to three types of music simultaneously. One was the folk music of Ibl al-Saqī, the village of my birth in southern Lebanon, music that was performed by shepherds, Gypsies, and local farmers, at weddings and other festive occasions. Another type of music was the urban largely pan-Arab style. In this case, the modes of learning included listening to the radio, to my parents' 78-rpm-disc phonograph, to older amateur musicians including my mother and two maternal uncles who all performed either on the violin or ʿūd, and to one highly skilled buzuq player and maker from the same village. Meanwhile, I experienced Western music through a wide variety of means, including taking private lessons on the violin and listening to recordings. In fact, the phonograph discs I heard at home included such varied items as qaṣā'id by Shaykh Amīn Ḥasanayn of Egypt, early film songs by Muḥammad ʿAbd al-Wahhāb, tango hits, and symphonic classics.

In Beirut, my musical education was similarly multifaceted. There, I continued to receive Western musical training by taking music courses at the American University of Beirut, receiving music lessons at one of the city's private academies, and attending classes at the Lebanese National Conservatory. My Arab musical skills, however, were further developed through direct exposure to established local artists and by performing with various mainstream musicians in private and public venues, including Beirut's television stations.

[23] From a conversation I had with Simon Shaheen in Maine in the late 1980s. Incidentally, during the last twenty years or so I have performed with this artist frequently. Shaheen has produced a number of CDs, including *Turāth*, which features Near-Eastern instrumental classics. He has also performed on the CD *Taqāsīm*, which, released by Lyrichord Discs Inc., contains improvisation duets for the ʿūd, by Shaheen, and the buzuq, by Ali Jihad Racy.

My assimilation of the ṭarab culture occurred through informal musical encounters, some of which left lasting impressions. During the early 1960s my brother Khaled and I met frequently to play music with two highly talented friends, also brothers themselves, a violinist, and an ʿūd player. During our musical "jam sessions" at their house, our friends' elderly father, himself a retired performer, always sat quietly in a somewhat dim and distant corner of the room virtually unnoticed except for an occasional glimpse of his bald head and thick white mustache. Following our inclinations as young musicians, we played what was fashionable at the time, including Westernized introductions to the then current songs of Umm Kulthūm. Soon after we started to play, we usually heard a murmur from the dark corner. As the sons explained, the father was saying: *Qassim*! which literally meant, "Play taqāsīm!" or "Improvise!" To fulfill the father's requests, which we accepted with an odd combination of humor and respect, we took turns at playing traditional modal improvisations. But eventually we would slip back into our modernized renditions, soon to hear the murmur again. For us, the father embodied the ṭarab culture. Reaffirming the value of modal improvisation, he also represented a musical link between his generation and ours. His mediating role gave us direct access to a musical tradition that valued critical listening, spontaneous music-making, and direct interaction between performer and listener. Indirectly, it also commented on the multifaceted nature of Beirut's music in the 1960s.

Musicians' jargon

The traditional musical jargon provides insights into the ṭarab learning-process and sheds light on ṭarab entertainers as a professional group. Reminiscent of, and apparently rooted in, the earlier guild culture, the jargon is craft-based and essentially presents music as a type of manual labor. For example, it embraces such expressions as *shughl* which literally means "work," but denotes performing music especially in professional contexts. *Yimsuk ālah* or to "carry a tool," may also mean "to play an instrument," especially in a less formal, or "make-shift" performance, or when the performer is less skilled on the specific instrument being played, for example when he is asked to play an instrument that is not his main specialty. *Fīhā shughl*, or "it has work" is said of a musical piece with intricate workmanship. *Naḍhīf*, literally, "clean," describes a flawless rendition of a musical piece. The jargon also identifies the instrumentalists through craft-related expressions that point literally to the mechanical aspect of working or to the working tools themselves, for example: a *raqqāq* for a riqq player, a *qānūnjī* for a qānūn player, *nāyātī* for a nāy player, and so forth. In these expressions, the suffixes are similarly used in words that refer to the practitioners of manual professions in general.

Other usages may reflect a historical correlation between music and speech. For example, singing is referred to as "*qawl*," literally "saying." Similarly, the expression *yaqūl jumlah*, which is used for "singing a short musical passage" literally means "to utter a sentence."[24] The profession oriented words *muṭrib* (male singer) and *muṭribah* (female singer) are favored by the professional performers. These two expressions may be used by nonmusicians to ridicule or stereotype professional entertainers. However, they imply due recognition of the "learned," or professionally established, ṭarab vocalist. In fact, they are preferred over such potentially offensive designations as *mughannī* and *mughanniyah* which mean, "male singer" and "female singer" quite literally and are usually connotative of the less sophisticated or pedestrian public entertainer.[25]

The musical jargon promotes cohesion within the professional ṭarab community. It also establishes symbolic boundaries between two distinct yet mutually dependent groups, the musicians and the general public. Through specialized speech, the performer can reinforce his or her status of professional insider. By comparison, a person who uses ordinary speech or reacts to music through such passionate or romantic expressions as "beautiful," "sweet," "I could listen all night," may be recognized by the musicians as an outsider, but also as someone who is professionally nonthreatening, and in a more positive vein, as a faithful follower or supporter. Incidentally, the diehard musicians tend to be circumspect in their verbal, or for that matter, physical reactions to music, unless such reactions are shown out of politeness to encourage an amateur musician. Highly demonstrable gestures are usually the prerogative of the listening connoisseurs, and as such they tend to differentiate the ṭarab receiver from the ṭarab provider.

In recent decades, however, the musical jargon has lost a great deal of its consistency and currency. Not all young musicians seem accustomed to, or familiar with, the various in-group expressions. Furthermore, indigenous theoretical terms, such as the Arab and Persian names of the modal steps, are now intermingled with Western terminology, for example the European note-names. Also becoming indispensable are such designations as "bass," "treble," "reverb," and "echo," that are inspired by the ubiquitous technology of recording and sound amplification.

[24] Incidentally, in other Near Eastern traditions the song-speech correlation is prevalent. For example in Iraq, the term *qāriʾ*, literally, "one who reads" or "recites," describes the singer in the Iraqi maqām tradition, a usage that reminds us of the Persian term *khāndan* which refers to both reading and singing.

[25] For more information on these and other musical expressions and their connotations see Racy 1986.

Musical manners

In the ṭarab culture, artistry must be refined through proper socialization. Ideally speaking, performers and listeners are expected to observe what is generally known as *ādāb* (singular, *adab*), translated roughly as "manners" or "codes of behavior." Prescribing desirable conduct and emphasizing moral or professional virtues, ādāb rules have appeared in conjunction with various professional and religious groups, particularly Sufi orders. In the latter case, the ādāb have set behavioral guidelines, for example in relation to samāʿ and wajd.[26] Musical ādāb in particular, have addressed both the musicians and the listeners.

Musicians

The notion of a socially fit musician has deep historical roots. In the ʿAbbāsid era, the court singer was expected to possess qualities that made him a perfect social companion. On the basis of al-Iṣfahānī's *Kitāb al-Aghānī*, George Sawa points out that such an artist was appreciated for his role as a *nadīm*, or "close-companion." Quite often, he amused the ruler or patron and educated him about various aspects of life. He had to be knowledgeable, sociable, and entertaining.[27]

Concern about the performers' behavior was later expressed in a nineteenth century musical treatise written in Egypt by Muḥammad Shihāb al-Dīn (1795–1857) followed in the early twentieth century by a chapter on the subject in al-Khulaʿī's all-encompassing book on Arab music.[28] In this latter source, the author criticized what he described as the morally deplorable behaviors of musicians and listeners. He also lamented the musical entertainers' bad image in the eyes of the Egyptian public during and before al-Khulaʿī's time, a phenomenon incidentally well-observed by Edward Lane some seventy years earlier. Furthermore, the Egyptian author outlined what

[26] For such Sufi codes see al-Ghazālī (n.d.: 236–269), namely his chapter titled Kitāb Ādāb al-Samāʿ wa-al-Wajd (The Book of the Manners of Listening and Ecstasy) and al-Suhrawardī's *Kitāb al-Murīdīn* (*A Sufi Rule for Novices*) in Milson 1975. For a more recent version by Salāmah ibn Ḥasan Salāmah (b. 1867), founder of the *Ḥāmidiyyah Shādhiliyyah* order in Egypt, see Gilsenan 1973: 208–241.

[27] Sawa 1989: 119.

[28] Al-Khulaʿī's chapter (ca. 1904: 78–83) was titled, "Faṣl fī Ādāb al-Mughannī wa-al-Sāmiʿ" (Chapter on the Manners of the Singer and the Listener). Here, as in other parts of his book, al-Khulaʿī borrowed generously from ancient and medieval sources. He also refered to the discussions on *ādāb al-nadīm*, "the manners of the close companion" in Shihāb al-Dīn's earlier work. Notably, al-Khulaʿī's book appeared around the time when Salāmah compiled his Sufi rules.

he considered to be desirable social, moral, and musical attributes of musicians and audience members. Among the traits that he detested were the musicians' bitter professional jealousies and the prevalence of intoxication, especially among a group of performers known as *ṣahbajiyyah* (from *ṣahbāʾ*, a generic name for wine, or alcohol). The author similarly chided those who entertained at *qahāwī al-ḥashīsh*, or "ḥashīsh coffee-houses," a category of artists he considered particularly vulgar and ignorant of the principles of the musical art. Meanwhile, al-Khulaʿī addressed the composers whom he implored, among other things, to learn *muwashshaḥāt*, *bastāt*, and *adwār* (traditional compositional genres) in a variety of maqāmāt, to know the rhythmic modes well, and also to learn to appreciate the compositions of the foreigners, or *al-ajānib*, a term that basically refers to Westerners. "That will make it possible to tell what is good and what is bad in their music" (ca. 1904: 81).

The modern ṭarab culture tends to embrace comparable performer related ideals. Obviously now, and probably at al-Khulaʿī's time, practicing musicians learned about such ideals not from books and manuals but rather through extended processes of socialization. Furthermore, these standards may not be universally followed or lived up to, and may very well be exceptions to the rule. In reality, they may have always represented the less-common, albeit idealized, decorum. Nevertheless, they can be studied as part of a broader worldview, a prescriptive behavioral and moral ideology that comments on the visions, tensions, and contradictions that characterize the ṭarab culture.

The contemporary public, or more specifically the ideally minded listeners, embrace a variety of artist related criteria. Visual appeal is important. Elegance and fashion have played a noticeable role in the careers of leading singers and movie stars such as Muḥammad ʿAbd al-Wahhāb. Statements praising good conduct appear quite often in musicians' conversations, and similarly voiced are criticisms of bad behavior. Often bemoaned is greed over money and the musicians' attempt to undercut one another. In various gatherings it is common to hear such phrases as *al-mūsīqá akhlāq*, "music is good manners," and *al-fannān lāzim yakūn muʾaddab*, "the artist must be polite," or "well mannered." Likewise, a good muṭrib must be *ʿazīz al-nafs*, "of high morals," or "dignified" and *muḥāfiḍh ʿalá karāmtuh*, "preserving his own dignity." An immoral artist is said to constitute an *ihānah lil-fann*, "an insult to the art."

Likewise, generosity and self-negation are highly praised. Indeed many stories are told of singers donating their salaries to humanitarian causes or supporting needy fellow musicians. By the same token, a reputation of being stingy or tight-handed (*bakhīl*) can give an artist notoriety in artistic circles, although many famous ṭarab singers are known for their materialistic passions. Another common and frequently praised trait is wit. Modern artists, particularly instrumentalists tend to show great fondness for humor, and often possess a vast repertoire of jokes. Joke-telling, like jargon, tends to function as a mode of bonding among members of the same ensemble and among musicians in general. Sometimes, musicians are also lauded for their religious piety or reserved behavior. According to one of his elderly admirers, the early-twentieth-century qānūn player Muḥammad al-ʿAqqād (Sr.) was so conservative that he often became uncomfortable if he noticed a woman in the audience.[29] Many become more religious later in their lives, a phase during which their religiosity may inspire aversion to, and ultimately abandonment of music, at least as a professional pursuit.

Among the musical virtues is also good rapport with the audience. The singer, for example, must understand that his role is to please and provide ṭarab, as the word "muṭrib" clearly suggests. Musicians' behaviors and verbalizations betray a certain hierarchy of roles. Usually, the patrons are ranked on the top and then come the patrons' guests, particularly those distinguished by social or economic rank, although tacitly a good portion of the performer's attention is directed toward the listening connoisseurs in the audience. Within the performing ensembles, the muṭrib, who is typically the most highly paid, enjoys the main prerogative and responsibility of communicating with the listeners or of shaping the content of the performance in ways that satisfy the audience as a whole.

The above social hierarchy notwithstanding, ṭarab musicians may not always fulfill the wishes of their listeners and patrons. For example, a celebrated muṭrib may resent being asked by an audience member to perform a song by a rival artist or by a lesser singer or even to sing a song that is totally incompatible with his own style. Some musicians expressed a great deal of respect for one highly established Syrian singer because he refused to honor the request of a politically influential yet musically uninitiated listener to perform one of the later hits of Umm Kulthūm. The singer politely declined on the basis that he only sang his own *lawn*, or "style" (literally, color). Accomplished musicians may also proclaim that they are "amateurs," or *huwāt*, in order to show that they perform only for their own gratification and furthermore to justify their refusal to perform in less dignified contexts.

Indeed, certain artists have been viewed as role models to be emulated and admired. The medieval epochs have presented us with numerous such exemplars. And similarly, the last hundred-and-fifty years have witnessed many highly attractive personalities, the musician written about most proverbially being the Egyptian ʿAbduh al-Ḥāmūlī.[30] As portrayed by music historians, ʿAbduh fits the profile of the gentleman musician. His personal

[29] From personal conversation with Maḥmūd Raʾfat in Cairo in 1972.

[30] For writings on al-Ḥāmūlī, see al-Khulaʿī ca. 1904, Rizq ca. 1936 and ca. 1938, Mansī 1965, al-Jundī 1984, and Kāmil 1971.

Egyptian singer ʿAbduh al-Ḥāmūlī (1841–1901). From al-Khulaʿī ca. 1904.

attributes, the auspicious milieu he lived in, and his musical abilities all made him a legendary figure for the succeeding generations. We are told that he became a favored court companion to Khedive Ismāʿīl (r. 1863–1879), whom ʿAbduh accompanied on some official visits to Istanbul, where this celebrated singer reportedly sang before the Ottoman Sultan. He possessed charisma and physical charm and appeared fashionably dressed in a modern Western suit usually with the traditional fez, or headdress. He was pious, conservative, and self-respecting, having once resisted the Khedive's insistence to have the celebrated female singer Almaḏḥ, by then ʿAbduh's wife, sing at the court. Furthermore, he was generous, chivalrous, and supportive of his fellow musicians. He was also endowed with phenomenal musical talent and a powerful voice that exerted tremendous emotional effect upon the listeners. ʿAbduh was both a prolific composer who had to his credit dozens of adwār, and a musical innovator known for having introduced new maqāmāt into Arab music. Al-Ḥāmūlī was the subject of numerous elegiac essays and poems by Aḥmad Shawqī, Khalīl Miṭrān and others.[31] Furthermore, one of Cairo's streets was named after him.[32]

Comparable attributes have distinguished more recent artists. In her extensive study on Umm Kulthūm, the Egyptian author Niʿmāt Fuʾād attributed this artist's successful career to her exceptional personality, as well as to her musicianship. Accordingly, when Umm Kulthūm entered the public arena, she was a model of female decency. As a woman, her conservative religious background, the image of chastity she projected, and the full protection of her own family all accorded her great respect. Accordingly, "when she stood up to sing, there was in front of her an invisible sign that read 'Do not touch!'" (Fuʾād 1976: 174). She was learned and cultured, refined and faithful to her art in ways that differentiated her from the female singer Munīrah al-Mahdiyyah (d. 1965), who reportedly had frequently returned to the public their admission fees because "she was not in the mood for singing" (*mā lahāsh mazāj*) or because the number of attendants was too small. Umm Kulthūm, whose career was associated with great composers and lyricists, was also known for supporting various national causes, and on a personal level, for being remarkably witty.

Listeners

The idea of promoting a cadre of good listeners has concerned the musicians and the musical critics alike. In the early twentieth century, al-Khulaʿī

31 Some of these elegies are included in Rizq ca. 1936: 77–92.

32 Kāmil 1971: 44.

stressed that the public must be cognizant of the musicians' needs, how they feel when they perform and what circumstances are best suited for their performing. He also emphasized that such knowledge is only useful when combined with good listening habits and a positive outlook toward music and musicians.

More specifically, the listeners were implored to refrain from disrupting the performances by voicing their musical requests. As he explained, when performing the musician becomes deeply attuned to the maqām of the performance, a clear reference to the state of salṭanah, or modal ecstasy. Therefore, a request would be improper, particularly if the requested piece was in a different maqām. Accordingly, requests must be made before the instruments are tuned.[33] Al-Khulaʿī added that the singer does not have time to fulfill everybody's demand, and moreover, "if the singer was not possessed by ṭarab himself he would not be able to instill ṭarab in anyone" (ca. 1904: 83). Further, criticism was directed against false pretense. In other words, audience members should refrain from pretending that they know "the fundamentals of the modal science," for example, saying, "please repeat (*Allāh kamān*) this phrase in [mode] Jahārkāh, when in reality that phrase is in [mode] ʿIrāq" (ca. 1904: 83). Similarly, al-Khulaʿī spoke against audience members who merely pretend that they are enjoying the music, a stance that reminds us of al-Ghazālī's displeasure with those who display disingenuous ecstasy.

Furthermore, al-Khulaʿī deplored drunkenness among the listeners, the vulgarity of "mediocre poets" who interrupt the performance by reciting bad poetry, the duels of curses and ridicules that "our people call joking (*tankīt*)," coming to the performance merely to show off one's apparel or jewelry or to gaze at windows, through which women may be noticed in their privacy, and showing lack of interest in the music, for example, "bothering to bestow upon the singer every half an hour an utterance of *āh*! [a gesture of appreciation] totally out of context" (ca. 1904: 84). On the contrary, as the author maintains, the listener has an obligation to take into consideration the feelings of the performer, and to instill within him the right mood through affectionate words of approval. "That is what gives the singer the sense of comfort and the right disposition to engender ṭarab within you inasmuch as God [at the moment] has enabled him" (ca. 1904: 83).

Modern critiques of the public are not very different from those outlined by al-Khulaʿī. Often lamented is the patrons' indifference toward, or disrespect of, the musicians, or their reluctance to remunerate them adequately.

[33] The sudden introduction of a new mode would have been technically difficult since, at al-Khulaʿī's time, the qānūn did not have tuning levers and had to be tuned ahead of time to the mode of the performance to come. Further information on the qānūn and its tuning is included in the discussions on pitch in Chapter 4.

A. Toscanini

Also bemoaned is a general ignorance about the exigencies of music ma In musicians' circles it is frequently said that the listeners need to be [illegible] appreciative of the performers' need to have an ambiance appropriate for producing affective music. Often cited is the lack of truly active performer–listener communication and the domination of one of two extremes: apathy (the worst enemy of ṭarab according to most musicians) or excessive excitation, often marked by drunkenness, dancing, clapping, and singing loudly with the muṭrib, antics that may stifle the delicacy of the musical process and annoy those interested in a finer level of listening. Once I asked a famous violinist from Lebanon why he did not play taqāsīm in public anymore and instead presented medleys mostly of metrically animated popular tunes that the public often dances to. His answer was that in the old days when he used to play, people used to listen attentively and cry, but now they "listen through their feet."[34] In a related vein, one Egyptian musical connoisseur described to me Umm Kulthūm's disappointment with her audience when she sang somewhere in North Africa. According to the description, she sensed right away that the audience was by and large "not with it," because it exploded with cheers and whistles at times uncalled for from the musical point of view. The audience also showed no noticeable reactions precisely when such reactions would have been musically and emotionally pertinent, for example, at a climactic point following a powerful cadence.[35] As implied by the report, proper listening requires the display of reactions that are both genuine and idiomatically correct.

The performers' self-image as public entertainers tends to embrace a certain duality. This is most notable in recent decades, at a time when the Arab musical scene has been dominated by new, popular-oriented styles. Typically, ṭarab musicians accommodate the public's common musical denominator, but also express such sentiments as "that is what they want," or "that is what goes (*māshī*) these days," or "we have to satisfy the needs of the market (*al-sūq*)." As they do so, they tend to live in two separate worlds: professional reality marked by what may be perceived as artistic expediency, and an ideal or imagined world of music making. The latter world is lived somewhat vicariously through memorable past experiences, or virtually through conversations, reminiscences, and at times informal jam sessions with other musicians who share their artistic worldviews.

[34] From an informal conversation that took place in Los Angeles in the early 1980s.
[35] From an informal conversation in Doha Qatar in 1988.

The Sammiʿah

The colloquial word *sammīʿah* (singular, *sammīʿ*) refers to the diehard ṭarab listeners, or literally, those who listen well.[36] Derived from the verb *samiʿa*, "to hear" or "to listen," this usage underscores the symbolic importance of listening in Arab and Near-Eastern civilizations in general. Musicians usually praise audiences and individual listeners through expressions that are linguistically and conceptually related to listening. Among such expressions are *biyismaʿū*, "they listen," and *biyismaʿ kwayyis*, "he listens well." By the same token, a good listener may politely ask a musician to perform by using listening-related expressions such as *sammiʿnā*, "allow us to hear," or something like "delight our ears," and *kullinā sāmʿīn*, or *kullinā samaʿ*, both meaning "we are all listening" or "attentively ready to listen." As part of the musicians' jargon, the concept of sammīʿah appears frequently in musicians' conversations and represents one of the most important entities within the ṭarab culture.

As theaters, radio stations, and record companies provide the economic base for ṭarab making, the sammīʿah form the emotional and artistic lifeline of ṭarab artistry. Although the dividing line between them and the rest of the public is not always clear cut, the sammīʿah tend to share certain recognizable characteristics. Generally, they constitute a minority within the ṭarab public. They may either cluster together as a substantial constituency in a small musical gathering or may be "sprinkled" as individuals or small "pockets" of individuals within large audiences at public performances. They may come from different social backgrounds as well as include some amateur performers. However, in terms of their common interest and comparable levels of musical initiation, the sammīʿah can be viewed as an in-group, somewhat like members of a Sufi order, or brotherhood.

A sammīʿ is believed to have a special talent for listening, a gift that has been developed through musical exposure and proper polish. He or she is considered naturally predisposed to feeling and responding emotionally to the music, an attribute symbolically illustrated by al-Khulaʿī's aforementioned anecdote about the sage and the babies. The sammīʿ's unmistakable proclivity toward listening can be illustrated by the following example. A young man from Lebanon spoke to me about business trips he made to Egypt with a business partner. As he put it, whenever they walked across the crowded Taḥrīr Square in Cairo, at times when religious chanting was being broadcast through loudspeakers he would stop and listen very attentively. He explained that for him, the experience was profoundly transforming.

[36] The feminine of sammīʿ is sammīʿah, which is also the plural form, either masculine or feminine.

"Although he and I are from the same culture, my business partner totally ignored the chanting and never stopped. I used to lose sight of him completely and end up walking alone."[37]

The sammīʿah tend to be musically informed. Many, for example, are totally familiar with the main performance genres, and take full notice of the technical maneuvers that musicians make, although much of their knowledge is intuitive rather than theoretical. For that matter, those who do not perform may not recognize the various maqāmāt by name. Furthermore, the ability of the sammīʿah to listen and feel is manifested in a culturally established vocabulary of gestures, facial expressions, body language, and verbal exclamations, that all express their genuinely felt ṭarab sensations.

In context, the sammīʿah put their musical knowledge into practice. Forming the basis for meaningful performer–listener interactions, their knowledge leads to higher musical expectations and thus prompts the artist to excel. Describing to me the relationship between the informed listener and the performing artist in earlier decades, the celebrated Aleppo singer Ṣabāḥ Fakhrī (b. 1933) used a phrase commonly heard in ṭarab-related conversations, namely *muḥāsabah*, which means "following attentively and judiciously."[38] A listener who exercises muḥāsabah through appropriately communicated gestures is considered musically connected, as well as ecstatically involved.

Furthermore, cognizant of the performer's mental and emotional needs when performing, the sammīʿ may either refrain from making musical requests or may voice such requests politely and at musically opportune times. During an informal gathering of friends to honor the late Egyptian-trained Tunisian singer ʿUlayyah al-Tūnisiyyah (d. 1990), I was invited to play the ʿūd. As soon as I picked up the instrument, one young man in the group requested that I perform something by Farīd al-Aṭrash. However, that person's request drew an immediate, but polite admonition from ʿUlayyah herself. As she put it, "you don't tell the *fannān*, or "artist," what to play. You let him play what is on his mind [or agreeing with his disposition, *illī bi-mazājuh*]."[39] This reference to the artist's tendency to perform best and most comfortably music that agrees with his mood at the time of performing, reminds us of al-Khulaʿī's advice to young listeners some eighty years earlier and underscores the ecstatic implications of good listening habits.

Finally, the ecstatic reactions of the sammīʿah may vary in intensity and in the manner in which they are expressed, depending upon the music itself, the context of listening, and the disposition of the listener himself or herself. However, when they listen, the sammīʿah usually display distinct musical

[37] From an informal conversation in the middle 1980s.

[38] From an interview with Ṣabāḥ Fakhrī in Los Angeles on January 24, 1990.

[39] This musical gathering took place in Los Angeles toward the middle 1980s.

focus. They also seem genuinely to feel the music and to express what is felt in ways that enhance the creative flow of the performance. Their mode of responding to the music reflects a certain composure and betrays an equilibrium between emotional expressivity and rational control. Their demeanor is not unlike the mystical trait that al-Ghazālī had extolled, namely to be serene on the outside, yet from the inside, to be agitated by the flame of divine love.[40]

[40] Al-Ghazālī, n.d.: 266.

3 Performance

Throughout Arab history, musicians, philosophers, theologians, biographers, and mystics have for various reasons expressed interest in the musical process: where music is performed, when, for whom, and on what occasions. It may be sufficient to browse through the writings of al-Iṣfahānī, al-Ghazālī, and al-Khulaʿī and in the popular music magazines of Lebanon and Egypt to sense the centrality of the performance event in the ṭarab culture. To a large extent, the visions of those who have prescribed ādāb for listeners and artists, or who have explained how music affects different individuals, have been directed toward the performing process. Whether at an ʿAbbāsid court, or a modern Cairo nightclub, the performance event is recognized for its multiple connotations, as well as for its distinctive social and artistic character.

Early venues

In the late Ottoman Period, which extended into the early twentieth century, the musical life of cities such as Cairo, Damascus, and Aleppo centered around a few typical performance venues. Sufi groups, usually with leading vocalists, accompanying choruses, and in some cases instrumentalists, performed on various religious holidays. Secular performances were also prevalent. Some were hosted by wealthy individuals or local government officials. Reminiscent of the medieval court performances, these musical events shared some overall characteristics. They tended to be exclusive, being attended mostly by the patrons and their families and friends, and taking place within the confines of the patrons' homes or the rulers' palaces or courts. In some instances, the musicians were the protégés of the patrons and enjoyed their direct financial and moral support. Often such events occurred in contexts of festivity, for example, wedding parties, circumcisions, religious holidays, and receptions of officials. They entertained music lovers and added glamour and prestige to the patron's assembly, or *majlis*.

Ṭarab making was also enjoyed on a more popular level. It was often featured at the *sahrah* (or evening musical party) typically held as part of a faraḥ, or wedding celebration. A prime arena for Egypt's guild performers, the sahrah was closely associated with takht entertainment. The patron or host was not necessarily a musical connoisseur himself and neither was the hosting family necessarily musical. In addition, the interactions between the patron and the musicians may have been indirect, and based on the intervention of a guild master, although often the musicians, who traditionally performed in small (takht) ensembles, were well-known to their clients. Held either in the open courtyard of the client's home or in a colorful, cloth tent (*khaymah*, also called *sirdāq*, or *shādir*), specially erected outside the client's house, the performance was not strictly private or exclusive and tended to attract individuals from surrounding neighborhoods. Thus, the musical parties were likely to include non-sammʿīah, or even individuals who displayed the types of conduct that al-Khulaʿī had bitterly criticized. In fact, this Egyptian writer stated clearly that, to his displeasure, such behaviors were predominant at wedding parties.

On the other hand, the wedding provided ideal conditions for ṭarab making. As a collective celebration marked by socializing and feasting, it generated an atmosphere of elation (*basṭ*, or *kayf*) perfectly suited for producing and listening to ṭarab music. Also physically, the courtyard or the tent constituted a relatively self-contained setting for the ṭarab process, thus facilitating intimate contact and direct communication between the performers and the listeners. Furthermore, the wedding performances were not devoid of sammīʿah, many of whom followed the musicians faithfully from one performance to another. For example, the famous nineteenth-century Egyptian singer Shaykh Sālim al-ʿAjūz, who lived for over a hundred years and continued to sing throughout the later years of his life, maintained a group of sammīʿah who came with him to his performance locations throughout Egypt.[1] Such a practice was followed by most early twentieth-century celebrities, Munīrah al-Mahdiyyah and others. Older musicians and music historians speak proverbially of such sammīʿah, particularly of their high level of musical initiation and positive influences upon the performers. In the same vein, writers such as Qisṭandī Rizq and Aḥmad Abū al-Khiḍr Mansī, both of whom had witnessed the zenith of the so-called *qadīm* (literally "old") musical tradition of late nineteenth- and early twentieth-century Cairo, used highly laudatory, sometimes poetic, language to describe the captivating musical renditions created by ʿAbduh al-Ḥāmūlī and others at wedding parties.

It is difficult to ascertain the frequency of wedding performances in pre-World-War-I cities such as Cairo, Damascus, and Aleppo, or whether all weddings had ṭarab music, or even professional musical entertainment

1 Fuʾād n.d.: 158.

Early recording-artist Shaykh Yūsuf al-Manyalāwī (1847–1911), front center, and his takht ensemble, with a phonograph in the background. To the front right is Muḥammad alʿAqqād (Sr.) holding a qānūn, which used no tuning levers; to the front left is Ibrāhīm Salūn holding a Stroh violin, which was specially designed for acoustic recording. A publicity photo.

altogether. In fact, weddings were known to be seasonal and irregular. Reportedly, in order to have more access to performing and thus to keep his voice from getting "all rusted," Shaykh Yūsuf al-Manyalāwī (1847–1911) volunteered every Tuesday night to sing at a *ḥadrah*, or Sufi ceremony, held at Sitt Fāṭimah al-Nabawiyyah in one of Cairo's quarters. Accordingly, the wedding was "the outlet for everyone, sammīʿah and ṭarab singers alike" (Fuʾād n.d. 157). Furthermore, the wedding was the main arena for the *ʿawālim*, or female entertainers, whose performances are known to have incorporated ṭarab, as well as folk and popular song and dance entertainment. As indicated by a number of nineteenth-century Western travelers,[2] the female wedding performances were no less lively and ecstatic than the men's.

Another context prevalent in the large cities, was the *qahwah*, or coffee house. Toward the mid-nineteenth century, Lane described the Cairo coffee house as a popular place which males of modest social and economic backgrounds had frequented. In it, the shāʿir, a poet-singer, typically accompanied himself on the *rabāb al-shāʿir*, or "poet's fiddle,"[3] as he sang traditional epics, such as the one about the medieval Arabian hero Abū Zayd al-Hilālī. By the end of the century, there were numerous coffee houses that presented ṭarab related repertoires and had attracted a certain segment of the ṭarab public.

Although fulfilling specific social needs, the *qahāwī* (plural of *qahwah*) were portrayed negatively by critics such as al-Khulaʿī. To begin with, music coffee-houses were public and often located in less prestigious, or morally suspicious quarters of the cities. Furthermore, the entertainers included female singers and dancers, who were frequently stigmatized as prostitutes.[4] Such considerations would have given these establishments a dubious image within the sexually segregated society of the time. Furthermore, the coffee houses, within which alcohol was often consumed, were considered unbecoming of respectable performers. It is not surprising that some celebrated

2 See for example Lane 1860/1973: 355 and Ebers 1879: 316.

3 In nineteenth-century Egypt, the *rabāb* was an upright fiddle that had a quadrilateral soundbox with the front side covered with skin. The poets are known to have used one string on their instrument, whereas the singers used two, their instrument being identified as *rabāb al-mughannī*, "the singer's rabāb." Incidentally, by the early twentieth century, Egyptian folk musicians had abandoned the quadrilateral fiddle in favor of the *kamanjah*, a spike fiddle that was originally used by the urban musician; see Lane 1860/1973: 356. The adopted instrument was renamed *rabāb* or *rabābah*, after the older folk instrument. Meanwhile, the Western violin had already replaced the *kamanjah* as an urban (takht) instrument and usurped its name.

4 As Karin van Nieuwkerk shows, the female staff of the Cairo café-chantant, or early nightclub, usually sat with male customers and enticed them to purchase alcohol. Although many were not really prostitutes, they had to contend with the public image of them as fallen women (1995: 43–99).

takht musicians refrained from working in the coffee houses except out of dire financial necessity. [5]

During the early twentieth century, the domain of public entertainment was expanded. In Egypt, which was under British control between 1882 and 1922, the Azbakiyyah Garden was a prime location for open air military-band performances and European-modeled nightclubs. Furthermore, in addition to the traditional coffee houses, the city witnessed the rise of Western style theaters, some of which were managed by women and had held weekly matinee performances for female audiences.[6] Presenting various music and dance genres including ṭarab, musical comedy, and vaudeville, these places usually carried such modern and somewhat formal designations as *masraḥ* (theater), or *tiyātrū* (from Italian for theater), *kāzīnū* (casino), and *ṣāla* (hall, or auditorium).

These were some of the main venues that dominated the ṭarab world before and during the early twentieth century, but continued to exist in one form or another in later decades. Other venues must have also existed. There is no reason to exclude such less formally structured events as the intimate musical gatherings of connoisseurs and the private performances of the amateur musicians and apprentices.

Ṭarab, ḥashīsh, and alcohol

Studies on social and artistic life in the nineteenth and early twentieth centuries reveal a certain association between music making and intoxication. By exploring this association, we may gain insights into the nature of the ṭarab process, and for that matter, dispel some of the stereotypical misconceptions about ṭarab music. According to various historical accounts, ḥashīsh use in the region is centuries old and is known to have existed among members of certain Sufi orders.[7] Referred to as, "the poor man's wine," it was eloquently described and often praised by poets, especially in

5 For example, one Egyptian biographer was saddened that Amīn al-Buzarī, a celebrated nāy player, at one time member of al-Ḥāmūlī's takht ensemble, was obliged to perform in a coffee house due to pressing economic need aggravated by the gradual loss of his eyesight. We are told that al-Buzarī, who came from a Christian background, was the son of an eminent ministry-of-foreign-affairs official who was in turn a companion to Khedive Ismāʿīl. Al-Buzarī's grandfather was the Khedive's special physician (Mansī 1965: 250–253).

6 See Danielson 1991a.

7 For example, we are told that in Egypt the use of ḥashīsh became established toward the middle of the twelfth century, during the Ayyūbid period, through the arrival of mystics from Syria. See al-Maghrabī 1963: 56–59 and Khalifa 1975: 199. Similarly, it is said that in Islamic history hemp has been somewhat tolerated because many Muslims have felt that, unlike alcohol, it was not explicitly outlawed by Qur'anic law (Zakī 1986: 189).

the Sufi literary circles of the thirteenth century.[8] Similarly, Lane noted the prevalence of hemp and to a lesser extent opium, especially among musicians.[9] Moreover, in Egypt the local ḥashīsh culture has been linked to a type of "folklore" that incorporated humor, poetry, and music, as well as interactive drug-related etiquettes.[10] In fact, ḥashīsh was the topic of numerous popular songs, particularly in the 1920s and 1930s, a period that witnessed an increase in the use of drugs, including cocaine and opium.[11]

Ḥashīsh songs embraced a variety of characteristic themes. Usually speaking on behalf of the *ḥashshāshīn*, or ḥashīsh users, they described this social group's carefree lifestyle and portrayed the drug and its effect in delightful, often humorous ways. For example, in a song by Shaykh Sayyid Darwīsh, presented in one of the plays of the famous comedian Najīb al-Rīḥānī, a group of actors who play the role of ḥashīsh addicts appear sickly and poverty stricken, but sing gleefully about ḥashīsh and intoxication. Furthermore, in this song, criticism of the political and social system, as well as vows to give up ḥashīsh, are voiced.[12]

Comparably, in Arab literary history alcohol became the topic of a poetry genre called *khamriyyāt*, roughly, "wine poetry," from *khamr*, a generic name for "wine," or "alcohol." In popular culture, the consumption of alcohol has occurred in conjunction with music making and within a variety of contexts, ranging from medieval ʿAbbāsid circles, as al-Iṣfahānī's portrayals testify, to modern nightclubs. Lane mentioned that although alcohol was forbidden by Islam, a few Egyptians drank it discreetly and that a local liquor called *buza* (or *būḍḥah*) was typically consumed by the Nile boatmen and other members of the lower classes. He added that the male professional musicians (*ālātiyyah*) of his time tended to drink excessively:

> They are people of very dissolute habits; and are regarded as scarcely less disreputable characters than the public dancers. They are, however, hired at most grand entertainments, to amuse the company; and on these occasions they are usually supplied with brandy, or other spirituous liquors, which they sometimes drink until they can no longer sing, nor strike a chord. (1860/1973: 354)

The above associations between intoxication and music foreshadow al-Khulaʿī's admonitions against musicians' drug abuse. They also anticipate the present-day link between music and the use of mind altering substances. In the modern ṭarab culture, ḥashīsh and alcohol are sometimes used in connection with music-making. Listeners, particularly in festive musical

8 al-Maghrabī 1963: 56–57 and Ḥusayn 1964: 171–175.
9 Lane 1860/1973: 335.
10 al-Maghrabī 1963: 56–59 and Khalifa 1975: 199.
11 al-Maghrabī 1963: 155.
12 Ibid.

gatherings, may treat such substances as part of the overall listening "ritual" and use them to promote a feeling of *basṭ*, or elation. [13]

In certain ways, the intoxicative and the musical experiences are comparable. For example, the typical ḥashīsh smoking session, like a musical gathering, is collective and attended by individuals sharing compatible interests and inclinations. In essence, both are "in-group" activities. Also, in general ways, the two processes are patterned and marked by distinctive group behaviors and interactions.[14]

Moreover, both experiences are highly transformative, and may produce a variety of physical, mental, and emotional reactions. For example, despite the prevailing sense of togetherness, the state of ḥashīsh intoxication prompts a wide gamut of individual behaviors, thus reminding us of the musical anecdote about the babies related by al-Khulaʿī to describe the various inborn reactions to music. Stating that the participants' innate personality traits and tendencies are emphasized when intoxication occurs, al-Maghrabī mentions several types of responses: elation (*inbisāṭ*), melancholy accompanied by wandering thoughts (*shurūd*), and others.[15]

More specifically, an experiential link seems to exist between ḥashīsh and music as an auditory experience. As various studies indicate, the linkage is manifested in three related ways: 1) the intoxicated individual experiencing an urge to sing or perform music; 2) the intoxicated person similarly experiencing a strong desire to listen to music; and 3) that person developing altered perceptions of what he performs or listens to. These transformational modes seem to explain the often heard concept of *aghānī taḥshīsh*, or "ḥashīsh-using songs." This term generally points to a loosely defined musical trait found in songs which may or may not have been created or performed under the influence of ḥashīsh. What is implied here is that the drug causes the melody to become more fluid, or metrically and accentually more flexible, so as to "shadow" rather than rigidly follow the underlying meter or accent. And similarly, the textual delivery becomes somewhat slurred. Reminiscent of, or perhaps induced by intoxication, such musical looseness is known to generate irresistible ecstasy.

Furthermore, the two worlds share certain verbal expressions. In both ḥashīsh and ṭarab cultures, elation is described through such key words as *baṣṭ* and *kayf*.[16] Also, the modern ṭarab public utilizes a number of

13 According to Khalifa (1975: 203), modern ḥashīsh users look down upon the consumers of alcohol and various hard drugs on the basis that the consumption of these substances becomes an addiction and causes people to lose their mind and their respect, not to mention also, alcohol is strictly forbidden by Islam.

14 For details on the typical ḥashīsh-smoking session, or *jalsat al-ḥashīsh*, see al-Maghrabī 1963: 154–156 and 283–321.

15 al-Maghrabī 1963: 155.

16 According to Lane, the word *basṭ* was used to describe a type of ḥashīsh preparation (1860/1973: 333–334). Similarly, the word *kayf* is used to describe a certain type of ḥashīsh.

intoxication related metaphors to describe the ṭarab state. Accordingly, both ḥashīsh and ṭarab music are felt physically as well as emotionally. Music that instills profound ṭarab sensations is sometimes described as *bitʿabbī al-raʾs*, or "it fills the head," an expression also used for describing the effects of intoxicating substances, especially the smoking of ḥashīsh. Such parallelism underlies Muhammad Asad's poetically engaging description of a takht performance he had attended in Damascus. The author discussed the intoxicating powers of the music, albeit in a symbolic or mystical sense:

> It rather seemed to me that I was not so much listening to a musical performance as witnessing an exciting happening. Out of the chirping tones of the string instruments there grew up a new rhythm, rising in a tense spiral and then, suddenly, falling down – like the rhythmic rising and falling of a metallic object, faster and slower, softer and stronger: in dispassionate persistence, in endless variations, this one uninterrupted happening, this acoustic phenomenon which trembled in a restrained *intoxication*, grew up, spread out powerfully, *went to the head*: and when it suddenly broke off in the midst of a crescendo (how early, much too early!) I knew: I was imprisoned [italics mine]. (Asad 1954: 142)

However, despite such parallels and overlaps between the two realms, ṭarab is not necessarily drug bound or intoxication based. Whether out of religious observance or mere physical and mental aversion, the ṭarab culture embraces a distinctly purist and drug-free approach to the creation and appreciation of music. Islamic mysticism, as demonstrated by the authoritative writings of al-Ghazālī and others, have focused the novice's attention on the power of samāʿ, in other words, on religious ecstasy that is musically induced. And similarly, the various themes and images of wine and intoxication are treated primarily as metaphors for spiritual transcendence. For that matter, we may look at the puritanical anti-drug stance of al-Khulaʿī, an accomplished musician and composer himself. Biographers and elder musicians point out that many late-nineteenth- and early-twentieth-century artists were totally averse to mind altering substances. Muḥammad al-ʿAqqād (Jr.) recalled that as a rule early-twentieth-century music masters drank just enough to establish a condition of basṭ. He explained that "if you are in an elated mood you do not get drunk easily, but if you are not you are more likely to get drunk and lose control of the music." Establishing a distinction between "emotional conditioning" and outright drunkenness, al-ʿAqqād also indicated that those who refrained from drinking were viewed as noteworthy exemplars.[17]

[17] From the conversation with Muḥammad al-ʿAqqād, in Los Angeles in 1984. ʿAqqad's statement can be illustrated by a specific incident humorously described by the late well-known Egyptian composer and singer Sayyid Makkāwī. Accordingly, a well-known early-twentieth-century singer consumed hemp oil before performing at a wedding tent and consequently completely forgot the words of the song as his chorus members kept waiting for him to start singing. From a conversation I had with Mr. Makkāwī in Los Angeles on May 30, 1994.

In today's culture, the same holds true. Indeed, a large number of well-established singers and instrumentalists do not use alcohol or ḥashīsh, and in a few cases do not drink coffee or smoke tobacco. Many stress that although alcohol and drugs may reduce inhibition, they also pose a threat to concentration, particularly when the performer must render precomposed works accurately and in full coordination with other members of the ensemble. One young violinist adds that music is capable of producing its own "high." Notwithstanding the historical connections and metaphoric links between music-making and intoxication, it is basically shown that the musical experience stands on its own.

Modern contexts

Since the 1920s, the contexts of performing have become increasingly varied. Furthermore, through the modern media networks they have grown more interconnected. The different venues have fed into one another, and typically artists who have performed at live events have also recorded commercially and in some cases appeared in film. Obviously, listening to ṭarab music has extended beyond the conventional contexts of music making. The media have created new and unprecedented settings for listening, and in significant ways have changed the overall ṭarab practice, including the live music.

The informal gathering

In cities such as Cairo, Beirut, Damascus, Aleppo, and Baghdad, performing and listening to ṭarab music may take place in intimate social settings. Musicians and listeners speak of a *jalsah* or *qaʿdah*, both meaning "a sitting" or "get together," or *jalsat ṭarab*, roughly, "ṭarab gathering."[18] In some ways reminiscent of the musical sessions that took place in the confines of the medieval courts, jalsah gatherings have certain common characteristics. They may occur regularly, for example, on a certain day of the week or month, but often take place irregularly and without much preparation, as friendly encounters in which music "happens to occur." A *jalsah* usually takes place in the evening – in this case, it might be called sahrah, or "evening party." It is safe to say that ṭarab events are largely nocturnal. The consumption of food, appetizers, and sometimes alcoholic beverages is very

18 The word "*jalsah*" comes from *jalasa*, "to sit," and is linguistically related to the word *majlis*, namely "place of sitting," or "assembly."

common. Usually consisting of no more than ten or fifteen men or women, and in many cases both, a jalsah group typically meets in a private home. The group members may either take turns in hosting the event, or may gather primarily in the house of a music-loving, relatively well-to-do host. The attendants may come from a variety of social and professional backgrounds. In some cases, however, they are united mainly by family ties or by vocational affiliations, factors that do not always guarantee compatibility in the levels of musical initiation and may even dampen the overall musical atmosphere, as illustrated by the following example.

One gathering I attended in Cairo in 1971 took place on a late afternoon at the home of a man who pursued a highly respected nonmusical profession, but was also an accomplished performer on the buzuq. The group consisted of about a dozen individuals, including other professionals, government employees, and one music theorist who also played the ʿūd. The jalsah conversations touched upon a variety of social and intellectual issues, but also tangentially upon topics related to music theory and instrument making, and were followed by a performance of taqāsīm by the host. The musical performance may have occurred partly due to the presence of the theorist-musician, who had brought me along and who introduced me as a music performer and researcher. It was clear to me that the attendants, whose relationship to the host was based on professional rather than musical collegiality, were mostly non-sammīʿah. Indications that the ambiance was tilted toward polite, non-interactive, and non-ecstatic "listening" were made obvious through the reserved demeanor of the guests and through the performer's own behavior. After starting to play his instrument, the host stopped every few minutes to make brief comments. His verbalizations, covering issues related to the philosophy of music and to the history of the instrument he was playing, may have been prompted by a desire on the host's part to maintain some form of polite communication with his musically uninclined guests. However, during that same year, I heard a recording of a live performance that the host himself had given at a small theater at the Cairo Music Academy. The recording captured an outstanding display of artistry before a lively audience that responded with well-synchronized verbal exclamations and had clearly incorporated a large contingency of sammīʿah.

Ideally, at musical gatherings, the participants listen attentively and appear totally immersed in the process. Furthermore, the performers are able to determine or negotiate the times appropriate for them to perform and to choose repertoires they feel inspired or prepared to perform with relatively little interruption from the listeners. The performances emphasize small ensemble or solo playing. The instrumentalists may take turns in playing, or may perform together, for example when accompanying a singer. Traditional, especially improvisatory, genres are frequently chosen.

Moreover, the typical atmosphere of the jalsah is amicable. For one thing, the performers tend to feel at home while performing nonprofessionally within their own circles of friends, admirers, students, and family members. The event itself may become a memorable experience, one that the individual participants talk about or remember for years. At the end of one lively musical evening that took place in my parents' house during the early 1960s, one elder music lover commented: "these moments will go with me to the grave." In the aftermath of such a performance the attendants may give music even deeper philosophical or universal meanings. After a musical gathering in Cairo, the celebrated Egyptian riqq player Muḥammad al-ʿArabī explained to me that music was love in the broadest sense, love for one's wife, love for one's family, love for everybody. He added that "love is everything and that if the artist did not love he would be nothing," an explanation that conjured distinct mystical overtones.[19] After a performance in Los Angeles, a percussionist from Syria explained to me that if there were more sammīʿah in the world there would be less evil and fewer wars. At the end of a musical jalsah in Baghdad, an event during which I played the buzuq and nāy for a number of intellectually sophisticated and musically initiated listeners, I encountered a number of noteworthy reflections. One person attributed the love of music to a natural predilection of the human soul, an attribution clearly reminiscent of al-Ghazālī's eleventh-century writings on samāʿ, while another person made reference to Aldous Huxley's *The Doors of Perception* (1954), in which the author's own intoxication presumably caused him to undergo a deep mystical state.[20]

In its entirety, a jalsah event tends to embody a sequence of gradually unfolding and organically linked phases, an order of events that contributes significantly to the jalsah's transformative purpose. In Cairo, I have attended a few informal music sessions at the home of a local composer and music aficionado. These sessions usually took place either in the late afternoon or evening in a rather small reception room where ʿūds, nāys, and riqqs were hung on the wall, and which constituted a self-contained enclosure furnished with sofas, coffee tables, and ashtrays, thereby providing an ambiance that seemed physically and visually conducive to music-making. The gatherings occurred usually once a week and involved a more or less steady core of individuals, namely about a dozen local professional and amateur musicians and performing and nonperforming listeners, and occasionally a few visitors and guests such as myself. The attendants were basically all male but women could also sit in or listen in an adjacent living room. The ages of the participants tended to range from forty to seventy years, although one musician occasionally brought his son, who was in his twenties and was also a career

[19] From a conversation that took place in May 1989.

[20] This event took place in September 1989.

musician. The following is a rough description of one such jalsah whose internal sequential flow is typical, although by no means fixed or totally predictable.[21]

That event seemed to unfold in a gradual and seamless fashion. The guests began to arrive around nine o'clock in the evening. They greeted the host and each other. Some embraced. The first half-hour represented a carry-over from prior daily affairs and thus incorporated an ordinary exchange of platitudes and discussions of mundane concerns, especially benign ones such as: "I have tried calling you several times in the past few days. Is your phone out of order?" Reestablishing a sense of comfort and collegiality among the different group members, such preliminary exchanges were accompanied by other forms of mental and physical "conditioning": drinking coffee, tea, or soft drinks; smoking cigarettes; and so on.

This preparatory period eased itself smoothly into the performance proper. Toward the end of the mundane verbal exchanges, one celebrated singer and composer arrived and was warmly greeted and shown to his seat. At that time, a middle-aged ʿūd player had his instrument in its cloth bag leaning against the wall next to his seat. As he picked it up to move it to another place in the room, he explained that he had been taking it to the repairman to have the neck fixed and had hoped that this time it was fixed for good. His explanation led to further discussions on instruments, for example what plectrums and what strings were best and ended with the performer taking the instrument out of the bag in order to show the repairs to his eager colleagues and demonstrating what the ʿūd sounded like after the repair. The middle-aged musician played a few phrases that outlined the scale of one of the maqāmāt and seemed well-suited for testing his newly repaired instrument. The instrumentalist's demonstration, although brief, was met with verbal gestures of admiration from some audience members, who begged him to continue to play. The instrumentalist modestly declined and voiced such remarks as: "you don't want to have me take up the time since we are enjoying chatting this evening." Then one of the guests, a more or less steady member of the group, suggested that the attendants hear a friend of his, a young amateur ʿūd player who was visiting from another Arab country and was joining the group for the first time. Everybody applauded the idea and the young ʿūd player obliged. He played for about ten minutes, mostly skillfully rendered semi-improvised pieces, and received a good round of compliments at the end. Here, the musical discussions and the young musician's performance served as the final and major thrust into the main musical segment of the evening.

At this point, the guests begged to hear something from the singer, "whatever he wished to sing," and voiced their pleas through commonly

[21] This performance occurred on May 29, 1989.

heard polite expressions such as: *Athifnā*, "Cast your gems upon us;" *Tafaḍḍal*, "Grant your benevolence;" and *ʿĀyzīn nismaʿ*, "We would like to listen." Some members of the audience urged the middle-aged ʿūd player to start performing, as his music had to set the mood for the singer. The ensuing segment began with tāqāsim, during which the ʿūd player established one of the māqāmat and in the process drew many ecstatic responses from the audience members. The taqāsīm came to a natural cadence followed by a burst of complimentary responses and then started again, at this point basically serving as a prelude to the singing. Here, some of the exclamations addressed the singer by name, thus giving him added recognition and encouraging him to start. Subsequently, the singer began his performance which, incorporating a medley of several ʿūd-accompanied songs, lasted for about forty-five minutes. During the performance the listeners did not request songs outright, but at times discreetly slipped in the names of some of the songs that the singer specializes in singing, particularly when these songs were of the same maqām that was being performed at the time.

Moreover, the sammīʿah were truly "at work." During the song segment there were emotionally charged silences punctuated by animated and seemingly involuntary physical and vocal gestures. The various responses differed in their levels of intensity from one person to the other, but on the whole seemed genuine, as well as emotionally profound. They were also synchronized with one another, and seemed to instinctively emulate the climactic build-ups and resolutions of the musical phrases. The verbal exclamations were usually released toward the termination of, or after the *qaflāt*, or cadential motifs ending certain phrases. Sometimes these gestures were accompanied by raising a hand or lifting both arms and occasionally by nodding the head or laughing discreetly as a sign of admiring or "figuring out" an intricate modulation or an unusual qaflah. At times also, a man whose listening style was relatively more demonstrable looked at some others including myself and expressed his admiration of the singer through statements such as, "What is that?" "It is impossible!" and "He is a legend!" Others expressed their ṭarab in a somewhat subdued manner, without talking to each other or looking each other in the face. Here, as well, the variety of reactions displayed brings to mind al-Khulaʿī's illustrative anecdote.

As the vocal performance came to a stop, the ʿūd accompanist made a humorous comment as if to break the silence and prevent an anti-climactic feeling from setting in. The comment led to about a half-hour episode of joke telling by different members of the group. The jokes were not factual and did not mention any specific individuals, but instead poked fun at social stereotypes, particularly the Ṣaʿīdīs, or Upper Egyptians, whose alleged naiveté is the butt of numerous Egyptian jokes. These were short jokes, but had poignant punch lines sometimes ending in puns or double meanings. Jokes were told by practically all attendants except the singer and to some extent the ʿūd player, who both listened and seemed to enjoy the joking performance, which again was exhausted and in turn came naturally to an end. At that time, the host and two of the guests who all knew me well, and had heard me perform on the buzuq before, insisted that I play something. Since I did not have my own instrument, the host handed me one that he owned, but that needed repair. After apologizing for the condition of the instrument, I played a taqāsīm performance that lasted for a few minutes and aroused enthusiastic responses followed by lavish praise from the singer.

Subsequently, the group expressed interest in another musical "set" by the singer and his ʿūd accompanist. Obliging, these two performed again for twenty minutes or so. Then, after a momentary feeling of repose had set in, the host, an amateur ʿūd player as well as a composer, remarked humorously that since he owned the house and paid the utilities, he was therefore entitled to play at least one of his tunes. He picked up his own ʿūd and accompanied himself in a song that he had recently composed. Rather than reacting with the same emotional intensity exhibited earlier, the audience made their complimentary responses after the performance had ended and commended the composer for his clever compositional applications. In return, the host briefly discussed the background of his composition and linked his attempts to record it commercially to an earlier incident that was humorous and involved a specific person who was not present at the gathering but whom most of the guests knew very well. At that point, the samaʿ mood began to unwind, as the group members listened to and sometimes exchanged factual stories about that same person, stories that poked fun at his excessive frugality, his odd social mannerisms, and the like.

After these exchanges, the event seemed to come to an end. Some members glanced at their watches, and expressed their utter surprise at how fast time went by, how several hours were gone without being noticed. The guests also began to thank the musicians and the host and to note how important such evenings are, uttering statements such as "music is food for the soul." As the guests bid farewell to the host, who walked them to the outside gate, the conversation – despite a few additional exchanges of compliments and humorous remarks – included brief projections concerning the business that had to be pursued the following day.

As definable occurrences in place and time, jaslah events transform the participants both mentally and emotionally. Yet in order for that to happen, the various "players" must perform specialized but also complementary roles. Both listeners and musicians need to become part of an organic and a highly dynamic performative process. The transformational qualities of the jalsah also stem from the implicit ordering of micro-events, repertoires, and modes of behavior. In the case just described (see Figure 3.1), the jalsah began with an *ordinary phase* then gradually moved to an *entry phase*. A common behavioral mindset marked by mundane conversations progressed

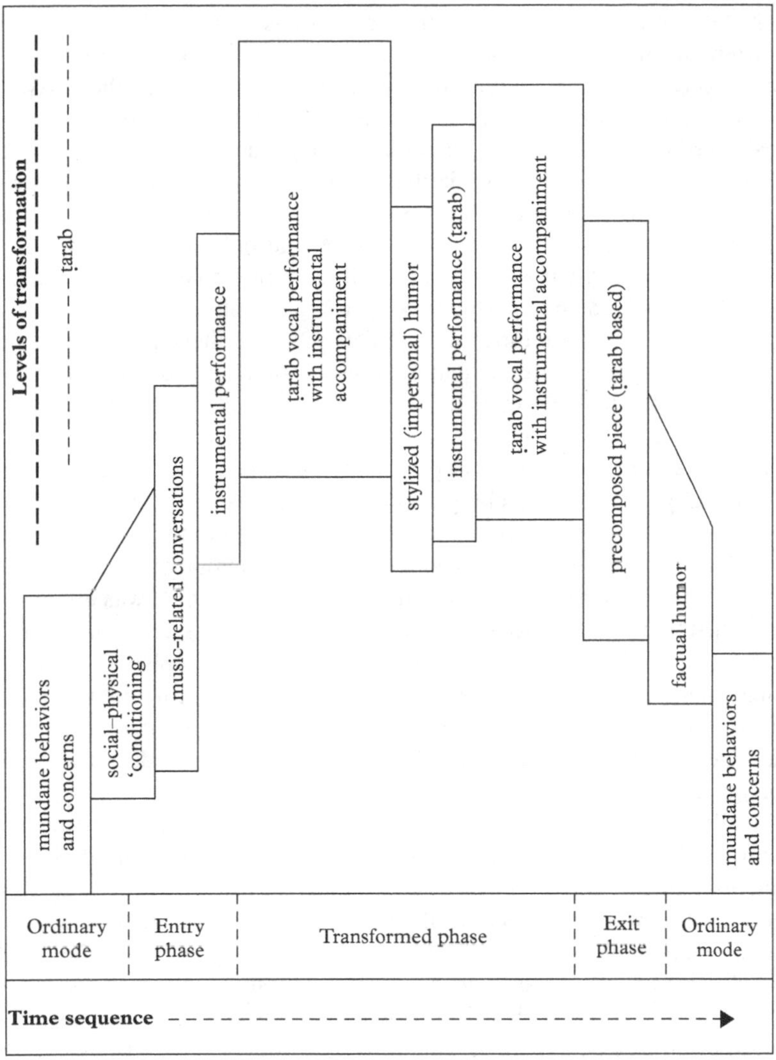

Figure 3.1 Analysis of a jalsah event

into a musically conducive state of physical and psychological preparedness. Furthermore, delving more deeply into the topic of music in their discussions, the participants recognized the presence of the less established guest ʿūd-player, and gave him a chance to participate. His performance provided a suitable segue to the *central phase*, namely the ʿūd accompanist's solo and the emotionally charged performance of the celebrated singer. Representing what may have been the highest point of ṭarab in the jalsah, this phase was marked by physical and emotional conditions that made the farthest departure from the participants' ordinary modes of consciousness. The musical performance, including the symbolic love themes of the texts and the abstract instrumental improvisations and vocalizations by the singer, transformed the behaviors and emotions of the group most radically.

The humorous verbal interlude that followed seemed to offer expressive variety, as well as "dramatic relief." Significantly, in the form of short depersonalized and stereotyped vignettes, the jokes did not seem to distract from the abstract transformational mood prevailing at this phase of the jalsah. In effect, they provided an opportunity for participants other than the musicians to "perform," as joke-telling in Egyptian social gatherings constitutes a communal verbal performance that requires a certain level of talent and skill, and as al-Khulaʿī had earlier stated (to his great displeasure), often surfaced in musical contexts. After that, the insistence that I perform on the buzuq may have served the double purpose of enabling the group to acknowledge me musically as well as socially and of providing further ṭarab before the second vocal set was presented by the singer and his ʿūd accompanist. In effect, the second set, which seemed less emotionally charged and less climactic than the first set, prepared for the *exit phase* which was effectively established by the host through his tactful and properly timed request of the guests to hear his new tune. Furthermore, the ensuing episode of humor, which employed factual subject matter, facilitated the participants' gradual return to their *ordinary phase* of consciousness. As this interpretation, or "thick description" (Geertz 1973: 6) reveals, the jalsah is delicately engineered, but also spontaneously and creatively played out.

Finally, in today's informal gatherings attentive and highly responsive listening is becoming less common. Quite often, jalsah events are dominated by non-sammīʿah, who may enjoy, or tolerate one or a few "listening-type" pieces by the musicians, but would soon convert the jalsah into a "sing-along," "clap-along" occasion. In such instances, the repertoire often veers toward the more "popular" and musically accessible songs or song fragments. The more established instrumentalists, who tend to become mere accompanists or whose playing would have to follow the party's collective musical flow, may feel reluctant to perform, or may even stay aside and just observe. Indeed, when true samaʿ events occur they are usually savored, cherished, and fondly remembered by the sammīʿah and the performers alike.

The public performance

Today, the word "*ḥaflah*," which roughly means "ceremonial gathering," or "celebration," is used to describe the large, publicly advertised ṭarab performance. At least conceptually, a ḥaflah is treated as a festive event and is linked to a nonmusical context, for example a religious or national holiday. However, in most cases, such linkage becomes perfunctory and is often forgotten or ignored by the ḥaflah goers.

In terms of ambiance and structure, the ḥaflah has a number of characteristic traits. For example, the program may feature several performing groups, a female dancer, a comedian, possibly a master of ceremony, and a number of vocalists, including one or more ṭarab singers. At times also, only one singer and his or her *firqah*, or accompanying ensemble, are presented. This was typical of Umm Kulthūm's *ḥaflāt* (plural of *ḥaflah*). Normally, the event takes place in the evening and would be introduced as *ḥafl ṣāhir*, or "evening festive gathering." It may occur at a theater, which was the usual setting for Umm Kulthūm's performances. It may also take place in a hotel ballroom, large restaurant, or public park, venues that most often have table seating and include food and drinks. Typically the audience is large, ranging from a hundred or so to a thousand or more. An exception is the private event (*ḥaflah khāṣṣah*), which is usually small and restricted to members of a specific organization or family and guests. Ḥaflah-goers usually come from different backgrounds. They may include rich patrons, government officials, military personnel, and ordinary citizens, both male and female.

Obviously, the public nature of the event and its celebratory connotations attract individuals of a wide variety of musical dispositions. This phenomenon was noted by Umm Kulthūm, who reportedly stated that around 1925 when she first launched her professional career she used to feel very nervous in front of the sophisticated sammīʿah of that time, but much later she developed greater confidence, and even began to find pleasure in facing her audience members, "as if I were at a school and the listeners were pupils" (Fuʾād 1976: 302–303). At the same time, she was able to study their personality traits, "as if I were watching an entertaining film" (Ibid.: 303), and to divide them into four main types, which she described with her own touch of satire.

Accordingly, the first type of listener is extremely tender and becomes wondrously transported. "I see him swim in a space of absent-mindedness (*shurūd*) and moan, then all of a sudden he comes back to his senses when he hears the others applauding and joins them in their applause" (Ibid.: 303). The second type displays fast changing moods. He is extremely tranquil, but as soon as he hears the singing he is overtaken by ṭarab and becomes highly excited. "He shouts between phrases and says: '*Kamān yā Sitt*!' (Repeat once more, oh Madam!), but is not satisfied with that as he jumps on top of his seat because of excessive elation (*nashwah*), and instead of showing his appreciation by applauding, like everyone else, he throws his *ṭarbūsh* (fez) up in the air" (Ibid.: 303). Umm Kulthūm presented one variation, namely the man who comes to the ḥaflah not wearing any headdress, but in a

Umm Kulthūm in performance. Photo courtesy of Dār al-Ṣayyād.

a

b

c

Photos a, b, c: Listeners at a performance by Umm Kulthūm.
Photos courtesy of Dār al-Ṣayyād.

moment of high excitement he grabs someone else's ṭarbūsh and throws it in the air. The third kind of listener likes to sing along somewhat strenuously, but with great passion. "So often when I stop singing suddenly before the end of a passage in order to see what he will do, I see him look around smiling as if trying to hide his embarrassment in front of his fellow listeners" (Ibid.: 303). The fourth type she called *muharrij*, or "clown," someone who comes to the performance probably not to listen to her but rather to attract attention. As she put it, this strange type of person does not clap like the others, but rather pounds a wooden stick against the floor or against his seat every time he is overcome by the elation of ṭarab (*intashá ṭaraban*). "He doesn't say 'repeat' like everyone else, but unleashes an extended ululation [high-pitched vocal cheer] that brings about laughter throughout the hall" (Ibid.: 304).

Umm Kulthūm added that these and other types of listeners, whom she had encountered throughout her professional career, are all part of an audience that liked her and in turn she had liked. We are told that this Egyptian singer was so inspired by some of her devotees, that she bestowed upon one of them, Ḥāj Ḥāfiḍh al-Taḥḥān, the title *al-Sammīʿ al-Awwal*, "The First Sammīʿ."[22] Appearing to dwell on the extreme manifestations of listening, these descriptions nevertheless illustrate the wide range of desirable or even tolerable listening behaviors, and again remind us of al-Khulaʿī's listening related anecdote.

The ḥaflah performer faces a typical set of logistical and musical challenges. For the pre-microphone takht singers, such as al-Ḥāmūlī, loudness of the voice was not only desirable but also necessary. Reportedly, in 1932 when a microphone was put in front of Umm Kulthūm at the Azbakiyyah Theater, she indignantly threw it off the stage.[23] Later, the introduction of sound amplification enabled the singer to entertain large audiences, and made it possible for him or her to be better heard against an ensemble that had increased significantly in size and had incorporated new string, percussion, and in some cases electronic, instruments. For the modern ḥaflah artist, the sound system has been an indispensable mediator.

Also in view of the "theatrical" atmosphere of the ḥalfah, the ideal muṭrib or muṭribah can benefit greatly from having appealing looks and commanding stage presence. Similarly appreciated are proper facial and hand gestures. It is often heard that an entertainer must not look *jāmid*, namely "frozen," or "expressionless," on stage. In addition to knowing a very large repertoire, the ṭarab artist must also possess exceptional physical stamina. The celebrated Syrian singer Ṣabaḥ Fakhrī is well-known for being able to

22 Fuʾād 1976: 300.
23 Fuʾād 1976: 157.

perform for up to ten hours without stopping.[24] Actually some performers sing long enough to outlast most of their listeners, except for the persistent sammīʿah who remain eager to hear them at their best, usually during the latter portion of their performance.

At a ḥaflah, the muṭrib's primary support comes from the sammīʿah. As Umm Kulthūm's description demonstrates, ḥaflah singers are fully conscious of the connoisseurs who inspire them through the active participatory role they play. However, given the public nature of the typical ḥaflah, the number of sammīʿah in the audience is quite unpredictable. For that reason, many modern ḥaflah singers have continued the earlier practice of bringing their own small entourage of faithful listeners to their own performances.[25] In the 1920s, Umm Kulthūm was reportedly surrounded by a clique of people who followed her to every ḥaflah she gave. Furthermore, before she accepted any performance contracts, she insisted that these individuals be allowed to come along even to the private ḥaflāt. We are told that those individuals instilled great confidence and comfort within her. Similarly, "their gestures became contagious and brought about great enthusiasm into the rest of the listeners, who in turn were encouraged to applaud and cheer" (Fuʾād 1976: 181). I witnessed a similar situation when I attended a specially arranged performance of Iraqi maqām by the late celebrated singer Yūsuf ʿUmar in Baghdad in 1975. Since most of the listeners were musically noninitiated, including polite and highly appreciative Europeans, Americans, and others attending an international music symposium in the city, the singer had apparently requested to have a few of his followers join the audience. As it turned out, these followers provided the appropriate musical responses and the interactive dynamism the event so urgently needed.

In turn, the singer needs to develop a general sense of who his listeners are and to establish good rapport with them. As he stands on the stage, he needs to look at the audience members and determine their overall level of musicality and general mood. In Fakhrī's words, "a muṭrib must also be a psychologist."[26] One of Fakhrī's vocal accompanists maintains that Fakhrī himself is well-known for his ability to "study" his audience. In order to create a comfortable *jaww*, or "atmosphere," the muṭrib may begin by saying a few words, usually familiar platitudes that prepare the listeners emotionally and arouse their enthusiasm.

[24] Fakhrī's endurance is spoken of proverbially. One Arab-American newspaper, *al-Akhbār* (32) June 20, 1997: 19, wrote that Fakhrī was noted in the *Guinness Book of Records* for having sung for ten uninterrupted hours at a Caracas theater in Venezuela, as he stood on his feet from ten at night until eight in the morning while performing for an Arab immigrant audience there.

[25] Some Egyptians refer to such "implanted" audience members sarcastically as *muṭayyabātiyyah* in reference to their uttered expressions of approval, namely *taṭyīb*, roughly "sweetening." In fact, one such expression is "*ṭayyib*!" which literally means "delicious," "healthy," "good-hearted," and "wonderful."

[26] From an interview with Mr. Fakhrī in Los Angeles on January 24, 1990.

Particularly in the large ḥaflāt, the muṭrib also needs to locate the sammīʿah, or clusters of sammīʿah in the audience and to maintain direct visual and musical contact with them. In order to achieve that, he may make a few musical trials. As Ṣabāḥ Fakhrī explains, his ḥaflah really does not begin until after about one hour of singing has passed, because until that time, he would have been trying pieces in different styles, muwashshaḥāt, qudūd, adwār and others to help him ascertain the existence and location of the sammīʿah, as well as to sense the dominant tastes and inclinations in the audience as a whole. Fakhrī adds that such musical scanning is accompanied by continued visual surveillance, which enables him to constantly monitor the audience's reactions and to fashion or adjust the repertoire accordingly.[27]

Once a healthy rapport is established, the artist attempts to keep the audience emotionally engaged. He would present his repertoire in such a way as to prevent the ṭarab momentum from slackening or dissipating. For example, if the singer felt his mawwāl was becoming too long he would follow it immediately with a highly animated metric song. In the process, he may introduce what I call "signal pieces," essentially well-known songs of a "lighter" character, for example certain *qudūd* (plural of *qadd*, an Aleppo-based strophic song with a colloquial text). Such songs function as ecstatic capsules, or musical "aphrodisiacs," whose associative energy throws the audience, particularly the non-sammīʿah, into an instant participatory frenzy. Signal pieces are often treated as climactic "treats," but also many singers resort to using them as "crutches," for example, if they are not very skilled or whenever they are physically exhausted or uninspired. The typical responses, clapping with the beat, dancing, and singing along, are usually triggered as soon as the signal piece is begun or even when it is still being verbally announced by the singer. Essentially, the Western notion of background, or soft "dinner" music is alien to the ṭarab culture, whose practitioners tend to view direct and continued interaction between performer and listener as a prime condition for good entertaining.[28]

In the process of selecting their repertoires, the performers try to navigate through widely ranging musical tastes and backgrounds. Consequently, the musical items are often quite varied and the order in which the material is presented is rather unpredictable. However, in Ṣabaḥ Fakhrī's own performances, the evening usually opens with an instrumental prelude followed by

[27] From the same 1990 interview. For that matter, at a ḥaflah held in the same year in a hotel ballroom in Los Angeles, Ṣabaḥ Fakhrī reacted firmly against the routine dimming of the lights in the hall. Consequently, the lights were kept on throughout the performance, thus enabling the singer to maintain visual contact with the audience.

[28] I suspect that the musicians' interest in keeping their audiences engaged at all times and their discomfort with performing for nonattentive, usually chatty audiences, are among the reasons why in many ḥaflaṭ, for example dinner parties, the musicians turn up the sound amplification to such a high level, making the music painfully difficult to ignore.

listening-oriented metric pieces, usually including muwashshaḥāt. Similarly, pieces whose content is more ecstatic, such as vocal improvisations, tend to appear sporadically, in alternation with lighter songs. Also, the more ecstatic pieces often become more prominent toward the end of the ḥaflah, supposedly when the muṭrib has reached a high plateau of salṭanah, typically late in the evening. When a number of artists are featured, the lighter presentations normally pave the way for the main ṭarab attraction. In some cases, a boisterous or musically unfocused atmosphere predominant during the early phases of a ḥaflah suddenly yields to a listening-oriented, jalsah-like mood as soon as the featured muṭrib comes to the stage.[29]

The nightclub

The modern Arab nightclub, known by such names as *kabarēh*, "cabaret" or *malhá laylī*, literally "a night place-of-entertainment," has provided another outlet for ṭarab music, as well as for other musical styles and entertainment genres. Today, Arab night clubs are found in various large urban centers such as Cairo, Damascus, and Beirut, and in Western cities such as Paris, London, and New York. They are usually located in special "red-light" districts, in tourist places, in summer-resort areas, and in large fashionable hotels. The nightclub audience tends to be transient, heterogeneous, and largely anonymous. The clientele is likely to include many uninitiated listeners, or sometimes curious foreign tourists.

The nightclub repertoires vary considerably and may incorporate a wide array of Western and local popular music and dance genres. However, certain presentations are typical. When included, the ṭarab segment is usually presented toward the end of the evening. As in the ḥaflah, it serves as an emotional crescendo or musical finale for the entire show. Whereas the earlier "light" portions of the program are usually attended by the casual onlookers or entertainment seekers, the later segment serves those who, motivated by their musical interest, may remain in the club for hours waiting for an admired muṭrib or muṭribah to appear, typically after midnight. Obviously, the club owners can derive added financial gains from presenting the featured celebrities at the end of the show. At the same time, the order of presentation as such demonstrates a certain recognition of ṭarab as a late-night activity whose time becomes ripe after a long period of

[29] For example, this was the case at a variety performance during which I played the nāy as part of an ensemble that accompanied Sayyid Makkāwī. The event took place in Los Angeles in 1994. When this blind celebrity was brought to the stage, an unmistakable listening mood prevailed.

musical preparation accompanied by eating and drinking.

At the nightclub, ṭarab musicians may apply the same skills and strategies they use at the ḥaflah. A singer may talk to the audience members in order to establish basic rapport with them. He or she may also use the first few musical "numbers" to assess the listeners' musical orientation and to determine the existence and size of the sammīʿah contingency among them. Detecting the presence of the sammīʿah, a female singer may, for example, introduce an Umm Kulthūm song classic or a vocal improvisation. Otherwise, a singer may present a "lighter" repertoire of songs for the general audience to sing or dance to or even just listen to passively while eating, drinking, and chatting.

The physical atmosphere of the nightclub adds a peculiar dimension to the ṭarab experience. The nightclub ambiance relies on intensified levels of stimulation, for example through bright colors and striking decors, including those portraying Orientalist Arabian themes, psychedelic stage lighting, dimmed or candle floor-lights, and thick cigarette smoke. These factors complement or conceivably enhance, the purchase and consumption of alcohol, yet another medium of stimulation. Such diverse interventions are reinforced by staging effects: various, and sometimes fast changing, numbers; dazzling beaded attire; colorful dance costumes; sexually suggestive clothing; exaggerated facial make-up; stylish hairdos; colorfully dyed hair; lavish display of jewelry; and others.

Such modes of stimulation serve different functions. On a certain level, they provide a sensory vehicle for stirring up an audience that is highly transitory and diversified: customers who may not know the performing musicians or may not be directly interested in the music per se. Simultaneously, the music itself may become "sensationalized" by emphasizing the percussive component, utilizing electronic instruments, and performing at a high level of sound amplification. In effect, ṭarab is experienced and appreciated, at least by some, as part of a visual, gastronomic, erotic, and intoxicating package. The resulting musical–sensory revelry may modify the customers' immediate awareness of time and place. It may also inspire them to forgo ordinary social and even economic scruples and consequently indulge more freely in the overall ecstatic process, as well as spend more liberally on food and alcohol and generously tip the entertainers, waiters, and cloak-room attendants.

For the musical purist, the club experience may seem socially and emotionally contrived, and even aesthetically compromised. Of the three main contexts discussed, the nightclub event is probably the least memorable, despite its high level of excitation. The musicians tend to conduct their nightclub performances merely as work, often describing it as being tedious if not demeaning and thankless, and similarly some audience members may think of the event as yet another night out. Nevertheless, for many the club provides a unique context for experiencing ṭarab music and its emotional affect. It also offers musicians, composers, and producers a primary arena for both economic gain and artistic creativity.

Performing for oneself

Ṭarab performances do not have to be group events; playing alone is extremely common. The immediate reasons for playing without the physical presence of an audience are numerous. The phenomenon of "practice," as we know it, for example through the use of scalar or melodic patterns in Western art music, or the regimen of *riyaz* (from Arabic *riyāḍ*, meaning "exercise") in classical Indian music, seems to play a minimal role in the ṭarab experience. Similarly, systematic drilling or technique building is atypical of ṭarab artists, except for the virtuosity-minded. Instead, performance dexterity is usually developed through actual musical work or by playing at a *brova*, namely a work session or rehearsal.[30] However, a musician may play alone in the guise of doing something else. An instrument-maker may perform in his workshop to try out a new instrument he has made. A qānūn player may play to "break in" a new set of strings or to repair certain defects with the tuning levers. And an artist may perform for the conscious purpose of composing. Riyāḍ al-Sunbāṭī (1906–1981), who composed some of Umm Kulthūm's best admired songs, is said to have played his ʿūd alone in his bedroom with a small tape recorder intended to capture the tunes that may emerge.[31] And of course, musicians play alone in order to satisfy an urge to play, or simply perform for their own pleasure.

Ṭarab musicians realize that playing in socially constructed musical contexts is "the real thing." For example, they recognize that the stringent technical demands posed by formal performances can be tremendously beneficial. A Lebanese nāy maker offered me a piece of advice that I found quite valuable as a nāy player. He insisted that in the final result you can best determine the quality of an instrument by playing it in a formal performance context, with an ensemble and for qualified listeners. Presumably in such a context the player faces emotional and musical exigencies that challenge the very mechanics of playing and expose the true limitations and capabilities of the instrument. The nāy maker added that for him the nightclub where he used to work provided a perfect ground for testing his newly made instruments.[32]

30 It is not known exactly when the term "brova," from Italian *pròva*, namely "proof," or "rehearsal," became part of the local musical parlance. Incidentally, the word is also locally used to mean "film negative."

31 I learned this about al-Sunbāṭī from the late ʿAlī Reda (Riḍā, d. 1993) in the early 1980s.

32 From a conversation in Beirut in the early 1980s.

Nevertheless, playing for oneself can be extremely creative. Being alone with an instrument or with one's own voice offers the performer, especially the improviser, an opportunity for experimentation without external interventions. In such a context, the musician is able to allow more room for his intuition, as well as to explore the potentials of his instrument or voice, or for that matter, of his musical mind. Being alone can free the artist to be his or her "feeling" self.

Moreover, playing alone can be profoundly ecstatic. It entails a certain "built-in" feedback within the performer, as a musician and listener at the same time. Lone music makers tell about the deep absorption they experience and indicate that they lose track of time and feel somewhat detached from their immediate surroundings. Similarly, they describe the jarring sensations that occur when others intrude. Accordingly, as soon as an "external" listener becomes involved, the performance may completely change direction, or depending upon the listener's musical disposition, or personal "energy," the performer's level of ecstasy may decrease drastically or vanish altogether. The emotive efficacy of playing for oneself seems embedded in the artist's ability to function as one's own musical springboard. The performer who plays alone appears to set in motion a relatively undisturbed cyclical process within himself, a dynamic through which the music is directly felt and generated.

Ecstasy and sound recording

In the modern history of Arab music, one of the most significant developments has been the appearance and proliferation of sound recording. By the turn of the twentieth century, the invention of the phonograph enabled some ṭarab artists to make their own home recordings on wax cylinders and soon after, some cylinders became commercially available. Around 1904 the prerecorded flat disc began to dominate the Arab market. In the first few decades of the twentieth century, millions of 78-rpm discs were produced, advertised, and disseminated by major European and Near-Eastern record companies. Large international business firms such as Gramophone (later His Master's Voice) of England, Odeon of Germany, and the locally owned Baidaphon became a major source of income for many musicians. Creating a massive record audience through rigorous advertising and dissemination strategies, they dramatically enhanced the popularity of certain ṭarab singers, Shaykh Yūsuf al-Manyalāwī, Shaykh Salāmah Ḥijāzī, Shaykh Sayyid al-Ṣafṭī, Ṣāliḥ ʿAbd al-Ḥayy, Umm Kulthūm, and many others throughout the Arab world.[33]

[33] For more information on the history of recording in the Arab world, particularly Egypt, see Racy 1976 and 1977.

The Egyptian musical film first appeared in 1932, and was inaugurated with a production that featured the actress and female ṭarab singer Nādirah. Subsequently, Cairo witnessed impressive growth in its motion picture industry, as Egypt's musical films played throughout the Arab world and featured singers such as ʿAbd al-Wahhāb, Umm Kulthūm, and sister and brother Asmahān (1912–1944) and Farīd al-Aṭrash (1915–1974). After World War II, the Arab cinema continued to present well-known male and female vocalists, although the singing styles of many film stars became further removed from the traditional ṭarab stream. The radio provided another channel. In the late 1920s and early 1930s, Cairo's private radio stations broadcast live performances as well as played available commercial recordings. Later, the official Egyptian Radio Station, established in 1934, offered various types of music, including *waṣlāt* (plural of *waṣlah*), specially prepared for the station by well-known ṭarab singers, Ṣāliḥ ʿAbd al-Ḥayy (1896–1962) and others. More recently, Arab radio stations, specifically those run by local governments, have introduced and recorded music by various artists and have generally kept their own archives of old and new recordings. Among their regular payroll staff have been singers, composers, lyric writers, and instrumentalists, as well as musical producers, announcers, and sound engineers. The mainstream music has been broadcast regularly from different Arab radio stations, although some stations have also featured weekly programs devoted to the *qadīm*, or early ṭarab repertoire.[34]

The period extending from the 1950s through the 1970s witnessed the rise of the LP and the 45-rpm discs and the proliferation of television, which began largely as a localized medium for broadcasting various musical and nonmusical programs. Similarly, the reel-to-reel magnetic tape became the primary medium for studio and home recording. During the last decades of the twentieth century, the cassette tape emerged as one of the most effective media of musical dissemination, largely because cassettes are relatively cheap to buy and easy to duplicate, store, and transport, or for that matter to bootleg.[35] The 60- or 90-minute cassette tape has been used widely to record live ṭarab performances and to copy songs from radio or to duplicate available recordings, an advantage that the present digital technology continues to provide.

Within the ṭarab culture, the ability of the record medium to communicate ṭarab feeling has been a topic of concern. When sound recording first appeared, there was a general feeling in the Arab world, as well as in the West, that the "talking machine" was a delightful novelty and a scientific

[34] One of the most remarkable examples is a regular weekly program that has been broadcast from Cairo for at least the last twenty-five years. Titled *Sahrat Alḥān Zamān* (An Evening of Tunes from the Past), it is prepared by the well-known music historian Maḥmūd Kāmil and presented by Hālah al-Ḥadīdī.

[35] See El-Shawan 1987.

marvel, but not a viable musical medium. In a chapter on acoustics, Kāmil al-Khulaʿī included a footnote in which he differentiated between listening to live music and listening to the wax cylinder, and considered phonograph records as inferior replications of reality. He criticized the phonograph precisely because of its acoustical limitations and because the exigencies of recording deprived the performer of both the appropriate human ambiance and the physical comfort needed for creating ṭarab. In his words, "listening to the phonograph is like eating with false teeth" (ca.1904: 24).

At the same time, al-Khulaʿī's judgment left open the question of whether or not the concept of recording per se was objectionable. Thus, had it not been for the technical barriers and artistic limitations confronting the performers, could recorded sound be enjoyed outside the traditional contexts of listening, without seeing and interacting with the performers directly? During the early decades of the twentieth century, the ṭarab culture gradually came to accept the record as a musical medium. The attitudes of the artists and the listeners, and the staggering disc sales showed that: recorded music, especially with improved acoustical fidelity, can communicate tremendous musical affect. Equally important, the communicability of ṭarab feeling is possible if the original performance had been ecstatically charged to begin with. In other words, musical ecstasy, generated through a feeling of salṭanah on the part of the recording vocalist or instrumentalist, could somehow be sensed or decoded by the musically initiated record buyer.

The channeling of ṭarab was enhanced by the early recording artists' attempts to create emotionally conducive climates amidst uninviting recording conditions. For one thing, the recorded vocal exclamations punctuating the various performances were intended to inspire the performers and may have been voiced by an intimate group of sammīʿah or by the record companies' local staff. Most often, these added gestures appeared genuine, well-timed, and musically well-deserved, although in certain instances they seemed exaggerated or contrived, gimmicks that remind us of the "canned" laughter heard on American television comedies. Meanwhile, some artists may have conducted musical warm-ups before recording or may have rehearsed the material with their takht accompanists so as to create a better mood for performing.

Especially in the 1920s, the competing record companies made systematic efforts to commission, copyright, and record vast numbers of original musical works. Their efforts contributed to the ascendancy of a type of song that was short (78-rpm-disc length) and fully precomposed, most often in a "lighter" strophic format. Thus, the record content shifted further away from the live ṭarab aesthetic, as precomposition had begun to overshadow context-bound flexibility. By the mid-1930s, with the gradual disappearance of recorded exclamations and the elimination of the celebrities' pictures from disc labels, a feature that was originally intended to evoke the live presence

Egyptian singer and composer Muḥammad ʿAbd al-Wahhāb (ca. 1901–1991), seated in front, recording for Baidaphon Company in an ornate tent in the early 1930s. A publicity photo.

of the recording artists, many ṭarab songs became fixed media "pieces." Among these were the works of Muḥammad ʿAbd al-Wahhāb, who exemplified the media-conscious ṭarab artist. Such pieces, as represented for example by ʿAbd al-Wahhāb's disc songs and his short often programatically conceived film songs, gained their own place within the contemporary ṭarab aesthetic. Indeed, many media-inspired, musical compositions are appreciated for their emotional content, as well as for the intricate technical workmanship and the modern features they often display.

Certainly, the culture's predilection for the live musical experience continues to prevail, as best illustrated by the large number of live recordings in the ṭarab market today. Such recordings, including many by Umm Kulthūm, sometimes carry the descriptive title *tasjīl ḥayy muṭawwal*, "extended live recording." In addition to these commercially available releases, the connoisseurs are known to exchange tapes of live recordings, some being cassette duplicates of older reel-to-reel tapes. Such recordings are highly prized, especially those that connoisseurs consider rare or commercially unavailable, as the home recordings of Zakariyyā Aḥmad, (1896–1961), one of Umm Kulthūm's major composers who also sang occasionally, or those of ʿAbd al-Wahhāb singing informally with his own ʿūd accompaniment. Particularly cherished are those made when the performers had been in a state of salṭanah and had performed renditions that are exceptionally ecstatic, for example some live performances by the late Syrian singer Muḥammad Khayrī. The connoisseurs may attribute the exceptional affective power of a live recording to the desirable setting in which the performance had occurred. In the case of a recorded jalsah, some of the attending sammīʿah may be recognized by name, and similarly acknowledged may be a musically initiated patron in whose house the performance had taken place. A recorded ḥaflah may also be identified with the place in which it had been presented. A live recording by a certain singer may be highly acclaimed because the recorded performance had occurred in a city such as Aleppo, traditionally known for its musically sophisticated public. Some ṭarab vocalists and instrumentalists may collect tape copies of their own performances during which they were highly inspired, largely due to the existence of a good and highly interactive audience.

Furthermore, live recordings are often appreciated as extensions of the original live events. This is reflected in the order in which recorded pieces are sometimes listened to. Customarily, local radio stations have presented "light" non-ṭarab pieces in the mornings and perhaps early afternoons, but typically assigned to evening hours the ṭarab proper, as the live ḥaflaṭ of Umm Kulthūm, Ṣabaḥ Fakhrī, and Muḥammad Khayrī. Often, members of the public have structured their listening accordingly. When Radio Cairo used to broadcast Umm Kulthūm's live performances in the evening of the first Thursday of each month, millions of Arabs planned to be by their radio sets. In Beirut in the early 1960s I remember seeing taxi cabs stopped by the street sides, as the drivers and other nearby enthusiasts listened to these broadcasts on the car radios. One Palestinian woman described to me that at the times of these broadcasts her father followed certain ritual-like observances, as he sat and listened with a glass of *ʿaraq* (a local alcoholic beverage) and *māzah* (appetizers that are traditionally served with ʿaraq).[36] When hearing ṭarab music on recordings, the connoisseurs may display familiar live-performance antics, such as facial gestures or signs of deep absorption, although perhaps in a less demonstrable manner. They may also try to avoid interruptions. One ṭarab lover indicated to me that he cannot fully enjoy an ecstatically moving recording in the company of individuals who do not know how to listen or to feel the music.

By the same token, many listeners concede that at some level, recordings are not as ecstatic or at least not as engaging as live performances. Media experts generally attribute such a discrepancy to a variety of factors. Live performances provide the opportunity for direct performer–listener interaction; they are physically self-contained, thereby focusing the listeners' attention directly upon the performance; they impart a certain collective "energy," an infectious mood that engulfs the entire audience. Moreover, the customary live setting tends to allow for an extended and gradual process of mental and musical conditioning that is likely to intensify the listening

[36] From a conversation in Los Angeles in the middle 1980s.

experience. For that matter, one Arab listener indicated to me that his rich uncle, a diehard sammīʿ, used to take a plane from Beirut to Cairo to attend Umm Kulthūm's monthly performances live, even though these performances were broadcast across the entire region. [37]

However, ṭarab remains unmistakably potent as a mediated experience. For one thing, sound recording has broadened the scope of the listening experience and added to it new emotional or physical nuances. A professional musician who lives in New York City and spends a great deal of time on the road states that he finds listening to ṭarab recordings most enjoyable when he is driving on the highway late at night, but adds that he would not listen to such recordings while battling the traffic in downtown Manhattan.[38] For the introspective listener, recordings may even take precedence over live performances, in which a variety of extraneous distractions, including noisy gesturing and rowdy conduct, may prevail.[39] Recorded performances also allow the listeners to create their own images of the original live contexts or even to reduce such contexts to mere impressions or abstractions. In the case of many recent ṭarab recordings, the original context is little more than a "high-tech" studio or a mixture of digital soundtracks.

[37] From a conversation in Los Angeles in the early 1980s.

[38] From a conversation in the late 1980s.

[39] In public performances, fights sometimes occur, as when those interested in listening ask noisy audience members, who often are under the influence of alcohol, to be quiet.

4 Music

In Arab culture, the concept of ṭarab brings to mind a certain musical idiom, or musical style. Similarly, it implies special musical applications or interpretations. In a large measure, musical evocation can be explained in terms of the "what" and "how" of music making. Whether it is al-Iṣfahānī describing a medieval court performance or Muḥammad al-ʿAqqād reflecting on the musical mastery of his grandfather, those who speak about music and its influence allude to both substance and style, form and expression, craft and feeling. In this chapter, I similarly explore both the general fabric of ṭarab music and some of the basic processes that enable the music to "speak," or impress emotionally. Understandably, it is difficult to distinguish between the idiom as such and the individual emotive application since the two work together as part of a broader affective syntax.

The links between the contemporary practice and the pre-World-War-I musical legacy are extremely significant. For modern composers and performers, takht music has served both as a model and a point of departure. As summed up by Sayyid Makkāwī (1926–1998), who is known for his ecstatic singing and his musical compositions for Umm Kulthūm and others, the old (*qadīm*) style is the foundation (*asās*).[1] From the takht tradition, which incorporated Sufi vocal elements and various indigenous and Pan-Ottoman secular ingredients, the modern musical ensemble has borrowed its basic Arab instruments. Similarly, the modern practice has derived from takht music basic ecstatic techniques, especially those related to mode and modal improvisation. Obviously, modern departures from the older expression have been extensive. Nonetheless, as a musical model, the takht not only represents the musical aesthetic of the late nineteenth and early twentieth centuries, but also informs us about the dynamics of ecstatic evocation in ṭarab music in general.

1 From the conversation with Mr. Makkāwī on May 30, 1994.

Abstraction and lyricism

Ṭarab music tends to be abstract; its substance is neither inherently programmatic nor necessarily evocative of entities (such as visual images, mythical plots, pantheons of saints and spirits) outside itself. Although programmatic allusions are often made, especially by the Western-minded composers, the intrinsic message is usually nonreferential. This trait is best illustrated by the modal improvisations and the various bashraf and samāʿī compositions, which are identified primarily by their generic names, the names of their composers, and the maqāmāt in which they are composed.

Given its individual-centered emotionality, ṭarab music is also highly lyrical. Although manifest in the various musical genres, its lyricism is epitomized by the vocal component, namely ṭarab songs that impress through self-referenced amorous themes and images. In combination, abstraction and lyricism appear to orient the music more directly toward the listener's realm of feeling. The resulting affect is usually expressed through the self-reflexive exclamations that punctuate the musical performances. As a rule, such gestures do not analyze or make evaluative statements about the music or objectify the technical–emotive ability of the performer, except indirectly. Essentially, they erupt as symptoms, or manifest "side effects," of the ecstatic condition and feed back into and energize the musical–evocative process. In short, the music's proclivity toward abstractness and lyricism highlights its emotive core and grants its ecstatic message certain centrality and directness.

Individuality and togetherness

Ṭarab music gives prominence to individuality and collectivity, two complementary dynamics that contribute to the music's ecstatic efficacy. Individuality is clearly illustrated by the role of leadership that the singer usually assumes within the traditional ensemble. It is also displayed most vividly when an instrumentalist leads or improvises either alone or against other accompanying instruments. In some respects, individuality streamlines the ecstatic performance and brings the emotionally evocative material to the forefront. Similarly, the individual artist who creates music on the spot appears to convey his ecstatic message most directly. His manner of delivery is likely to grant him added maneuverability as a ṭarab maker.

Notably, the aesthetic of individuality is consistent with timbral specialization within the traditional ensemble. The takht specifically is a collection of *khāmāt ṣawtiyyah*, "sound timbres," that are individually distinguished as well as imbued with ecstatic connotations. Incorporating one of each type of instrument, for example one ʿūd, one qānūn, one nāy, one violin, and one riqq, the takht amounts to a few layers of discernible timbral–acoustical lines. Thus, it can be contrasted with such "unitimbral" but register-separated combinations, such as Europe's Renaissance recorder or viol consorts, or for that matter the classical string quartet.

To illustrate, the ʿūd, a fretless short necked lute, often given highly impressive epithets such as *amīr al-ṭarab*, or "the prince of ecstasy," is particularly praised for its affective sound quality. Recognized as an *ālat naqr* (plucked instrument), the ʿūd produces a relatively low register, in Western theoretical terms the bass clef, an octave lower than the treble register of the violin. In this case however, the individual register of the instrument must be interpreted as a factor of sonic definition rather than as a function of harmonic specialization.

Like the ʿūd, the *qānūn*, a type of plucked zither, enjoys a distinctive timbre in part because of its open triple-courses of nylon and metal-wound-silk (formerly all gut) strings, and because its bridge rests upon spaces over which pieces of thin fish skin are stretched. Most often, it is played in the treble register by the right hand while the left hand frequently echoes the melody on the bass register an octave lower. The strings are plucked by two horn plectrums, each individually held against an index finger through a metal ring. Praised by al-Khulaʿī for its superb ability to produce ṭarab,[2] as well as noted for providing clear tonal references through its open, essentially unstopped strings, the qānūn is the preferred instrument for accompanying singers during their vocal improvisations.

The violin, a nineteenth century Western import, is highly prized for its emotional expressivity and resemblance to the human voice.[3] Spoken of as *ālat saḥb* (an instrument of sustained sound), it provides yet a different tonal quality. The bowing gives it the ability to produce long notes, while its fretless neck as well as its conventional Arab tuning enables the player to produce tonal nuances with great agility.

The nāy, an open-ended, obliquely held reed-flute, is another instrument of sustained sound, one that enjoys special emotional powers. Spiritually significant, it has been used in some Sufi rituals. Also, when properly played, it is associated with overwhelming ṭarab sensations. As one young Syrian musician puts it: "This instrument defines us as a culture."[4] The nāy is distinguished by its breathy, or reedy timbre, its characteristic trills, and its highly ornate style. It plays mostly in a pitch level an octave above the treble register.

2 al-Khulaʿī ca. 1904: 55.

3 For further historical information on the violin see Chapter 3, Note 3.

4 From a formal pre-performance presentation by qānūn player Sāmir Faraḥ in Los Angeles on December 6, 1998.

Similarly, the riqq, a small, but relatively heavy tambourine with five sets of brass cymbals and thin fish skin (more recently plastic), produces a variety of timbral effects that are used to form the beat patterns, namely the *īqā‘āt*, or "metric modes." Traditionally, the strokes are discretely produced, yet projected as crisp and distinctly heard taps on the skin. They constitute complex acoustical effects that combine the membranophonic skin sounds with the idiophonic vibrations of the cymbals, which are indirectly activated by the tapping, although sometimes are also hit directly. Also called *daff*, the riqq is the ṭarab percussion instrument *par excellence*. Today, especially, in the more popular groups, the riqq is joined by the *ṭablah*, a vase-shaped single-headed drum directly related to the folk *darabukkah*, which in Egypt has been associated with folk music that usually accompanied female dancing. The introduction of the loud, high-strung modern ṭablah has created a new sound aesthetic that shifted riqq playing somewhat from the artful subtleties of the takht-based style toward a more percussive approach that gives more prominence to the brass cymbals. Incidentally, such added percussive layering has coincided with an overall growth in the size of and instrumental variety within the typical urban ensemble.

The same form of acoustical differentiation can be extended to the singing voice. Obviously, singing gains special definition through the uttered text, as well as through the distinctive timbral quality of the voice itself. Furthermore, in the presence of an accompanying small chorus, for example, as part of the takht performing group, the muṭrib's voice usually stands out through its dynamic prominence, interpretive freedom, and higher level of ornamentation and complexity. Similarly, in religious choral groups, the munshid may occasionally switch registers, for example rising an octave above his accompanists.

Togetherness contributes to the ṭarab effect in a number of ways. The collective modalities of performing give individuality a suitable framework or contextual reference, for example when ensemble passages prepare for or alternate with solo passages. Moreover, togetherness allows the various performance components mutually to enhance one another. Collectively, members of a performance group may experience a creative synergy that manifests itself within the overall musical product. Additionally, the collective musical process enables the role of leadership to shift from one musician to another whenever desirable.

Togetherness is achievable primarily because the performance media are technically and dynamically compatible, as well as timbrally and acoustically differentiated. In a sense, the takht is a confluence of congruous musical means and abilities. Ṭarab instruments, with the exception of the riqq, which is sometimes referred to simply as *īqā‘*, namely "beat" or metric pattern, share with the singer's voice and with one another, basic stylistic properties. The ‘ūd, nāy, qānūn, and violin are all equally equipped to perform as solo instruments, for example rendering self-contained performances of taqāsīm. They are also well suited for interpreting a vocal composition instrumentally and for accompanying a featured singer individually or collectively. Depending on the musical context, each single instrument may assume the role of a leading soloist or may accompany less conspicuously, for example, by holding a drone or producing an ostinato in the background. Similarly, the violin, ʿūd, qānūn, and nāy are all capable of playing essential ṭarab ornaments and microtones, although perhaps not on the same level of agility and versatility. For that matter, apart from the riqq, the takht model includes no instruments that are purely for accompaniment such as the drone-producing *tambura* in Indian classical music. The ʿūd, violin, qānūn, nāy, and riqq also possess comparable levels of loudness, as well as individual timbres that complement and blend effectively with one another. Roughly speaking, the melodic instruments share the same working melodic range, about two octaves. In performance, these instruments play in tessituras that are either on the same pitch level or one or two octaves apart. In terms of both melodic range and tonal alignments, they are also compatible with the singing voice. In light of such compatibilities, it is not surprising that in the professional parlance, the instruments are treated as metaphors for the singing voice. As mentioned earlier, the verb *yaqūl*, "to say," also means "to sing" and by extension "to play" a melodic instrument, in a sense to "utter" the vocal material instrumentally.[5]

This combination of compatible yet differentiated entities can also be understood in human terms. Members of the takht ensemble, who often were individually recognized by the public, were also united by social rank, economic status, level of musical training, and performance experience. The very concept of "takht," literally, "platform" or "elevated area" upon which the musicians performed, can be viewed as a physical embodiment of the social, economic, and musical commonality among the takht members as a musical team.[6] In fact, the compatibility and reciprocity in the musicians' performance roles was linked directly to the ensemble's ability to perform effectively. During the 1930s, the Egyptian critic and biographer Qisṭandī Rizq, alarmed by what he viewed as an erosion of aesthetic finesse among musicians, made an urgent plea to Egypt's Royal Academy of Arab Music:

[5] For more information on these aspects of individuality and compatibility among the takht instruments see Racy 1988.

[6] It is not known when the Persian-Ottoman term *takht* became part of the Arab musical parlance. It appeared in al-Khulaʿī's book. A comparable term in Egypt was *dikkah*, which also referred to the raised area upon which musicians sat. Also, it is not clear when takht musicians began to sit on chairs, as they have done since the early twentieth century. Prior to that, Lane had shown drawings of performing musicians sitting cross-legged.

The Academy is entrusted not to give the takht directors (*ru'asā' al-tukhūt*) license to replace performers who have previously worked in their ensembles with new performers who are ignorant of these directors' playing methods. Each ensemble director has a particular style, special attributes, and a distinctive spirit. For example, the takht of Master (*Ustādh*) Muḥammad al-ʿAqqād never used to work except under the leadership of [the singer] ʿAbduh al-Ḥāmūlī . . . Each leader had a special takht with special players, as substitutions were obviously harmful because new musicians were unable to tune their instruments with equal facility and to perform in such a way as to allow the sounds to blend perfectly. (ca. 1936: 15)

As implied by the above plea, personal, artistic, or perhaps "spiritual" harmony among members of the same group is indispensable for effective music making. By the same token, the inclusion of one or more incompatible or incompetent performers is likely to affect the collective process of performing and consequently diminish the ecstatic quality of the performance as a whole.

Heterophony

As a cultivated form of artistry, heterophonic interplay is a primary feature of takht music. In practice, heterophonic texture exists in two closely related formats, an overlapping type and a simultaneous type. The first occurs when a leading musical part, typically a vocal improvisation, is accompanied, for example, by an instrument such as the qānūn. In this case, the accompaniment "echoes" the leading part at a slightly delayed pace, or in a rather "out of sync" fashion. The second type applies mostly when ensemble members produce slightly varied renditions of the same musical material at the same time. This happens when takht instruments perform the same basic composition together, but with each one rendering it differently through subtle variations, omissions, ornamental nuances, syncopations, anticipations, and so on. In the process, the performers produce interlocking melodic structures and intricate heterorhythms. A musical "note" may be deliberately dropped out by one instrument to be provided by another, or sometimes an instrument may play a certain portion of it, thus leaving it for another instrument to "pick up" the other portion. Realized spontaneously in actual performance, heterophony is a highly coordinated process rather than a mere confluence of isolated musical renditions or a collection of simultaneous variations of one fixed tune.

As an interactive process, heterophony is consistent with the intimate nature of the takht format. The takht ensemble is small enough to allow for its members to be heard and appreciated both as individuals and as a tightly knit musical group. For one thing, the timbral acoustic differentiation among the instruments enables the various heterophonic subtleties to be more discernible. Furthermore, the small performance-platform provides the individual musicians an intimate physical context ideally suited for establishing direct visual contact and exchanging various music related cues.

A trademark of the accomplished takht musician, heterophony has become less prominent in the modern musical mainstream. Heterophonic subtleties, which represent a small-group, or "chamber," aesthetic tend to be less obvious within, or perhaps less suited for, the typical post-1920s ensemble, which often performs fixed compositions and incorporates well over fifteen or twenty instruments. Within such a group, heterophonic nuances are likely to be muddled. More importantly perhaps, the emerging nonheterophonic relationships appear to coincide with further separation between the roles of the composer and the interpreter, and with an increasing sense of formality among the performers, whose stage seating is somewhat inspired by the European symphonic seating.[7] Less suited for heterophonic differentiation has been the duplication of instruments of the same type, epitomized by the use of several violins, often a dozen or more, and sometimes cellos and a double bass, in addition to various other instruments. This overall mixture has limited the timbral and acoustical transparency that typified traditional takht music. All of these factors have contributed to a somewhat evenly layered texture of parallel octaves and unisons that became well-established as an orchestral sound aesthetic.[8]

Heterophony constitutes a powerful tool of ecstatic evocation. It is generally felt that heterophonic interactions energize the musical content. In group performances, they give prominence to each of the individual parts, but also bind them together as an organic unit. In this respect, they represent an affective union between individuality and togetherness, or rather, individuality through togetherness. Furthermore, the ecstatic effect of heterophony stems from the textural fabric as such. The coordinated discrepancies among the individual parts, or differently stated, the performers' artful division of musical labor, generates a delectable sense of activity, a collective dynamism that is deeply enchanting.[9]

The direct relation between heterophonic interplay and emotional arousal

7 The rough resemblance appears for example in having a violin section to the left of the stage with cellos or a double-bass when available close to the right. However, conventionally the percussion is located at the extreme right, whereas the original takht instruments are placed in the middle.

8 It would not be totally accurate to say that the newer texture consists of exact parallel unisons and octaves. In effect, the unsynchronized bowing, along with some heterophonic nuances give the modern sound its characteristic opaque, or thick, quality, a new urban Arab texture distinct in itself.

9 Arab writers seldom conceptualize or analyze heterophony. However, it is briefly discussed by Samha Elkholy (Samḥah al-Khawlī); see Elkholy 1978. For additional information on the role of heterophony in takht music see Racy 1988.

is demonstrable on a vast number of early 78-rpm recordings. For example, impassioned verbal gestures are voiced in the middle of dawr performances, when the leading singer takes obvious heterophonic liberties or improvises several variants against reiterations by the chorus and the rest of the ensemble. Similarly illustrative are recordings of group instrumental genres such as the taḥmīlah, in which artists, typically of comparable stature and ability, produce complex heterophonic textures thus prompting a plethora of animated and distinctly heard vocal exclamations.[10] Further representations are displayed in Umm Kulthūm's live recordings from the 1940s and 1950s. In certain middle sections during which heterophonic activity becomes particularly prominent, a suspenseful and musically focused mood engulfs and audibly moves the singer's avid admirers.

The art of leading

In ṭarab music, certain hierarchies shape the musical content and render it more effective. In musical terms, the role of leadership is manifested in two basic formats, linear and vertical. In the linear format, the leading part, for example a singer's voice, is given prominence through the sequential order in which the musical material is presented. To illustrate, the leader's performance proper is usually prefaced by either precomposed or improvised, solo or ensemble instrumental preludes. Similarly, interludes, which tend to occur profusely throughout the performance, provide the featured performer with a sense of musical reference without undermining his or her role as the center of musical attention. In a vocal improvisation, a *tarjamah* (literally, translation), namely an improvised instrumental interlude that largely emulates a preceding vocal phrase, grants the leading vocalist suitable moments of repose between the improvised vocal phrases. It also reinforces his ecstatic message without disturbing his creative train of thought. Similarly, in a metric piece, for example in some compositions from the 1920s and 1930s, the *lawāzim*, or short instrumental "fillers" (singular, *lāzimah*)[11] add emphasis to the main beat and quite often outline the melodic structure of a preceding phrase by the leading artist. In some instances, a lāzimah may serve as a *kubrī*, or "bridge," as it moves toward a new tonal center or a new maqām, thus paving the way for the featured performer to make a full-fledged tonal shift or modulation. Typically however, the leading artist, who

[10] For a detailed analysis of a taḥmīlah performance see Racy 1988.

[11] The term *lāzimah* is related to the verb *lāzama*, namely to "accompany" or "stick to faithfully," and to the verb *lazima*, "to be needed." The abstract noun *mulāzamah* refers to the act of keeping company, and similarly the word *mulāzim* (feminine, *mulāzimah*) refers to someone or something that is retained, or perhaps constantly reintroduced.

represents the forefront of the ecstatic process, is granted the prerogative of a musical vanguard. Particularly in improvisatory genres, he or she is expected to initiate the various modal phases of the performance, to explore the new tonal areas of the mode, to introduce modulations to other maqāmāt, and to usher the return to the original mode of the performance.

The vertical format appears when heterophonic patterning enables the leader's individual musical line to stand out. More specifically, this happens when the heterophonic support provided by the rest of the ensemble is relatively subtle or sparse, particularly while the leading artist is actually performing. In turn, the leading artist tends to figure prominently on account of both the complex features of his performance and the greater fluidity of his creations vis-à-vis those of the accompanying ensemble. For example, in Sufi choral groups, a munshid may sing more ornately and melismatically than the rest of the group. He may sing only intermittently and momentarily "pull away" from the accentual pattern maintained by the rest of the ensemble. Similarly, a ṭarab singer may gain emphasis by improvising somewhat freely against a drone (or intermittent drone effect) or against an ostinato pattern.

Essentially, the role of leading demands a high level of group consciousness. Although it grants the featured artist considerable creative license, it requires good musical rapport within the entire ensemble. Healthy synchrony between the leader and the accompanists is a prerequisite for affective music making.

The art of accompanying

When called for, musical accompaniment plays a crucial role in the evocative process. Basically, an accompanying performer must be musically effective without being too prominent or obtrusive. Musicians usually describe good accompaniment as *tawrīq*, a term that implies subtlety and evokes the image of filling spaces somewhat sparsely with ornamental leaf designs (as in the case of calligraphy), or covering something with a thin film of paper or plaster. For example, a qānūn player accompanying a layālī and mawwāl performance must resist the temptation of competing with the muṭrib. He must refrain from moving ahead of the singer by anticipating the higher tonal areas of the mode, or playing more loudly than the vocalist, or producing melodic lines that are technically more complex or more ornate than those being accompanied. It is often stated that the accompanist must have *dhawq*, namely "taste" or "courtesy."

Ṭarab musicians devote a great deal of attention to the dynamics of accompanying particularly by praising the discreet and supportive accompanists and finding fault with those whom they consider musically self-centered, aggressive, and intent on soliciting attention. The latter type of musicians are criticized although their performances may be highly impressive from a purely technical point of view. Performers are often assessed in terms of their level of sensitivity as accompanists. During the 1930s the singer Muḥammad ʿAbd al-Wahhāb reportedly lost his patience with a well-known violinist for displaying excessive showmanship while accompanying him.[12] During one of his visits to Los Angeles, the elderly qānūn virtuoso Ibrāhīm Salmān was invited to listen to a young qānūn player perform, as the latter accompanied a local Arab singer. Asked about his impressions, Salmān described the young musician as having good technique, but his main problem was as follows: *bīqūl kathīr maʿ al muṭrib*, literally "he says too much with the singer," a jargon-based expression that referred to the younger musician's excessive performing when he accompanied.[13] Musicians in Los Angeles describe the impertinent showmanship of a young violinist by citing a specific incident, which they often reenact in order to make their point clear and to poke some humor. Accordingly, when a visiting vocal celebrity sang a layālī phrase, perhaps a short one in Rāst, one that began on the tonic, ascended to the fifth and cadenced back on the tonic, the violinist's "tarjamah" moved quickly to the fifth note then advanced to the octave note above the tonic. Also while descending, the violinist "threw in" a few accidentals, for example flattening the upper subtonic and momentarily raising the fourth step, before dropping to the lower tonic through a "flashy" qaflah more elaborate and quite different from the one that had been performed by the singer. Not surprisingly, such exhibitionism reportedly offended the singer and was suddenly noticed and scoffed at by the rest of the musicians.

It is generally felt that such display is disrespectful of the artist being featured. As it usurps his or her prerogative as a principal ṭarab initiator, it violates an established musical hierarchy. Certain anticipations by the accompanist, for example, leaping into a new pitch level ahead of the muṭrib or modulating to a new maqām, are sometimes called for by the composers. However, particularly in improvisatory contexts, such liberties could indicate that the accompanied performer is being rudely treated or looked at as being musically incompetent.

Most significantly perhaps, the manner of accompanying affects the ecstatic quality of the performance as a whole. Positively speaking, good accompanists inspire the muṭrib by instilling within him a feeling of salṭanah and helping him maintain that feeling throughout the performance. They furnish musical support that is succinct, yet stylistically eloquent and

[12] From an interview I conducted with Muḥammad al-ʿAqqād in Los Angeles in the summer of 1984. Reportedly, the violinist concerned was Sāmī al-Shawwā.

[13] Salmān, who is blind, is an Iraqi Jewish performer now living in Israel. He enjoys phenomenal technical mastery and outstanding ability to evoke feeling on the qānūn.

ecstatically conducive. In a sense, a good accompanist is a creative minimalist who utilizes his musical means economically to achieve the maximum ecstatic impact. His craft calls for finding the ideal balance between brevity and efficacy, correctness and aesthetic excellence. As qānūn player Muḥammad al-ʿAqqād explained, early takht musicians seemed to possess magical powers. Through their highly effective executions of short preludes, such as the *dawālīb* (plural of *dūlāb*), they were able to instill in the recording artists an immediate sense of modal transformation, thus enabling them to produce highly ecstatic performances.[14] By the same token, many recordings by brilliant singers have been ecstatically compromised, and for some connoisseurs even ruined, by the detrimental effect of one or several over-zealous accompanists.

In the course of performing, accompanying with taste requires a great deal of musical perceptiveness and ability to receive and respond to various nonverbal cues. It also entails the careful implementation of performance strategies that are called for by specific performing circumstances. These aspects of accompanying are illustrated in actual musical terms by Michel Merhej Baklouk, a well established riqq player who performed and recorded widely in Lebanon, and was on the teaching staff of the Lebanese Conservatory during the 1960s and 1970s.

Mr. Baklouk maintains that the riqq player must keep the beat constantly. However, he adds that at certain times the percussionist needs to hold back, contrary to what theorists and notated scores tell you, namely that the down beat (*dumm*) must remain predictably or uniformly strong. He explains that he himself would soften the accents so as not to overpower the textual delivery of a leading singer, particularly when the latter is about to delve into a delicate and emotionally involved passage. Accordingly, "when rigidity is avoided the feeling comes out." As he further clarifies, when the muṭrib enters into a phase of *taṭrīb* (a term that means creating powerful ecstasy and implies the stretching out of syllables or pulling away in calculated ways from the regular beat pattern), or when he appears particularly overtaken by the feeling of the text he is singing, that is the moment to hold back. In his words, "the worst thing I could do at that time is to blast the singer with strong beats. Therefore, I resort to a more reserved mode of playing until the right moment comes for bringing back the full effect of the īqāʿ."

Baklouk admits that at times such discretion disturbs ensemble directors, who think that the beat must not be altered or softened, probably fearing that such interventions will throw them or some of the musicians off. However, he hastens to add that first of all, the riqq player is not a machine and that machine-like playing does not produce feeling. Moreover, when the muṭrib is in a deep emotional state he cannot be bogged down by a rigid or

[14] From the 1984 interview mentioned earlier.

excessively imposing beat pattern. In other words, a good percussionist knows when to offer the leading performer the "space" needed for moving into a profound ecstatic state, or "as a percussionist you have to give and take."[15]

In short, accompanying is an art that feeds into the ecstatic flow of the performance. Generally speaking, affective accompanying occurs in two related ways. Firstly, through a combination of sound musicianship and stylistic circumspection, the accompanist provides the leading performer with direct aesthetic stimulation before and during the performance without disrupting his or her internal creative process. Secondly, good accompaniment produces the basic rhythmic and melodic backdrop against which the creative leader can make synchronized digressions that in turn excite the ecstatically minded listener. In either case, the accompanist is an organic part of ṭarab evocation.

The role of ornaments

Ornaments, which some modern literary sources refer to as *ḥilyāt ṣawtiyyah* (or, "sound embellishments"), are among the most effective tools of ecstatic stimulation. The types of ornaments used and the frequency of their occurrence depends largely upon the musical style and the historical background of the ṭarab artist. Typically, early-twentieth-century singers such as Shaykh Salāmah Ḥijāzī, Munīrah al-Mahdiyyah, and Fatḥiyyah Aḥmad tended to use ornaments profusely. In more recent decades, certain types of ornaments have practically disappeared, and furthermore, the renditions of singers have generally become less ornate.

The evocative power of ornaments, although seldom articulated as such, is tacitly recognized and appreciated. When properly placed and executed, for example as part of a cadential motif or in the course of a prolonged note, ornaments tend to elicit observable listening responses. They appear to draw the listener's attention closely to the music, as well as to qualify the performer as a "genuine artist." Rendered either vocally or instrumentally, embellishments exist in a wide variety, ranging from subtle grace-note effects to long held tremolo-like gyrations. They may also coexist with various other effects, such as the subtle portamento (or sliding between notes) and the wave-like manipulation of individual notes, in contrast to the

15 From a conversation with Mr. Baklouk (Mīshāl Mirhij Baqlūq) on Sept. 1, 1997. Having worked extensively with the Raḥbānī Brothers and the singer Fayrūz in Lebanon, Baklouk now lives in New Jersey. In this report, Baklouk attributes his strategy to the legendary riqq player and renowned Umm Kulthūm accompanist, Ibrāhīm ʿAfīfī, with whom he had conversed at an earlier time about the "secrets" of good accompanying.

rapid classical-European vibrato, which in the context of ṭarab music would be considered inappropriate or even distasteful.

The use of ornaments reflects both individual preference and established convention. We are told, for example, that among the secrets of Umm Kulthūm's success early in her career was her judicious use and careful timing of ornaments, a trait that granted her ṭarab delivery a refreshing sense of structure and refinement. When guiding a traditional Lebanese female singer toward the path of professional success, Muḥammad ʿAbd al-Wahhāb is said to have advised her to be more circumspect in the use of ornaments. Nevertheless, the role of embellishments in the process of ṭarab making remains quintessential. Having reminded some medieval writers of the melancholic singing of the nightingale, ṭarab ornaments entail various sorts of tonal, rhythmic, dynamic, and timbral applications. When properly executed, they generate irresistible aesthetic stimulation, delectable agitation that is highly ecstatic.

The vocal ethos

In the ṭarab culture, the *ṣawt*, or "voice," is recognized as a supreme medium of evocation. In a short but highly indicative statement appearing in a chapter on the acoustical and stylistic properties of musical instruments, Kāmil al-Khulaʿī wrote:

> You must keep in mind that the best mode of musical execution is the human voice. It is the most magnificent of all musical media (aʿḍhamuhā). Suffice it to say that when it is available, instruments can be dispensed with, and that instruments are in need of it. Moreover, it delivers to the mind meanings in the form of sung lyrics. It also causes great musical enchantment and produces more ṭarab than do other performance media. It is also more supple than the others in view of its ability to fulfill various technical needs and to do so with great mastery. (ca. 1904: 59)

Ṭarab voices share particular musical characteristics, but also vary within a certain margin of acoustical acceptability. In the early twentieth century, the voices of the male singers were by and large strident and relatively speaking high pitched. The female voices, for example that of Sakīnah Ḥasan, tended to be low-pitched as well as strongly projected. In terms of timbral variety, Munīrah al-Mahdiyyah for example was famous for her "seductive" husky voice and characteristic *baḥḥah* (literally, "hoarseness"). The more contemporary male voices range from being brilliant and relatively high-pitched (as illustrated by the voice of Syrian singer Ṣabaḥ Fakhrī) to being mellow and relatively low-pitched (for instance the voice of Egypt's Muḥammad ʿAbd al-Wahhāb later in his life). Such variety is to some extent applicable to the

Singers and composers Wadīʿ al-Ṣāfī (b. 1921) and Farīd al-Aṭrash (1915–1974) performing informally in Beirut in 1970. Photo courtesy of Dār al-Ṣayyād.

modern female singers. Similarly, ṭarab listeners today may savor the charming rasp of such late singers as Ṣāliḥ ʿAbd al-Ḥayy and Muḥammad ʿAbd al-Muṭṭalib, or the "weeping" vocal quality of the late Farīd al-Aṭrash. Comparably, one connoisseur explained that the late Syrian singer Muḥammad Khayrī sang in an enchantingly "grainy" voice that shifted and developed progressively as the performance went on. Accordingly, his voice had a kind of roughness and variability that made it ecstatically irresistible.[16]

Certain types of vocal production are considered basic to ṭarab singing. Underlying the various timbral profiles is an affinity for the "natural" vocal register for either women or men. What is traditionally valued can be roughly described as a full, somewhat throat-controlled chest voice, in contrast to the "head," or falsetto voice (*ṣawt mustaʿār*, literally, borrowed or

[16] From a conversation in Los Angeles in the early 1980s.

artificial voice), which in ṭarab singing is deemed aesthetically objectionable, or at least recognized as being alien to ṭarab vocal artistry.[17]

Furthermore, modern ṭarab listeners cherish voices that are supple and able to produce ornaments and various rhythmic and tonal effects with full ease. In the musicians' jargon, the expression *fīh ʿurab*, roughly "it has microtonal nuances," is used to describe the voice of the ecstatically engaging singer, specifically the ability to render the various microtonal inflections accurately and with great mastery. Also praised are singers who seem to enjoy an exceptionally wide melodic range. Historians recount somewhat proverbially that in the course of one performance ʿAbduh al-Ḥāmulī continued to ascend melodically until his qānūn accompanist threw up his hands in utter amazement as he "ran out of strings."[18] However, it is extremely important that the voice maintain its richness and timbral consistency in both low and high registers. As musicians put it, a good ṭarab singer needs to be good in both the *qarārāt*, the lower-octave notes, and the *jawābāt*, the upper-octave notes. A further, and no less significant advantage lies in the singer's ability to enunciate the sung text properly. As in the Islamic religious tradition, the ṭarab culture places a high premium on clear utterance. Indeed, clarity of textual delivery, as well as the correct pronunciation of classical Arabic consonants, are among the trademarks of an effective ṭarab singer. [19]

To close, the efficacy of ṭarab singing is multidimensional. The voice produces an extraordinary impact through its distinctive timbral quality, melodic fluency, and intonational flexibility. Furthermore, it enjoys special symbolic significance as a supreme religious medium and an auditory link between the secular and the mystical realms. Ultimately, it combines an emotive literary idiom with an affective message that is purely musical.

Textual stretching

As a rule, the sung lyrics are sparse. A muwashshaḥ which takes five or more minutes to sing often has no more than a few couplets of text. A mawwāl that

[17] Influenced by Western classical pedagogy, which upholds the European operatic paradigm, a certain falsetto quality is noticeable in the delivery of some young female, especially Lebanese, singers. This phenomenon has drawn criticism from traditional music connoisseurs and performers.

[18] From al-Jundī 1984: 42.

[19] When using classical Arabic, singers (and for that matter public speakers), especially in Egypt and among the Lebanese urbanites, sometimes mispronounce certain consonants, specifically by changing the "*th*" sound into an "*s*", the "*dh*" into a "*z*", and the "*ḍh*" into a "*ẓ*", Such conversions tend to disturb the linguistically trained ear and detract from the ecstatic flow of the vocal performance.

could last for more than ten minutes usually consists of seven or fewer short lines of poetry. In the late nineteenth and early twentieth centuries, a qaṣīdah singer sometimes based his entire performance on a few selected lines from an older and much longer love poem. The hundreds of Egyptian adwār, each of which could have taken more than forty-five minutes to perform in a live context, generally incorporated no more than a handful of poetry lines each. In these various genres, the sung texts are stretched out musically by the composers and performers.

The stretching of texts acquires different forms. To begin with, in the actual vocal performance, a variety of instrumental preludes and interludes are interjected. In the singing proper, vocal stretching is represented to a large extent by the profuse application of vocal melismas, or the singing of many notes per single syllable of text, usually a vowelled consonant (as compared to syllabic singing, when only one or a few musical notes correspond to a single textual syllable). As ṭarab devices, melismas prevailed in the Egyptian dawr, which developed into a highly sophisticated musical genre in the late nineteenth century, but gradually died out in Egypt after the 1920s. Toward the middle of the dawr performance, melismas were best represented by the several vocalizations on the sound *āh* by the singer and the chorus, passages that were known collectively as the *āhāt*. Accordingly, the singer led the chorus members into a sustained note against which he created his own vocalizations. He then led them into another sustained note, typically one step higher upon which he vocalized again, and so on.

Melismatic stretching also occurs in the layālī, which is one of the prime improvisatory genres in ṭarab music. Typically preceding and leading seamlessly into the mawwāl, which is similarly improvised but has a regular poetical text, the layālī performance consists in its entirety of vocalizations, on a minimal number of syllables, in particular *yā layl*, or *yā laylī*.[20] In a single phrase, for example, it is typical to stretch the yā syllable across a large number of notes and then to end with the word *layl* less melismatically.

Textual stretching also stems from the practice of inserting into the original texts certain verbal fillers. Usually referred to as *tarannumāt*, or *tarannum* (from the verb *rannama*, roughly, to chant devotionally or to sing in an enchanted manner), these additions include such expressions as *amān*, *lallī*, *layl*, and word combinations such as *lallī aman*, *yalā lallī amān*, *amān yā lā lallī*, and *jānim amān*. The tarannumāt are most typically used in the metrically complex, precomposed, muwashshaḥ genre. Structurally

[20] The literal meaning of *yā layl* or *yā laylī* is "oh, night!" or "oh, my night!," and that of another often used expression, namely *yā ʿayn* or *yā ʿaynī* is "oh, eye!" or "oh, my eye!" Contrary to some popular theories that explain the use of these expressions solely in terms of their literal meanings, the prevalence of such utterances as *layl* and *laylī* and the comparable expression *lallī* may have to do with their singable quality and highly enchanting sonic effects.

speaking, they serve as tools for stretching out the sung phrases. As such, they give the compositional process greater elasticity in terms of fitting texts in specific poetical meters to metric modes of determined lengths. Usually melismatically rendered, the tarannumāt add a great deal of emotional efficacy to the composition. Musical theorists and critics often correlate these and other, mostly nonlexical, devices directly with taṭrīb. Being semantically less descript, they also provide temporary relief from regular textuality, and perhaps enable the text proper to make more impact when it reappears in the course of singing. Furthermore, such standard expressions impress through their inherent auditory properties. As sung utterances, they possess a certain flow that makes them distinctly enchanting.[21]

Texts are also stretched through fragmentation and repetition. Sometimes the same textual phrase would be repeated either with slight melodic variation or in a different melody altogether. Also, a singer (or, in the case of precomposed vocal works, a composer), may repeat a certain poetical fragment, word, or even syllable more than once. Breaking the text into fragments of different lengths was quite common in the large middle section of the dawr, particularly in the passage (or passages) known as the *hank*. Here, the leading vocalist sang a textual fragment, usually one or two words, then "tossed it" to the chorus members to be reiterated throughout several call–response, or solo–chorus exchanges. In these exchanges the singer was free to create melodic and even modal variations in alternation with, or sometimes against, the choral responses.[22]

To conclude, textual sparsity and elasticity contribute to the ecstatic efficacy of ṭarab vocal music. Representing a deeply rooted aesthetic, word economy establishes a workable balance between textual–semantic evocation and vocal–musical stimulation. This balance precludes the stifling effect of excessive wordiness or extreme semanticization, thus giving the music more space to "breathe." Similarly, textual stretching enables the composer to break away at least momentarily from the rigidity of the poetical meters and the verbal patterns of accentuation. It grants him freedom to plot his own melodic, metric, and accentual path without deviating totally from the overall textual framework. Contrastingly, when singing is syllabically confined or textually saturated it tends to move away from the evocative mode of taṭrīb, although it may still be appreciated for its declamatory

21 In recent decades, certain music transcribers and chorus leaders in Syria, Lebanon, and Egypt have attempted to rid the muwashshaḥāt of "the reminiscences of Ottoman influence" by purging out such tarannumāt as *amān*, *jānim*, and *ʿimrim*, and replacing them all with layl or yā layl. In pure musical terms, such symbolic and largely politicized practice compromises the evocative richness of the idiom and leads to a form of redundancy that tends to encumber the vocal expression and limit its overall ecstatic impact.

22 The word *hank* may be related to the Persian-Ottoman word *āhang*, namely "tune" or "something tuneful or harmonious." For more information on the dawr structure, see Note 60 below.

"energy." Indeed, the use of brief but musically stretchable texts grants ṭarab singing tremendous ecstatic fluidity. In a sense, it allows the music to be more musical.

Interpretive liberties

The ability to create one's own rendition of an existing musical model is highly praised. The concept of *taṣarruf*, which usually refers to the taking of legal or literary liberties, or simply to the practice of individual discretion, is also applied to the music. Taṣarruf constitutes an artistic skill that a genuine ṭarab performer applies intuitively and effectively at the time of performing. By the same token, takht composers tended to leave room for the interpreters' input, and probably expected them to add their own nuances and embellishments to the composed works. Although particularly common in the Egyptian dawr, interpretive liberties occurred in various vocal and instrumental genres. An integral part of the final compositional product, such liberties made the difference between a dull performance and a highly engaging one.

Recent decades have witnessed an increasing preference for fixed compositional format. Similarly, with the dominance of Western-based pedagogy and the prevalence of large performing groups, fewer young performers seem interested or fully competent in the art of taṣarruf. Nevertheless, interpretive liberties are still displayed by the traditionally trained ṭarab musicians. When interpreting a musical score, for example, performers may add their own ornaments and melodic and rhythmic nuances. In this case, their reading is truly a process of "translation," or conversion of the notation into music. As some musicians explain, the added nuances bring to the music "sweetness" (*ḥalāwah*) and feeling. It is said that after the performers had fully learned his composition from a musical score, the famous composer Zakariyyā Aḥmad told them, "from now on take the notation away and give me *mazāj*," roughly "mood" or "feeling."[23]

In technical terms, when musical works are flexibly interpreted several evocative devices are at work. Performing with taṣarruf implies adding certain ornaments, inserting slurs between the notes, producing prominent heterophonic variations against other musical parts, lengthening or shortening some syllables, de-emphasizing or shifting the position of some accents, and creating a sense of drama by momentarily switching to a more

[23] This was conveyed to me in September, 1998 by Salīm Saḥḥāb, a Lebanese conductor who currently leads an Arab choral group in Egypt. Accordingly, the incident happened when the performers were learning the song *Yā Ḥalawt id-Dunyā*, sung by Zakiyyah Ḥamdān.

declamatory style of delivery or adding subtle but expressive dynamic inflections. The performer may also temporarily break away from the regular meter, or in the case of vocal music may substitute a word or expression in the lyrics with another of his own, often to add a touch of humor or to create a startling twist to an all familiar text. In extreme cases, the practice of taṣarruf veers more closely toward outright composition. The singer for example may improvise or compose an entire new section within an existing work.

To conclude, flexible musical interpretations produce tremendous ecstasy through the use of highly evocative musical devices. Basically, they convert the mere act of reproducing music into an instantaneous and contextually inspired mode of recasting it creatively and evocatively. In the course of performing, an ecstatically conceived musical composition may both realize its full ecstatic potentials and gain new efficacies. Furthermore, such interpretations render the overall compositional process more dynamic while preserving its collaborative essence. More specifically, it accommodates both the "work" as a prior musical design and the interpretation as a spontaneous and individualized, artistic endeavor. The interpreter teases out the compositional form without breaking it, tantalizes musical expectations without totally violating them, and presents refreshing departures without obfuscating their essential points of reference. In all, the manipulation of preconceived structures renders the musical message more potent. Ecstatically speaking, it brings out the "real music."

Improvisation as evocation

Improvisatory genres are primary vehicles of ecstatic arousal. Created in performance, improvised music follows the overall melodic designs embodied in the various melodic modes, namely the dozen or more maqāmāt that are commonly employed today. Improvisations, whether instrumental or vocal, are: typically through-composed, in other words, nonstrophic, or devoid of verse-like repetitions; solo-oriented; and nonmetric, or "rhythmically free," although in some cases, for example when ostinato-accompanied, they may display noticeable metric patterning. Improvisations can be heard as separate pieces or in conjunction with other nonimprovised genres. Traditionally, improvising is viewed as a highly sophisticated art, an affective expression that requires extraordinary skill, talent, and inspiration.

In recent decades, improvising has become less prevalent. A case in point is the diminished role of vocal improvisation in the repertoires of Cairo's modern-minded and media-conscious artists. As Egyptian musicologist Samha Elkholy explains, the gradual decline of the takht tradition after

World War I, the importation of Western musical values, and the preference for large ensemble formats all had an adverse effect on modal improvisation, as well as on the traditional practice of heterophony.[24] These developments notwithstanding, modal improvisation continues to exist, especially among the more traditionally oriented ṭarab performers. In Egypt, both improvisation and heterophony are also common in certain dance related instrumental genres and in the performances of some urbanized folk ensembles.[25]

The extraordinary emotional impact of modal improvisations is often quite observable. During a taqāsīm or layālī performance the serious listeners' attention tends to be exceptionally focused. Similarly, their verbal gestures seem profound, as well as perfectly synchronized with the musical content. In religious contexts, such responses have been noted for example during the masterful Sufi qaṣīdah and tawshīḥ performances of Shaykh Ṭaha al-Fashnī. In secular events, they may punctuate the *mawāwīl* (plural of *mawwāl*) of renowned vocalists, Ṣabaḥ Fakhrī, Wadīʿ al-Ṣāfī, and others.

The distinct emotional efficacy of modal improvisation has also been articulated by members of the ṭarab culture, music educators, theorists, and sammīʿah alike. Toward the middle of the twentieth century, the Syrian theorist, composer, and violin virtuoso Tawfīq al-Ṣabbāgh (1892–1964), criticized the Western-trained local musicians whose improvisations fail to create true feeling, and added that "the taqāsīm are the most sublime component in instrumental performing in general" (1950: 104). This view was echoed by another Syrian scholar some forty years later. According to Maḥmūd ʿAjjān "good taqāsīm have a magical effect and are considered among the most beautiful, tender, and desirable types of instrumental music." He added that this artistic expression is "among the most ecstatic (*aktharuhā ṭaraban*), and among the dearest to a healthy connoisseur spirit" (1990: 69). These and other similar statements testify to the ṭarab culture's premium on modal improvisation, especially the taqāsīm, as a medium of ṭarab evocation.

The manner in which improvisation creates ecstatic feeling is complex, partly because improvised performances utilize a large variety of components: tonal, intervallic, temporal, and structural. Generally, the improviser appeals to his or her listeners in two closely related ways. The first can be described as the artful use of familiar modal material. In this case, the

[24] Elkholy 1978: 11 and 24.

[25] In Egypt today, these musical techniques may be found in the so-called *titt* music, which is folk-dance oriented and may utilize the accordion and some brass instruments, in addition to a few local instruments. Also both improvisation and heterophony are predominent in the performances of urbanized folk ensembles that play a combination of timbrally diverse instruments, including the *rabābah* (spike-fiddle), the *arghūl* (chanter-and-drone double-pipe) and the *mizmār* (double-reed instrument). These ensembles retain a style of playing that reminds us of the earlier takht music.

improvisatory practice offers the performer "a kind of table of contents of the mode" or a set of ingredients that are "at least to a degree obligatory" (Nettl 1974: 12, 13). In specific terms, it provides access to such phenomena as typical beginning notes, stylized cadential motifs, likely sequential patterns for ordering the shorter and longer phrases, and common overall progressions, for example those displaying gradually ascending then gradually descending contours. In addition there are characteristic intervallic structures, notes of emphasis, and likely modulatory scenarios. On a finer level, improvisations also incorporate a vast number of small motivic structures that reappear in numerous variations from one performance to another, and to some extent, from one mode to another.[26]

The ways in which such familiar components are introduced and manipulated to create powerful emotions can be observed through the listeners' gestures vis-à-vis the improvising performer. In her study on Qur'anic chanting in Egypt, Kristina Nelson indicates that typically, the highly responsive listeners implore the shaykh to fulfill certain expectations:

> Listeners would also shout out their requests, and these were particularly revealing of their expectations: "Again, so we can memorize it!" "How about the higher register?" (ig-gawāb), "Give us (maqām) Shūri!" "(maqām) Ṣaba! By the Prophet, we're waiting for Ṣaba!" Where there were musical references to other reciters, knowledgeable listeners would shout out the name of the reciter quoted in delighted recognition, with such comments as, "He's taken us back thirty years!" (1982: 43)

Nelson adds that reciters rely on their audiences for guidance in such matters as dwelling on certain modes or moving to others that the listeners happen to like or to request. She also notes that reciters who respond to the listeners and recognize them as a source of guidance and inspiration are those whose musical delivery is more moving.

The second mode of evocation requires introducing components that are novel, as well as aesthetically fitting. In other words, the improviser must avoid structures that are extremely redundant or predictable. In a number of Arabic sources we encounter direct correlations between ecstatic feeling and improvisatory freedom. For example, al-Ṣabbāgh writes:

> A *taqsīm* [singular of *taqāsīm*] is a tune that is nonmetric and improvised (*murtajal*). It is the fruit of the performer's imagination and taste and therefore is unlimited. The taqāsīm performance is the litmus test of the performers' talent, a medium through which their ability and scope of imagination can be ascertained. It is the greatest thing in all music. If the performer is skillful in the taqsīm and possesses strong feeling (*iḥsās qawī*), broad imagination, and healthy taste he can evoke in

[26] Nettl and Riddle (1973) show for example that the taqāsīm vary in such areas as performance length and may or may not incorporate modulations, but display considerable unity in the use of detailed melodic and rhythmic motifs and sequences.

the listener the magical influence of the most magnificent orchestra in the world. (1950: 140–141)

The author elaborates even further upon the direct correlation between novelty and ecstasy, as he stresses that if the improvisation is less imaginative and less novel, in other words less improvised, it loses its emotional value considerably. Similarly, ʿAjjān recognizes the direct connection between flexibility and ṭarab feeling. "The taqāsīm must be created at the spur of the moment (*min waḥī al-khāṭīr*) and improvised according to the performer's own inclination." He adds that the taqāsīm, which "express the artist's inner emotional tribulations (*infiʿālāt*), attest to the breadth of his knowledge, and reflect the ambiance surrounding his performance, can generate superb influence and pleasurable reactions" (1990: 70).

Musically, the manifestations of improvisatory freedom are both extensive and diverse. For example, it is generally felt that good improvisers must avoid sounding too stereotypical. Accordingly, "a musician who wishes to create ecstasy (*yuṭrib*) must not limit himself to customary or familiar modulations. He has to include unfamiliar surprises, which in turn arouse the enthusiasm and admiration of the audience" (Qūjamān 1978: 87).[27] The same can be applied to other components, such as melodic progressions and the use of accidentals and cadential patterns. Such surprises are appreciated for being ecstatically moving, as well as for being witty or clever. Needless to say, what differentiates a successful surprise from an unsuccessful one is not always easy to pinpoint. Similarly, the task of presenting modally convincing and ecstatically moving surprises can be musically challenging and even risky. However, excessive redundancy and the absence of creative novelties can rob an improvisation of its ecstatic potentials or render it emotionally static.

To close, improvisation operates on a variety of compositional, performative, and symbolic levels. The improviser presents the common modal vocabulary in ways that satiate, as well as tantalize, the listener's modal expectations. He also seeks to introduce novelties that stretch out the idiom's artistic potentials. By and large, he produces ecstasy by skillfully combining the notion of what *is* with the realization of what *can be*.

Modality as ecstatic substance

Modal stimulation derives impetus from the modal substance itself, namely the individual ingredients and microprocesses that make up the actual modal

[27] For specific information on modulatory patterns see Marcus 1992.

compositions. In other words, the modal "building blocks" (Nettl 1974: 12–13) are known to possess certain emotive relevancies, or as Habib Hassan Touma explains they constitute the "raw material" through which "the Arab musician creates emotional climates . . ." (1976: 33–36). Accordingly, the musical vocabulary can be viewed as ecstatic stuff.

Individually, the building components operate in a variety of ways. For example, "tonal fixation," or the treatment of a specific note as a tonal base, provides the performance with a tonal anchor, a *qarār* or "tonic," literally "place of repose" or "stopping." On a certain level, tonicity generates mental resonance that in modal terms is both delectable and compositionally stimulating. In the mind of the modally experienced artist it can offer both a sense of tonal referentiality and a certain urge for potential melodic creations to unfold. Providing tonal footing for a vast number of melodic-progressional possibilities, it tends to induce and ecstatically charge the linear, or melodic drive. In turn, linear motion, in other words the fleshed out intervallic-scalar track, embodies aspects of both tonicity and tonal variety. If tonal fixation stands for the vertical grounding that gives the modal performance its resounding focus, movement represents the horizontal flow that grants the modal work its engaging kinetic energy.

In its most basic, or least contrived form, modal movement is temporally flexible, in other words devoid of metricity. Similarly, it can be textless as well as "tuneless," that is to say, compositionally "neutral," or unbound by a specific preset tune.[28] In certain theory books, the *sayr*, literally "path," namely a brief written sketch describing how each mode unfolds, clearly implies that the most direct realization of the essential modal design lies in the realm of "pure" melody, or flexible melodic motion epitomized by the taqāsīm. Although far from being rhythmically, motivically, or structurally amorphous, modal improvisation appears to gain tremendous efficacy from its meterless, declamatory fluidity.

Comparably, textlessness may grant the melodic dimension added versatility. Although sung lyrics add their own type of emotional affect, their absence tends to highlight the modal substance itself, whose brand of ecstasy seems to have paramount appeal to the trained ṭarab ear. Indeed, genres that are textless or in which texts are used minimally, for example the layālī, the

[28] The notion of modal improvisation as being "tuneless" or compositionally "neutral" safeguards religious texts from the imposition of external, or humanly contrived, compositional creations. Tuneless music allows the sacred words themselves to structure the performance, as well as to accommodate the desirable melodic embellishments of the talented reciter. In a similar vein, Sayyid Makkāwī mentioned that Shaykh ʿAlī Maḥmūd, who is best known for recording improvised Sufi qaṣāʾid, composed the music for one of ʿAbd al-Wahhāb's early strophic songs, *Khāyif Aqūl illi fī Qalbī*, but declined to take credit for it in order to avoid the spiritually unbecoming connotation of being a musical composer. From the conversation with Mr. Makkāwī in Los Angeles on May 30, 1994.

āh vocalizations of the dawr, and the stretched out tarannumāt within the mawashshaḥāt, are all considered prime vehicles for the practice of taṭrīb. Similarly viewed are the long and florid melismas that, when artfully displayed for example by Sufi performers such as the late Shaykh Ṭaha al-Fashnī of Egypt, tend to invoke a tremendous elative frenzy among the diehard listeners. Basically, textual sparsity and rhythmic flexibility give the modal artist added freedom of movement and direct connectedness to the melodic content. Less fettered by the various semantic and syntactic interventions, the inspired improviser is provided further room to reflect inwardly into his own stream of modal consciousness, a process of musical "soul searching" implicitly recognized through the verbal expressions commonly used to describe the improvisatory process. Accordingly, an improviser who is endowed with "great imagination" (*khayāl wāsiʿ*) and "strong feeling" (*iḥsās qawī*) (al-Ṣabbāgh 1950:14) receives his inspiration "from the realm of inner consciousness" (*min waḥī al-khāṭir*), experiences "inner tribulations" (*infiʿālāt*), and derives his musical ideas "from the depths of his psychic feeling" (*min aʿmāq shuʿūrihi al-nafsī*) (ʿAjjān 1990: 70).

Melodic motion benefits from other evocative devices, for example those related to phrasing, pauses, intonation, accidental notes, and cadences. The emotive potentials of these devices are usually recognized and at times debated by musicians and music critics. This is particularly true in the case of the basic microtonal steps found in some of the commonly heard maqāmāt, for example Rāst, Bayyātī, Sīkāh-Huzām, and Ṣabá. Frequently voiced is the opinion that maqāmāt with such "neutral" steps, embody ecstatic qualities that are extraordinarily potent.[29] Accordingly, these "genuinely Arab" or "Near-Eastern" modes (*maqāmāt Sharqiyyah aṣīlah*) are difficult to fathom and subsequently to reproduce ecstatically by the nonnative or nontraditional musician. Upon hearing that some Western students have been learning how to play Arab music, one Lebanese violinist asked a typical question: "Do they really feel the microtonal steps (or *arbāʿ*, literally 'quarter-tones')?" In other words, can they experience the emotive sensations of the neutral steps in order to play Arab music with feeling?[30]

[29] See, for instance, al-Jundī 1984: 16. Here, the concept of "neutral" is used to refer to tonal degrees that fall roughly in the middle between two diatonic steps, for example one intervening between the minor-third and the major-third steps. In modern theories, such neutral degrees are usually presented as notes lowered or raised by roughly a quarter tone. They are typically indicated by special half-flat and half-sharp signs. To illustrate, in relative pitch, the Rāst octave scale is generally represented as *c*, *d*, *e*-half-flat, *f*, *g a*, *b*-flat (or half-flat), *c′*; Bayyātī: *d*, *e*-half-flat, *f*, *g*, *a*, *b*-flat (or half-flat), *c′*, *d′*; Sīkāh-Huzām (or Sīkāh ʿArabī as al-Ṣabbāgh calls it), which is usually played more like Huzām: *e*-half-flat, *f*, *g*, *a*-flat, *b*, *c′*, *d′*, e′-half-flat. Sometimes Sīkāh proper (pure Sīkāh) is also played, in this case with the notes *a*-natural and *b*-flat (or half-flat), although most often the two formats Sīkāh and Huzām are blended together, thus forming what can be conveniently called "Sīkāh-Huzām."

[30] The word *rubʿ*, singular of arbāʿ, is sometimes used to mean a neutral step. Incidentally, this comment was made in Los Angeles in the early 1980s.

In a broader sense, the maqāmāt are represented as autonomous ecstatic packages. Performers and listeners generally view all the modes as being ecstatic, but also speak of them as individual emotive entities. They tend to give them dissimilar ecstatic profiles and even maintain that some are more ecstatically engaging than others. During an informal musical gathering, the late Tunisian female singer, ʿUlayyah al-Tūnisiyyah echoed a certain feeling among musicians that the modes Ḥijāz, Sīkāh-Huzām, and Ṣabá produce an extraordinary level of salṭanah, or modal-ecstatic domination over the performer and the listener.[31] Also, "popular" maqāmāt such as Bayyātī are thought to produce ecstatic influences that are more potent than those of other relatively more "academic" modes, such as Nakrīz and Nawā Athar, especially among the less sophisticated listeners. As the Egyptian music historian Maḥmūd Kāmil explains: "If you were to perform for a group of ordinary listeners you are more likely to choose such maqāmāt as Bayyātī, Rāst, and Ḥijāz, rather than something like Ḥijāz Kār."[32] Similarly, one Syrian singer from the city of Ḥimṣ remarked that, whereas Bayyātī appeals to ṭarab listeners in general, it usually takes a sammīʿ to truly appreciate Nahawand.[33] Meanwhile, asked why he relied so much on Bayyātī for evoking ṭarab, Muḥammad ʿAbd al-Wahhāb explained:

> Indeed, Bayyātī is more saturated with ṭarab than any other maqām. Providing the foundation for all the Eastern modes that we sing in, it has close connections with dhikr and other forms of religious song, whose deep effect upon us we cannot resist. Even when the mashāyikh recite the Qurʾān, they begin with the mode Bayyātī and close with it. (Saḥḥāb, Ilyās 1980: 88)

In a comparable vein, musicians may feel attracted to certain modes, or seem particularly vulnerable to their ecstatic effects. In one musical get together in Cairo, one ʿūd player who admitted having a passionate love for, and a constant urge to play in, Kurd explained that a friend of his, apparently a traditional sammīʿ, was annoyed at this ʿūdist's bizarre obsession with such a "relatively less ecstatic maqām."[34] In another context, a well-known Egyptian riqq player explained that he succumbs to a state of profound elation whenever Nahawand is performed. When asked why he reacted in

[31] In conventional listings Ḥijāz has the following notes: *d*, *e*-flat, *f*-sharp, *g*, *a*, *b*-flat (or half-flat), *c*′, *d*′. Ṣabá has: *d*, *e*-half-flat, *f*, *g*-flat, *a*, *b*-flat, *c*′, *d*′, (or *d*′-flat). This gathering, which was referred to earlier, took place in Los Angeles in the early 1980s.

[32] The octave scale of Nakrīz is usually described as: *c*, *d*, *e*-flat, *f*-sharp, *g*, *a*, *b*-flat, *c*′; Nawā Athar: *c*, *d*, *e*-flat, *f*-sharp, *g*, *a*-flat, *b*, *c*′; Ḥijāz Kār: *c*, *d*-flat, *e*, *f*, *g*, *a*-flat, *b*, *c*′. The quote is from a conversation I had with Maḥmūd Kāmil in Cairo in the early 1970s.

[33] The octave scale of Nahawand is presented as: *c*, *d*, *e*-flat, *f*, *g*, *a*-flat, *b* (or *b*-flat), *c*′. The comment came up in a conversation in Los Angeles on November 21,1986.

[34] The octave scale of Kurd (or Ḥijāz Kār Kurd) is usually defined as *c*, *d*-flat, *e*-flat, *f*, *g*, *a*-flat, *b*-flat, *c*′. This mode has a typical descending tendency. The above report comes from a conversation I had with the artist in Cairo in May, 1989.

this way he answered poetically, that when he hears Nahawand, he feels as if someone has laid on the palm of his hand a jewel of breathtaking beauty, thus causing him to become spellbound and unable to move his sight away from that jewel.[35]

Establishing modal feeling

In modal music, whether precomposed or improvised, the generation of ecstasy requires the creation of strong modal presence. The maqām must "reign" fully so as to move and engage the listener. Inherent in the conventional *sayr* progressions of the various maqāmāt, the idea of unequivocal modal feeling is usually referred to as *rukūz al-maqām*, "the stabilization of the mode," or *iḍhhār shakhṣiyyat al-maqām*, "bringing out the character of the mode." Implied is the establishment of a strong tonal center, for example by emphasizing the tonic through reiterating it, frequently going back to it, cadencing upon it, and in some cases sounding it as a drone. Modal presence also means that the intervals of the mode are produced accurately and that the modal progression is presented gradually rather than rushed through.

The correlation between modal stability and ecstasy is well recognized by the practicing musicians and their initiated listeners. In 1972 the late Egyptian qānūn player and maker Maḥmūd Ra'fat, who continued to perform on a qānūn without tuning levers, following the tradition of his late-nineteenth- early-twentieth-century "idol," qānūn player Muḥammad al-ʿAqqād (Sr.), performed for me an almost half-hour-long taqsīm that stayed in Bayyātī without modulating to other maqāmāt. Ra'fat explained that staying in the same maqām for a long time, if the music is executed properly, can have tremendous emotional power, adding that young musicians who are impatiently eager to modulate expose their weakness as well as fail to produce real ṭarab.[36] Ra'fat's criticism of premature or uncalled-for modulations is reminiscent of a report by a young nāy player regarding a performance he and his group gave in Buenos Aires before a musically initiated audience of Syrian Jews. When this nāy player made a fast departure from Rāst, the original maqām of a taqsīm he had been performing, to another mode, one well-seasoned sammīʿ provided him with friendly criticism: *Shabbiʿ al-Rāst bil-awwal*, literally, "First have Rāst fully satiated," in other words do not modulate so soon, before allowing

[35] From a conversation I had with the artists in Cairo in May, 1989.

[36] The performance of Mr. Ra'fat was at his home in Cairo in the summer of that year. At the time, Ra'fat was probably in his eighties.

the original maqām of the performance to take its full natural course.[37]

In fact, modulation is of great concern to critics and artists interested in the ecstatic dimension of ṭarab music. Frequently stressed is the importance of establishing the maqām fully before moving to other maqāmāt and eventually returning to the original maqām. Tawfīq al-Ṣabbāgh, who repeatedly argued that ṭarab is not a matter of mere technique or the outcome of mechanical display of versatility, explains that the maqām must be carefully nurtured before any departures are contemplated: "Indeed, the excessive change of modes and the abrupt shifting from one mode to another dispel the [modal] influence; As soon as you begin to savor a mode, another one comes and washes away its influence" (1950: 141). Accordingly, the modulations need to be properly prepared for, the modes modulated to must not be dwelled upon for too long, and moreover, the original mode of the performance must be occasionally returned to.

At the same time, excessive modal emphasis must be avoided. The artist needs to safeguard the modal creation against the adverse extremes of both understating and overstating. Y. Qūjamān presents some of the notions subscribed to by Iraqi Jewish musicians. On the basis of interviews with these musicians, who are totally at home with the mainstream ṭarab practice, the author reports on several approaches to modulation. According to one such approach, the performer must maintain the sense of salṭanah (or modal ecstasy) created by the original maqām more or less throughout the entire performance. In other words, when introducing a new modulation, a musician must resist the temptation of developing or elaborating upon the new mode to the extent of causing it to impose its own dominant salṭanah. Accordingly, if it does so, it diminishes or wipes out the salṭanah of the original maqām within the performer and the audience members. A rule of thumb is presented: one instrumentalist is quoted as saying that while performing in maqām Rāst for example, if the listeners utter the ecstatic exclamation *Allāh*! during a modulation, say to Bayyātī on the fifth degree, the performer must know that he has overstated the modulatory part. "If I play a taqsīm in Rāst I want the listener to remain in the atmosphere (*jaww*) of Rāst all the time, and to admire me basically as a performer of Rāst . . ." (Qūjamān, 1978: 88).

Modal emphasis is illustrated by a variety of traditional compositional structures. According to ʿAjjān, many of these structures aim primarily at evoking musical ecstasy, thus constituting what the author calls *ṭarab mubāshir*, or "direct ṭarab." We are similarly told that such designs follow psychological principles whose efficacy is demonstrable through scientific

[37] From a conversation with the nāy player in the mid-1980s. The performance took place in the early 1980s. When the nāy player asked the listener if he himself was a musician, the latter indicated that he was only a sammīʿ and that he was Argentinian born.

ion.[38] One outstanding example appears in the dūlāb. In view of tion this introductory ensemble composition encapsulates the ost representative features of the maqām. Characteristically, it phasis upon the central notes of the mode, presents the characteristic directional tendencies of the mode (albeit in an abbreviated form), explores the essential pitch areas, usually without extraneous accidentals, and then returns to the tonic through a firmly and unequivocally stated cadence. For this reason, the dūlāb is treated as a prime tool for instilling salṭanah.

Of a more elaborate structure is the *bashraf* (Turkish *peşrev*), an Ottoman-based genre admired for its structural beauty, majesty (*fakhāmah*), solemnity (*waqār*), and direct ecstatic effect (*tāṭrīb mubāshir*).[39] Musically speaking, the bashraf embraces aspects of both unity and diversity. Expected to bring out the character of the metric mode (*shakhṣiyyat al-īqāʿ*), in other words, of the rhythmic pattern that runs through the entire work, the bashraf consists of four variable sections (*khānāt*, singular *khānah*) each of which is followed by a reoccurring section, or refrain (*taslīm*). It has an overall rondo-like form that can be described as A x B x C x D x (with A B C D referring to the different verse-like segments and x to the consistently reappearing section).

As described in detail by theorists, including the Syrian ʿAjjān and others, the first khānah (A) establishes the character of the main maqām. Starting in a traditionally prescribed pitch area, it highlights the tonic or a similarly emphasized note or notes of the maqām, usually without introducing accidentals that may detract from the character of the maqām. The taslīm (x), which the first khānah must smoothly lead into, enhances the established modal feeling and explores it even further before coming to a natural conclusion. Stating that the taslīm should be played only once each time to avoid monotony (*ratābah*), ʿAjjān writes that the listener looks forward with anticipation to this refrain, because its attractive melody intensifies the listener's ecstatic feeling.[40] The second khānah (B) moves smoothly to a related maqām or may only make passing allusions to other maqāmāt before it reverts back to the main maqām. The third khānah (C) gradually explores the higher pitches of the maqām or may make an appropriate modulation to another maqām. Constituting a climactic modal phase, this section reaches a higher plateau of liveliness and complexity, at times posing special technical demands. We are also told that this section is usually filled with "heavenly ecstasy" (*nashwah ʿalawiyyah*) (ʿAjjān 1990: 86). Somewhat like a modal recapitulation, the fourth variable section (D) reestablishes the basic

38 ʿAjjān 1990: 70.
39 Ibid. 1990: 88.
40 Ibid. 1990: 86.

character of the maqām and "recaptures the gist of the melodic content of the bashraf in a ripe manner" (Ibid. 1990: 86), in addition to smoothly paving the way for the final statement of the refrain.

In its entirety, the bashraf, which in traditional Ottoman music serves as an introduction to a *fāṣil*, namely a compound or suite-like genre in a certain mode, constitutes a self-contained apparatus for producing modal feeling. In a section discussing the psychological foundations of the bashraf composition, ʿAjjān states that one of the aims of this genre is to establish the character of the maqām and to cause the maqām to take hold of the listener's psyche (*nafsiyyah*) in preparation for subsequent pieces, whether instrumental or vocal. "The bashraf enables the basic mode to be set firmly in the mind, thus augmenting the mode's influence (*ta'thīr*) and its power of ecstatic evocation (*taṭrīb*)" (1990: 87). Comparable modal applications are found in the samāʿī, which shares with the bashraf a basic rondo-like structure.

Further patterns of consistency and variety can be found in vocal compositions such as the dawr. Referred to by the late nineteenth- and early-twentieth-century Caireans as *sayyid al-sahrah*, or "master of the evening," the dawr was particularly known for its highly ecstatic content. Its opening section established the maqām of the performance and paved the way for a middle section that included numerous modal digressions and was in turn followed by a brief segment in the original mode. Somewhat comparable is the *muwashshaḥ*, a precomposed vocal genre that as a rule adheres to a specific metric pattern and musically follows a multisectional, often AABA, format. In this case, the restated A section presents a basic rendition of the maqām, usually emphasizing its tonal area. The B section, or *khānah*, tends to move gradually to other higher tonal areas and to modulate to a related maqām before gradually reverting to the original maqām, thus preparing for the recapitulatory final statement of the A section.

A similar pattern applies to a large number of modern instrumental pieces and songs, or *aghānī*. Examples include Umm Kulthūm's songs, especially those from the 1940s and early 1950s, a period that many view as the "golden age" of the singer's ṭarab career. We are told, for example, that Riyāḍ al-Sunbāṭī was fully conscious of the ecstatic function of modal satiation (*ishbāʿ al-maqām*). Accordingly, he was once surprised and disappointed to see one song he composed for Umm Kulthūm in 1943, despite its excellent lyrics by Aḥmad Rāmī and its fair amount of modal emphasis, overshadowed by the ecstatically evocative tunes (*alḥān taṭrībiyyah*) of Zakariyyā Aḥmad, who also composed for Umm Kulthūm at that time.[41]

[41] From al-Sharīf 1988: 122.

The magic of cadences

Cadential patterns, especially in improvised performances, constitute powerful ecstatic devices. Known as *qaflāt*, (plural of *qaflah*, literally, "closure") ṭarab cadences are recognizable motivic structures that mark the endings of major musical phrases and are typically followed by short pauses. In terms of overall stylistic content, the qaflāt seem particularly dense and dynamic. They often pack many short notes, exhibit intricate accentual, rhythmic, melodic, and ornamental nuances, and display a relatively high level of melodic activity. Although largely improvised, qaflāt tend to be highly patterned, or cliché-like.

These structures also vary in length, ranging from small motifs of one or a few notes, to more elaborate configurations that span an octave or more. They typically last somewhere from a few seconds to fifteen or more seconds. Furthermore, they inspire various degrees of finality or resolution. Some, for example, are suited for less conclusive or momentary stopping, whereas others, being associated with a powerful sense of finality, would characteristically end on the tonic note and mark the termination of a major section if not an entire performance. The effectiveness of a qaflah depends significantly upon its timing, the precision with which it is executed, and the novel ways in which it is rendered. At a premium is the artist's ability to produce qaflāt that are emotionally effective, yet not hackneyed or overused by the artist himself or by others.

Arab listeners, music critics, and theorists generally view the qaflah as one of the distinguishing traits of ṭarab music. Some even state that it is a uniquely Arab phenomenon,[42] while others describe it as an Egyptian trait *par excellence*.[43] Moreover, qaflah mastery is seen as the trademark of an emotionally effective artist. Umm Kulthūm's biographer Niʿmāt Fuʾād describes the female singer's consistent ability to execute good qaflāt as one of the reasons for her supreme status as a muṭribah. She refers to ʿAbd al-Wahhāb's comment that Umm Kulthūm's unfailing command of the qaflah is due in part to her artistic self-confidence when facing her audiences directly, a skill she had cultivated even before she had access to the microphone. At the same time, the biographer attributes Umm Kulthūm's mastery of the qaflah to her impressive grounding in the ṭarab tradition and her training under the major ṭarab singer Shaykh Abū al-ʿUlā Muḥammad. She contrasts Umm Kulthūm with a variety of singers whose cadential deliveries are either inconsistent or ineffective.[44]

[42] Such characterization is provided for example by ʿAjjān 1990: 7. Similarly al-Ṣabbāgh maintains that the Arab qaflah has no exact parallel in the Turkish taqsīm (1950: 141).

[43] For example, it is described as such by Egyptian composer and music researcher Sulaymān Jamīl, quoted in Fuʾād 1976: 402.

[44] Fuʾād 1976: 402, 404.

The qaflah is viewed as a magical device that charges the performance with ecstatic power. It is said, for example, that "the successful qaflah enhances the aesthetic quality of the taqsīm, and that no matter how correct a performance is, it can lose its artistic value if the cadencing (*qafl*) was not properly executed." Accordingly, the qaflah grants "the melody elegance, beauty, exuberance, and life; the listeners wait for it in order to receive new charges of energy, thus when cadencing occurs utterances of exclamation and admiration are strongly voiced" (ʿAjjān 1990: 71). Based upon his field interviews, Qūjamān provides similar testimony to the emotional impact of the qaflah upon the performance as a whole. Maintaining that the cadence is of crucial importance because it is the last portion of the phrase and the one that stays most vividly in the listener's mind, he explains that "an unsuccessful qaflah may cause the entire phrase to be forgotten or to be considered unsuccessful, and conversely a successful qaflah may cause the weakness of a phrase to be forgotten and may lead one to think that such a phrase was successful" (1978: 89).

In the course of performing, the cadences are artfully selected and utilized in order to stir the listeners' emotions. In her book, *The Art of Reciting the Qur'ān* (1985), Kristina Nelson describes the reciters' paramount interest in the qaflah, or *waqf* (literally stopping), which is considered "the real test of the reciter's (and musician's) melodic skill," (1985: 127). Indicating that while performing, some mashāyikh think ahead in anticipation of the qaflāt which the listeners eagerly wait for, Nelson identifies some of the commonly recognized qaflah types. There is the "calm" one, which basically uses no ornaments or melismas, and another, the "burning" type, which utilizes more notes and involves more artistic maneuvering thus creating tremendous emotional impact upon the listener. Stating that qaflāt are naturally found in the florid and highly melismatic *mujawwad* style of Qur'anic chanting, particularly in phrases that end with vowelled syllables, Nelson also describes two cadential procedures. The first brings back a melodic phrase to its emphatic tonal base, thus completing the symmetrical contour initiated by that phrase and releasing the tension generated by that same phrase. The second heightens tension by ending the phrase ambivalently on a note less central to the maqām or on a note shared prominently by another maqām, thus creating uncertain modal anticipation, a feeling that listeners appear to deeply appreciate.

Similar patterns are encountered in the secular expression. Although the longer, elaborately worked out qaflāt tend to have a very powerful effect, particularly upon ordinary listeners, the subtle qaflāt in the form of clever or witty gesturing are specially valued by the musical connoisseurs. Qūjamān reports a consensus among his informants that more effective, as well as technically more demanding is the subtle and succinct qaflah. Stating that the long qaflah is often seen as the attribute of a weak taqsīm, he describes a general feeling that a well-executed and intelligently conceived few-note cadence can generate tremendous ecstasy, as well as evoke a clear sense of finality.

Emotionally speaking, the qaflāt operate in certain patterned ways. As best illustrated in the more conclusive and more elaborate qaflah type, the underlying effect is one of momentarily heightened anticipation followed by resolution. Typically, the movement toward a final tonal station takes a circuitous, or briefly digressive path. For example, a taqāsīm player may rest on the tonic very briefly, but then quickly run up across the octave scale and down to end upon the final note in earnest. Thus, he would produce a tantalizing sense of delayed resolution but ultimately, an unequivocal repose on the final note. He may also create a feeling of anticipatory anxiety by temporarily stopping on, or dwelling upon, a less emphatic tonal station, for example the leading note or the second note above the tonic, before resting upon the final note. To close, as emotive microstructures, qaflah patterns energize the modal–melodic flow. Particularly in nonmetric improvisatory music, they grant the performance added structural definition but also make it particularly engaging.

Correct pitch and beyond

In ṭarab music, the ability to play or sing in correct pitch is another requisite for creating ecstatically effective performances. Essentially, few theoretical works describe the ecstatic role of intonation, despite the abundance of treatises and text-books that deal with tuning and modal scales. Furthermore, in such sources melodic intervals are most often presented in terms of the microtonally crude, largely Western inspired theoretical system of equal-tempered half-steps, three-quarter steps, whole steps, augmented seconds, and so on, intervals derived from a theoretical scale of 24 equal quarter-tones per octave. In actual practice however, ṭarab music exhibits an intricate and a highly patterned system of intonation. Proper intonation is usually acknowledged through common evaluative expressions, as well as through direct reference to pitch-related phenomena. For example, the concept most typically used to describe faulty intonation is *nashāz*, which roughly means "out of tune," "unharmonious," or "aesthetically offensive." Embodying the culture's intonational sensibility, this concept has a variety of derivative usages such as the verb *nashshaza*, "to go out of tune" and the noun *tanshīz*, "making intonational errors."[45]

[45] This word *nashāz* appears to come from Persian–Ottoman usage. Accordingly, the suffix *sāz* means "musical instrument," or "tune." Similarly, in Persian *nāsāz* means "out of tune" or "unharmonious."

Effective ṭarab music operates on a fine intonational level. Performing the "basic notes" may produce acceptable pitch correctness, or at times may seem barely passable or even outright nashāz. In fact, good intonation tends to cut across the artificial compartmentalization of equal temperament and to transcend the confines of fixed or gross tonal stations. The emotive role of microintonation as such is explained by the performance-minded and ecstasy-conscious Syrian theorist Tawfīq al-Ṣabbāgh. In his musical treatise *al-Dalīl al-Mūsīqī al-ʿĀmm: fī Aṭrab al-Anghām*, or "General Musical Guide into the Most Ecstatic Melodies (or Modes)" (1950), the author discusses the Arab modal scales with special attention to the ecstatic connotations of proper intonation. Stressing that equal temperament, or the system of 24 equal quarter-tones, is a contrived construct highly detrimental to the generation of ṭarab and to Arab music altogether, al-Ṣabbāgh proposes a more detailed microtonal system. Specifically, he uses the Pythagorean-based *comma* (roughly, one-ninth of a tone) as a measuring device, which he borrows from medieval Arab treatises and describes as a pitch unit found in Byzantine church modes. On the basis of dividing the octave into 53 commas, al-Ṣabbāgh specifies certain sizes for the whole-step, half-step, neutral-step, and augmented-step intervals, and by extension the larger intervals that consist of combinations of these intervals. Incidentally, al-Ṣabbāgh's analytical tools are comparable to those applied by Turkish theorists and by some of his fellow Syrian theorists, although he makes a special point of matching his maqāmāt in terms of structure and ethos with Byzantine counterparts, which he appears to have experienced musically and ecstatically first-hand. Here, al-Ṣabbāgh indicates that his renditions (for example the large whole-step consisting of 9 commas, the small half-step 4 commas, the perfect fourth 22 commas, the perfect fifth 31 commas, and so on) assure certain intonational correctness, or at least a minimum degree of ecstatic effectiveness.

Beyond this basic level, however, the author demonstrates that certain microtonal readjustments or modifications can raise the musical expression to a higher ecstatic level. Accordingly, these procedures are dictated by the musician's own aesthetical sense, as well as proven by al-Ṣabbāgh's own experimentations on the violin. Furthermore, they are determined not only by the maqām being played, but also by the specific tonal area being developed at the time of performing. To begin with, al-Ṣabbāgh identifies a few basic maqāmāt in terms of fixed steps. More specifically, he represents the essential notes through familiar Near-Eastern and European names, in some cases with specific accidental designations, for example, "flat and a quarter" (*bemol wa rubʿ*) to indicate a very flat note and "quarter flat" (*rubʿ bemol*) to indicate a note that is only partially flattened, and so on. He then specifies the exact number of commas for each of the fixed scalar intervals within these maqāmāt. And subsequently, he sets up this somewhat "tempered" but intonationally more detailed structure as a matrix within which he proposes small microtonal readjustments and describes their distinct ecstatic effects. The following is a selective illustration.

Ḥijāz Kār Kurdī (a mode with a scale that roughly resembles that of a Phrygian mode) is described as being: *c*, *d*-flat, *e*-flat-and-a-quarter, *f*, *g*, *a*-flat-and-a-quarter, *b*-flat-and-a-quarter, *c′*, or in terms of intervallic structure expressed in commas: (5, 8, 9, 9, 4, 9, 9). Al-Ṣabbāgh stresses that this mode does not cause ṭarab unless the performer is highly skillful. He also hastens to state that certain microtonal adjustments are of critical importance. Complaining that some musicians lower the second and third degrees above the tonic to such an extent that causes the listeners to be repelled by the mode, he maintains that if these two degrees were to rise slightly, "there would be tremendous increase in the ṭarab effect of the mode" (Ibid.: 44). He adds that judging by his own experience, it is preferable to raise the third step by one comma (in other words, to make the distance between the second and the third step 9, instead of 8, commas) during the regular sayr of the mode, but to keep that note in its regular position when used as a temporary point of repose (*rukūz*). As he explains: "those who try this specific procedure would experience more pleasure and ecstasy (ṭarab)" (Ibid.).

Comparable observations are applied to the mode Ḥijāz (*d*, *e*-flat, *f*-sharp, *g*, *a*, *b*-half-flat, *c′*, *d′*, or intervallically in terms of commas per interval: 5, 12, 5, 9, 7, 6, 9). We are told, "this is one of the most important and most ecstatic (*aṭrabahā*) of the Eastern maqāmāt, a mode that is very easy to comprehend, and one that enters into the make up of all other modes . . ." (Ibid.: 45).[46] Furthermore we are reminded that the second step (*e*-flat) in this mode is characteristically high and that special attention must be paid not to lower it, because if that note is lowered even very slightly (for instance by one comma, as for example should happen in some other modes using augmented seconds) the modal feeling of Ḥijāz would be lost. Al-Ṣabbāgh also calls our attention to the possibility of creating a deeply moving modal structure known as "Ḥijāz Gharīb," which is used widely by Turkish musicians and results from lowering the third step (*f*-sharp) by one comma and moving the already raised second step upward by one comma. In addition, he refers to a flattened fifth note (*a*-flat), which if used as an accidental and "touched" briefly at an appropriate moment, would have "an influence that is powerful and ecstatic" (Ibid.: 47).

Bayyātī (*d*, *e*-half-flat, *f*, *g*, *a*, *b*-flat-and-a-quarter, *c′*, *d′*, or in terms of commas: 7, 6, 9, 9, 4, 9, 9) is presented as one of the most prevalent maqāmāt. Accordingly, this mode, which is similarly incorporated in the rest

46 Notably, this view of Ḥijāz as a particularly ecstatic mode is consistent with the previously mentioned statement by ʿUlayyah al-Tūnisiyyah, regarding the exceptional ecstatic efficacy of certain modes.

of the modes, demands great precision.[47] More specifically, in order to bring out its character properly and to produce ṭarab in it, it is advisable that the third note be raised very slightly. Furthermore, if the notes are played for example on a violin string on which the fourth note can be conveniently stopped (rather than produced on an open string, as often happens in the case of the ʿūd) it is advisable to lower the fourth note (*g*) by a tiny bit. Accordingly, "that will produce an emotionally effective Bayyātī" (Ibid.). The author adds however that when a group of instruments (for example ʿūd, qānūn, nāy, and others) play together it becomes impractical to produce this slight readjustment of the fourth note.

Comparably treated is Ṣabá, which the author describes as "one of the emotionally moving and melancholic modes" (Ibid.: 48). Al-Ṣabbāgh presents both the fixed format (*d*, *e*-half-flat, *f*, *g*-flat, *a*, *b*-flat-and-a-quarter, *c*′, *d*′, or in terms of intervals by commas: 7, 6, 5, 13, 4, 9, 9), and another rendition with fine readjustments. He states for example that the emotional impact of Ṣabá is augmented when the third note (*f*) is raised slightly, a move that should occur temporarily rather than on a permanent basis. The author also explains that, when the melodic progression proceeds upward from a point of entry somewhere around the *f*, a note highly emphasized in Ṣabá, the upper note *d* is lowered to *d*-flat, but when the modal progression moves entirely into the upper-octave region, the lower notes of the scale (including the lower tonic, *d*, natural) are all replicated in the upper octave. Regarding the modes that could be temporarily shifted to while in Ṣabá, the author includes "two of the most intricate and ecstatic modes" (Ibid.: 49). The first, which he explains as being between Ṣabá and Bayyātī, is caused by raising the fourth note, or *g*-flat, a bit to make it a *g*-half-flat, adding that "it is impossible for any mode whatsoever to influence the soul as much as this one" (Ibid.). The second is described as being between Ṣabá and Ḥijāz.[48] Accordingly, one must not move from Ṣabá to Ḥijaz without passing through this modal configuration. We are told that both of these modal patterns are illustrated in one specific samāʿī in maqām Ṣabá.

Such treatment is extended to maqām Sīkāh ʿArabī, or "Arab Sīkāh," which al-Sabbagh equates with the Turkish Huzām and describes as being formed of *e*-half-flat, *f*, *g*, *a*-flat, *b*-quarter-flat, *c*′, *d*′, *e*′-half flat, or in commas: 6, 9, 5, 12, 5, 9, 7. Accordingly, this "beautiful" and "pleasant" mode can express joy, but also melancholy "through a few minor adjustments" (Ibid.: 50). Especially at the time of cadencing, the note (*d*) just

[47] The notion of one mode embracing or influencing the make-up of other modes seems to refer to the reappearance of some basic intervals or intervallic clusters of that mode within the scalar constitutions of those other modes. Also, some modes are known to derive their tonics (and by extension intervals) from the different tonal steps of the Rāst scale.

[48] The author does not specify how this intermediary mode is produced. Presumably, it results from slightly lowering the second note of Ṣabá and slightly raising the third note.

below the tonic, and sometimes the note (*d′*) just below the upper-tonic, has to be slightly raised. Al-Ṣabbāgh also lists a number of modal patterns that can be incorporated in this maqām. Accordingly, one is similar to Ḥijāz Gharīb, which if constructed on the *g* step and eventually cadences on *e*-half-flat, as typically occurs when Turks play Huzām, the overall outcome is profoundly ecstatic.[49]

A comparable discussion appears with Jahārkāh (*f*, *g*, *a*, *b*-flat-and-a-quarter, *c′*, *d′*, *e′*-half-flat, *f′*, or intervallically speaking: 9, 9, 4, 9, 9, 7, 6). Al-Ṣabbāgh begins by stressing that this mode acquires its distinctive character, which differentiates it from ʿAjam (a mode whose intervals resemble those of the Western major scale) through the use of the microtonal leading tone (the note called Sīkāh, namely *e*-half-flat). He also states that sometimes it is permissible to lower the third and the fourth pitches by one comma each, readjustments "that inject into the performance distinctive pleasure" (Ibid.: 51).

The author suggests comparable treatments for two other modes. One is ʿAjam ʿUshayrān (which is comparable to a major scale constructed on *B*-flat), a mode he describes as having more grandeur than compassion and emotion. The other is ʿIrāq (*B*-half-flat, *c*, *d*, *e*-half-flat, *f*, *g*, *a*, *b*-half-flat, or 6, 9, 7, 6, 9, 9, 7), which he says has magnificence similar to that found in ʿAjam. Accordingly, the latter (ʿAjam) occurs when the major-like mode is constructed on *b*-flat, rather than on *B*-flat, an octave lower (Ibid.: 52).

The above exposé sheds light upon a number of key issues regarding intonation and the ecstatic experience. Reflecting the sensibilities of a performing theorist, al-Ṣabbāgh's ideas may not be universally accepted or applied. However, they illustrate the direct relationship between emotional gratification and intervallic "fine tuning." Furthermore, his empirical observations are consistent with the experiences and intonational preferences of a vast number of musicians. For example, widely recognized is the profound ecstatic character of the Gharīb modal structure, which apart from al-Ṣabbāgh's allusions, is seldom conceptualized or analyzed as such in the more formal theoretical sources. One specific maqām that musical

[49] Al-Ṣabbāgh 1950: 51. In this context, the description offered is very terse and does not tell us exactly how the modal pattern specified above, which he calls *Sīkāh Gharīb*, might compare with Ḥijāz Gharīb on the *g* step. See also Note 50 below.

[50] The suffix *gharīb* literally means "foreign," or "strange," or "estranged." As indicated by the current practice, both Ḥijāz Gharīb and Sīkāh Gharīb (also called *Sīkāh Baladī*, literally "local," "country," or "folk" Sīkāh) share a certain "compressed" augmented-second between the second and third degrees. The "folkish" quality of the former mode is sometimes noted. Khālid Khalīfah, who comes from Aleppo and plays Arab music on the cello, recalls that this mode has been referred to locally as *Ḥijāz Nawarī*, or "Gypsy Ḥijāz," an appellation reminiscent of the Syrian Gypsies, particularly the manner in which they play the Bedouin *rabābah*, a single-string fiddle (from a 1998 conversation in Los Angeles). Musicians often confuse the two mode names or use them interchangeably, probably for a good reason since excessive narrowing of the augmented second of Ḥijāz can lead to a certain "Sīkāh-ish"

practitioners refer to as "Sīkāh Gharīb," and that appears in the songs of such major artists as Umm Kulthūm, ʿAbd al-Wahhāb and Wadīʿ al-Ṣāfī (usually as an inner modulation), is known to produce an overwhelming sense of salṭanah.[50] Similarly, the accidental lowering of the fifth note in Ḥijāz usually toward the end of a phrase or during the final stage of the performance is a widely occurring practice, one that verges on being an ecstatic cliché. A further illustration is the slight shifting of such seemingly stable intervals as the major third or perfect fourth and fifth for example by moving them toward the tonic note, which has a tendency to pull other notes toward it as long as it is used as the referential center of the melodic activity.[51] Such subtle and temporary readjusting, which belongs to an intuitively learned and applied intonational grammar is intended to grant the performance "sweetness" and to make it emotionally effective.

Conversely, bad intonation, in other words, the creation of nashāz, results either from a poor sense of relative pitch or from an instrument's lack of intonational versatility. In recent decades, the Arab qānūn has been one of the most serious offenders. This is somewhat ironic since historically the instrument has been cherished as a prime tool of ṭarab. In the early twentieth century, the qānūn, which lacked tuning levers altogether, enjoyed a basic level of tonal correctness since its strings were separately tuned to individual maqām notes as sensed by the discriminating ear of the performer. Such tonal fixation, a temperament of sorts, did not prevent the qānūn player from introducing accidental notes through the careful and aesthetically pleasing practice of stopping the strings with the thumb or middle finger of the left hand. Such stopping happened only sporadically, given the relative modal consistency that pervaded each of the self-contained waṣlah performances. Thus, the qānūn was ideally suited for: 1) having the entire gamut of modal pitches individually, albeit somewhat immutably, preadjusted; and 2) providing the ensemble, especially the muṭrib, with a referential set of modal steps that are tonally stable, as well as sonorously prominent. Such attributes may have rendered the instrument worthy of its name, *qānūn*, which means "law" or "rule," from the Greek word "canon." In fact, highly ecstatic

feeling. However, in the Sīkāh-Gharīb mode, strong emphasis is placed on the third note (as would happen in Sīkāh, rather than on the fourth as the case would be in Ḥijāz). Furthermore, in this particular mode the full step below the tonic is raised by slightly less than a full semitone. For example, if Sīkāh Gharīb occurs on *g*, the note affected would be the *f* below, which in its raised form (low *f*-sharp) would function as a leading tone. And similarly, the note further below would be a slightly raised *e*-flat. Among the well-known works that incorporate prominent Sīkāh Gharīb modulations are ʿAbd al-Wahhāb's song *al-Karnak*, and Umm Kulthūm's song *Shams al-Aṣīl*.

51 The same tendency applies to the less stable notes. For example the half-flat seventh note in Rāst, as well as the half-flat sixth note in Bayyātī and Ḥijāz, is usually pulled down into a regular flat when the melodic activity is strongly referenced by or directed toward the tonic. Conversely, this note is typically raised to its neutral, or half-flat position when it serves as a leading note or part of a leading-note cluster below the tonic or the upper tonic.

performances have been recorded on this instrument by pre-World-War-I artists, the senior Muḥammad al-ʿAqqād and others.

The modern instrument most often lacks the number of tuning levers (*ʿurab*) needed for producing effective modal renditions. A few skilled and ṭarab-conscious qānūn players utilize instruments that are equipped with elaborate lever-systems that enable them to raise or lower each course of strings by increments smaller than a quarter-tone each and to obtain some of the smaller microtonal inflections needed for affective ṭarab making.[52] Yet, the vast majority of Arab qānūn players today employ minimal tuning systems, quite often four working levers per string course, that change the pitch roughly by quarter-tone increments. Although on such instruments some of the levers are set in places that may suit certain common modes, the format as a whole continues to reflect the popular paradigm of equal temperament and to render certain intervals blatantly out of tune.[53] The same applies to the buzuq, which as generally played in the Arab world, uses a minimal system of basically stationary frets arranged in terms of half steps with a few neutral steps on certain typical degrees.[54] Obviously, such intonational inadequacies are becoming more striking with the recent proliferation and increasing prominence of keyboard instruments.[55]

Finally, the traditional intonational practice is eloquently exhibited in the vocal performance. Through its exceptionally pliable nature the voice is

52 Some musicians recognize two types of elaborate lever-systems. The *mākinah kāmilah*, or "full machine," incorporates between nine and eleven metal levers per string and is capable of producing various comma inflections. The other, namely *niṣf mākinah*, or "half machine," being intervallically less detailed, usually has five or six levers and provides the approximate quarter-tone steps in addition to one or two in-between (plus-one-comma and minus-one-comma) types of intervals. Applicable mostly to Aleppo musicians, this information was provided by Dr. George Sawa, an Egyptian-born scholar and an accomplished qānūn player himself.

53 In fact, al-Ṣabbāgh expresses extreme unhappiness about the typical microtonal shortcomings of the modern qānūn as he accuses the musicians of always opting for what is facile or superficial (1950: 171). Furthermore, he makes reference to the abandonment of the original left-hand stopping, which was more difficult but extremely pleasing if done well, and also to the sliding pyramid-like wood bridges that were introduced at one time. In reality, many modern qānūn players justify their adoption of minimal lever systems through such statements as "it makes it easier to insert accidental notes and to modulate rapidly," or "it makes the instrument more in tune with the accordion or electric keyboard instruments." Incidentally, the intervals that appear to suffer most are the "narrowed" augmented-seconds, for example those occurring naturally in Ḥijāz, or between the fourth and fifth notes in Huzām, or between the fourth and fifth in Ṣabá, or even more prominently, in the Gharīb modal structures.

54 On my own buzuq, I have over the years developed an extremely elaborate fretting system. For example, I have found it necessary to include several microtonal gradations on most of the main pitch degrees.

55 Although instantaneous microtonal readjustments are possible on certain electronic keyboard instruments, the performers quite often choose to play the various intervals, including the microtones, conveniently in the fixed equal-tempered tuning, usually to the detriment of proper intonation.

capable of producing the finer ʿurab that evoke ecstasy. Rendered most effectively by the trained vocalist, such microtonal inflections are particularly observable within the purely vocal genres, for instance Sufi hymns that are performed without any instruments. Embracing a similar level of intonational finesse is the unaccompanied vocal solo, the supreme example of which is Qurʾanic chanting, particularly the more elaborate mujawwad style as rendered by the masterful reciters. The primacy of the voice as an intonational model is stressed by Aḥmad al-Jundī, a practice-conscious Syrian biographer who defends the use of neutral microtones on artistic grounds and admonishes those who advocate abolishing such microtones on the grounds that they are not well-suited for Western instruments or do not fit certain arbitrary laws of physics. In his words: "Why don't we use as reference the human larynx, which is the first and eternal sound medium . . .?; Should we adjust our larynx to the inanimate instruments or should not the reverse be the proper thing to do?; Do we make clothes to fit the body or do we compress the body to fit the clothes?" (1984: 16).[56] In the same vein, it can be stressed that an affective ṭarab practitioner is someone who "plays out" the music's implicit intonational system beyond the confines of formal theoretical constructs.

Meter and motion

Meter, or the system of rhythmic modes known as *īqāʿāt* (singular, *īqāʿ*), or *ḍurūb* (singular, *ḍarb*), or *awzān* (singular, *wazn*), adds to the music a special ecstatic dimension. As ṭarab related writings indicate, meter appears to generate ecstasy in a variety of ways. As repeated self-contained structures, rhythmic patterns generate an orderly temporal flow. Furthermore, through their distinctive internal designs, they evoke certain affects. In the īqāʿ orientation, which is typical of Syria's muwashshaḥ tradition and to a large extent shared by Ottoman classical music, we encounter a wide array of cyclical patterns, each containing a specific number of *dumm* (or deep sounding, emphatic) beats, *takk* (or light, crisp) beats, and rests (or silent) beats.[57] Creatively embellished and fleshed out by the percussionist, each pattern resembles a unique architectonic design whose individual aesthetic quality permeates the entire performance. Al-Khulaʿī, who extolled the artistic value

[56] In performance, the singers tend to maintain certain intonational correctness even when the accompaniment is intonationally problematic. However, I have heard numerous artists, including established singers, compromise their own intonation in order to avoid sounding "out of tune" with their intonationally faulty instrumental accompaniment.

[57] In some Syrian sources, the rest is also referred to as *saktah* (literally, "silence") and especially in Egypt the word *iss* is used to indicate a rest. Meanwhile, in some earlier theories specific beat-combinations are recognized and syllabically represented.

of the Turko-Syrian rhythmic modes while lamenting the prevalent ignorance about this legacy among his compatriots, pointed clearly to the ṭarab effect this category of meters is capable of evoking.[58]

It is also known that the length and tempo of the pattern determine the quality of its affect. Accordingly, īqāʿāt that are more elaborate or move at a slower pace, for example those upon which many bashraf compositions are based, tend to evoke a stately presence, or in emotional terms, a profound "intoxicating" effect. In this regard, al-Khulaʿī mentioned that some musicians slowed down certain meters, for example playing the thirteen-beat Zurāfāt mode twice as slow "in order to augment the ṭarab feeling" (ca. 1904: 72). By comparison, short and fast meters are generally known to create an exhilarating sense of movement or to intensify an already existing ṭarab state and to carry it gradually toward an emotional climax.

Meanwhile, musical structures may gain special efficacy through the use of differing metric patterns. Despite the general emphasis on metric consistency, as typically illustrated by the muwashshaḥ and the bashraf, metric variety in the span of a full performance, or even a single musical work, is seen as an antidote to excessive repetitiveness, a phenomenon detrimental to the evocation and sustenance of ṭarab feeling. Metrically, the general pattern of statement-digression-restatement found in the samāʿī form, is a case in point. Here, the ten-beat Samāʿī Thaqīl meter is maintained throughout the samāʿī composition except for the fourth, or last khānah, which typically uses a triple or a six-beat pattern, before the final repeat of the refrain returns to the original ten-beat meter.

Furthermore, ecstatic buildup may result from metric intensification, specifically the gradual or progressively phased shifting from long and stately patterns to shorter and livelier ones. This procedure usually appears in the Syrian *fāṣil*, which consists of a medley of traditional genres in a certain maqām and incorporates a collection of muwashshaḥ compositions of various beat patterns. The same can be observed in the performance "sets" of some Sufi orders, or for that matter in the overall structure of many ḥaflah performance. In these and other contexts, this general pattern, although by no means always predictable or orderly, creates a sense of gradual intensification, an ascent that usually leads to a climactic conclusion.

Ecstatic stimulation may also stem from accentual reiteration, a phenomenon best exemplified by a fundamental metric principle referred to as *waḥdah* (or *wāḥidah*), which literally means "unit," "one," or "metric accent." Strongly associated with Egyptian music, the waḥdah can be described as a reoccurring accentual effect. Unlike the Syrian-Turkish cyclical patterns, which display a wide variety of essentially predetermined and succinctly structured beat designs, the waḥdah in its most elemental form

[58] al-Khulaʿī ca. 1904: 85.

is a unit of time marked by one downbeat, or dumm. Sometimes treated as a primal theoretical design, the waḥdah pattern exists in a variety of lengths or tempi and is given such descriptive epithets as large, medium, and small.[59]

Historically and aesthetically, the waḥdah principle is rooted in the local religious practice, specifically the Sufi dhikr. It is associated with the reiterative beat pattern, or *waḥdat al-dhikr* that permeates the typical Egyptian dervish performance, at one time a prime training arena for ṭarab singers. Typically, the dhikr performance embraces an encompassing accentual drive that combines repetitive swaying of the upper torso, rhythmically controlled breathing, reiteration of a religious verbal formula, and metric clapping by the shaykh, or religious leader. In some cases, percussion instruments may also be involved. This underlying metric, and sometimes melodic, activity usually provides an accompanimental ostinato (or *arḍiyyah*, literally, ground or foundation) for the leading religious vocalist. Similarly, the performance tends to engender a series of ecstatic high points that in some cases are carefully controlled. As Michael Gilsenan explains: "the shaykh, by clapping his hands in increasing tempo, builds up each of the series of climaxes to a high pitch, but stops abruptly before the danger of mass frenzy can be realized" (1973: 173).

In the secular practice, particularly in Egypt, the waḥdah has developed as a ṭarab meter *par excellence*. As various early recordings demonstrate, the relatively slow rendition, or Waḥdah Kabīrah, is characteristically heard in the metric qaṣīdah. It also appears in the dawr, particularly in the middle and highly flexible segment, which in turn is preceded and followed by sections that are compositionally more fixed and use the somewhat stately eight-beat pattern, Maṣmūdī Kabīr.[60] The waḥdah is also used in a variety of

[59] Modern theoretical treatises usually discuss the waḥdah as an accentually marked unit of time, as well as an īqāʿ, or metric-mode proper. Al-Khulaʿī presented four variants, namely: the *kabīrah* (large), that amounts to four counts (a whole note) and that twenty-five of which occur per minute; the *mutawassiṭah* (medium) that equals two counts and that fifty of which occur per minute; the *saghīrah* (small) that receives one count and that a hundred of which occur per minute; and *niṣf saghīrah* (half small) that equals a half count and that two hundred of which occur per minute. He added that in his time, the first one was used in the Egyptian dawr (ca. 1904: 64).

[60] Maḥmūd ʿAjjān's book (1990), one of the most detailed and reliable modern studies on ṭarab genres, discusses the dawr in its various historical stages and outlines the stylistic innovations that were introduced by major dawr composers, especially the highly esteemed Egyptian composer and singer Muḥammad ʿUthmān (1845–1900). As he describes it in its more standardized format, which prevailed since the late nineteenth century, the dawr began with an opening section (*madhhab*), which usually used the Maṣmūdī Kabīr meter and ended with a conclusive qaflah. Then came an elaborate section (*ghuṣn*), which commonly used the Waḥdah Kabīrah. It began with the opening melody of the previous section, but proceeded into a development-like segment that introduced new melodies, and allowed for considerable interpretive flexibility. Leading into *āh* and *hank* segments, this part finally closed with a brief section that typically repeated the concluding phrase of the opening section. See ʿAjjān 1990: 11–29.

instrumental and vocal works from different periods and in different genres, including Umm Kulthūm's classics of the late 1940s and early 1950s.

Like other metric designs, the waḥdah generates an enticing sense of motion. Whether in the form of tapping one's fist on the knee or rendering a rhythmic pattern on a percussion instrument, the mere flow of accents is capable of engaging the ṭarab musician's rhythmic sense, thus inspiring him or her to perform or compose. The Lebanese-born poet Khalīl Miṭrān (1872–1949) described how during a trip on a steamliner from Alexandria to Marseilles, at a time when he felt quite lonely, the beat of the ship engine kept him company as it served as a waḥdah against which he sang to himself a favorite dawr he had just heard from ʿAbduh al-Ḥāmūlī. He added that more than forty-five years later he continued to remember the dawr (*Mattiʿ Ḥayātak bil-Aḥbāb*) very well and, despite not having a good voice, to sing it occasionally to himself and to experience its profound ecstatic effect.[61]

Ultimately, the full impact of the waḥdah is brought forth by the artistry of the performer. When interpreted on a percussion instrument, most characteristically the riqq, the accentual pattern becomes generously embellished. In other words, it is furnished with a rich filigree of timbral and accentual nuances. The ability to "fill out the beat" as such is usually cited when praising the artistry of outstanding riqq players, the late Ibrāhīm ʿAfīfī of Egypt, the late ʿAbd al-Karīm Qazmūz of Lebanon, and others. The almost boundless variations, made possible through an elaborate vocabulary of sonorities and dynamic effects, render the waḥdah more attractive and safeguard it against oversimplification or tedious repetition. In an attempt to produce variety, percussionists may even briefly introduce, or gradually "modulate" to, īqāʿ patterns that fit the waḥdah cycle in length and overall accentual design. When musically appropriate, a longer waḥdah may be transformed into the so-called *Bamb* pattern or into another more familiar configuration (sometimes also referred to as Waḥdah) which, like Bamb is heard typically as an ostinato motif accompanying a taqāsīm performance.[62] The performers may also introduce some rhythmic mutations through substituting a short waḥdah for one that is twice as long, or vice versa, at a musically suitable moment. A riqq player may even skip the dumm beat momentarily in order to create tension or anticipation or may insert brief syncopations, for example creating dumm–takk reversals so as to generate suspense, as well as to display virtuosity and even musical wit. Moreover, if the musician being accompanied were to go off the beat (*yiṭlaʿ barra* literally, to go out) say for lack of competence, a dexterous percussionist may

[61] Miṭrān ca. 1938: 135.

[62] The Bamb metric ostinato, usually combined with a melodic ostinato, is frequently heard on early twentieth-century 78-rpm recordings. The similarly applied Waḥdah variant mentioned above resembles the Turkish Çifte Telli pattern.

cleverly cover up by subtly repositioning the beat so as to match the accompanied musician's metric track, a technique that drummers refer to as *talbīs*, literally "dressing up something" or "custom fitting."

Conversely, excessive liberties can interfere with the ecstatic efficacy of the waḥdah pattern. For example, shortening the duration of the cycle itself by converting a larger waḥdah into another one half its length may create a livelier temporal track but may also detract from the elative feeling associated with longer waḥdah cycles. Furthermore, frequent excursions into dance related or popular meters, for example the ubiquitous Maqsūm and Malfūf, may add certain energy to the performance, but may also replace the "intoxicating" or "spiritual" effect of the waḥdah with an atmosphere that purists may deem too "pedestrian" to suit serious listening. Accordingly, such alterations may project a mood of *tarqīṣ*, literally "making people dance" or *tahyīṣ*, "generating or displaying vulgar musical excitation."[63]

Indeed, the percussionist must strike a balance between variety and consistency. A good riqq accompanist must produce exciting fillers, variations, and mutations without losing control of the tempo or compromising the reiterative clarity of the accentual beat or beat pattern. Although, as indicated earlier, good accompaniment may at times call for extreme subtlety in the rendering of the metric accents, the basic beat pattern remains the prime pillar that supports the overall musical structure.

Playing around the beat

As an accentual pattern, the waḥdah grants the music rhythmic regularity without seriously encumbering its temporal fluidity. Unlike the Arab-Turkish metric mode, which furnishes the underlying rhythmic design for a musical work, the waḥdah beat tends to serve as an accentual grid that guides the overall performance. Thus, the waḥdah fits well within a musical tradition that encourages elastic, as well as metrically conscious melodic creations. More specifically, its overall referential role favors thematic deliveries that flow in a piecemeal fashion, as typically happens in modal improvisations. If treated as an īqāʿ proper, the waḥdah can inspire tightly worked out metric compositions, but when approached as an accentual

[63] In fact, serious listeners and fans of ṭarab music have complained that the commercially successful tunes that Muḥammad ʿAbd al-Wahhāb had composed for Umm Kulthūm later in her career, basically in the 1960s and early 1970s at the instigation of President Nasser of Egypt, veered toward the popular *tarqīṣ*, primarily through the frequent use of short dance meters. Also criticized have been the composer's dense orchestration and his allowing the singer very little room for individual interpretation. See Fu'ād 1976: 330–331 and 464–465, and Danielson 1997: 173–177.

device it can grant the performer, or ideally the improviser, a certain flexibility in determining the timing and the length of each melodic phrase. By the same token, the waḥdah makes it easier to slightly anticipate or delay a qaflah, as long as the execution maintains a certain degree of synchrony with the beat pattern. Differently stated, waḥdah accompaniment is perfectly suited for the process of taṭrīb, as it provides the creative performer basic temporal order, but also allows him or her a considerable margin of flexibility and compositional discretion.

These features are deeply rooted in the local religious expression, specifically the dhikr practice as generally encountered among Egyptian Sufi groups. Here, metric structure and rhythmic flexibility are carefully integrated. On the one hand, a certain order is sought: "As section of the dhikr succeeds section, all the action of the members should be in consort so that there is unity of performance in every aspect" (Gilsenan 1973: 175). On the other hand, the narrowly structured accent, or verbal–melodic ostinato, is used as a framework against which the leading vocalist may sing freely and make well-calculated rhythmic departures and returns. The waḥdah serves as "the lattice over which the munshid's music flows" (Waugh 1989: 171–172). This combination of metric definition and relative temporal freedom is viewed as a symbol of the mystical experience, in particular, the tension between realizing one's own transcendental visions and adhering to the norms of the Sufi order as set forth by the founding saint. In the case of the Ḥāmidiyyah Shādhiliyyah order, Gilsenan writes:

> Their ritual therefore contains a high degree of internal polar tension: between freedom and control, between unrestrained emotional ecstasy and formal regulation, between the individual and the group experience which must be one, though the first always threatens the second. In a sense this tension reflects a wider motif in tasawwuf as a whole. (1973: 174)

In the secular music, a comparable dynamic exists. Ṭarab artists demonstrate a striking proclivity toward moving loosely *with* the beat, as compared to performing strictly *on* the beat, for wandering about without losing track of the underlying temporal structure. They seek a desirable balance between metric orderliness and rhythmic freedom, a balance that Qūjamān describes as a test of the ṭarab performer's talent and skill:

> A weak musician makes the listeners feel that he is tied up, or awkwardly obstructed, by the meter. He concentrates upon rendering the metric beats on his instrument as if he is playing the rhythmic pattern rather than a taqsīm. In contrast, a good musician improvises without making the listeners feel that he is playing taqāsīm on the waḥdah, except when he brings the music to coincide with the meter, that is from time to time or from a musical phrase to another. He does not dwell on the metric strokes although he is truly bound by the meter and does not go off of it. (1978: 95–96)

The ability to feel the beat so strongly but also to "play around" it, a skill that some musicians refer to as *taṣdīr*, is occasionally cited when describing impressive ṭarab artists. Ṭarab connoisseurs for example have marveled at the metrically accompanied taqāsīm of the early twentieth century qānūn virtuoso, Muḥammad al-ʿAqqād (Sr.). In the realm of precomposed metric music, similarly noted have been the vocal renditions of the Egyptian composer Shaykh Zakariyyā Aḥmad and the various songs of Farīd al-Aṭrash and Muḥammad ʿAbd al-Muṭṭalib. Described as a true *waḥdajī*, or someone with a superb sense of meter, ʿAbd al-Muṭṭalib (1907–1980) combined melodic mastery with an almost declamatory style of delivery that became one of his distinguishing trademarks.[64]

To close, performing loosely on the beat requires talent, experience, and a great deal of ensemble coordination. As percussionist Souhail Kaspar stresses, for this to work, the accompanist himself must be absolutely steady, or stated differently, dependably unwavering.[65] The resulting ecstatic impact stems from the leading performer's ability to combine the best of two worlds, an overall sense of motion provided by the metric drive and individual freedom that transcends strict metric conformity.

[64] The ecstatic effectiveness of performing loosely with the beat was alluded to in the preceeding chapter when speaking of "ḥashīsh songs," although in such songs the looseness is probably more pronounced or even exaggerated.

[65] From a conversation with Mr. Kaspar in September, 1998.

5 Salṭanah

The generation of musical ecstasy is associated with an inspirational state that musicians recognize by a variety of names. Frequently heard in musical conversations, these names have different semantic nuances and modes of application. However, the most common and most specific in its connotations is the term *salṭanah.*

Unlike the concept of *ṭarab*, which assumes a rather broad meaning as it describes the overall transformative experience connected with the music, salṭanah and other related concepts usually suggest a specific music-related condition. In a salṭanah state, the performer becomes musically self-absorbed (*mundamij*), and experiences well-focused and intense musical sensations. Furthermore, whereas the concept of ṭarab characterizes traditional Arab music in general and connotes a trait permanently present in ṭarab works whether recorded or played live, salṭanah is most often a temporary state generated before and during the performance proper. Also, unlike the feeling of ṭarab, which extends to all participants in the musical process, especially the audience members, salṭanah typically applies to the musicians, specifically in connection with performing. Salṭanah is the condition that inspires affective music making. Although musically and emotionally part of the overall ṭarab experience, it is the "magic" that momentarily lifts the artist to a higher ecstatic plateau and empowers him or her to engender ṭarab most effectively. In this sense, salṭanah is creative ecstasy.

Moreover, compared to the concept of ṭarab, which is applied to the ecstasy emanating from the various components of the performance (timbral, textural, metric, melodic, and others), the concept of salṭanah is usually linked to the maqāmāt. Accordingly, each mode has its own potential salṭanah, as musicians are said to be in a state of salṭanah, for example in maqām Rāst, or maqām Bayyātī, or maqām Ṣabá. While in such a state, the performer finds himself captivated by the mode, particularly the intervallic and tonal components. He feels haunted by the tonic pitch and the intervallic structure, but is also fully prepared to evoke the powerful ṭarab effect of the mode. Thus, the strongly felt presence of an established tonic and related intervals and notes of emphasis makes it possible to view salṭanah as a form of modal, and by implication tonal and intervallic fixation, or essentially as modal ecstasy.

Finally, whereas the concept of ṭarab refers to the affect of all ṭarab music, whether precomposed or improvised, the condition of salṭanah displays strong affinities for the spontaneous creative process typical of the live performance. The state of salṭanah prepares the artist to improvise with feeling or to interpret or modify precomposed works in highly affective ways. In other words, salṭanah appears most valuable in the context of taṭrīb, described earlier.

Although part of the local musical jargon, the various concepts that refer to the momentary inspirational ecstasy of the artist appear to have parallels, and may have originated in, related mystical, literary, and artistic domains.[1] For example, the concept of *mazāj*, literally "mood," "disposition," or "temperament" reminds us of medieval cosmologies that establish interconnections among such diverse entities as the planets and zodiacs, times of the day, colors, sentiments, bodily organs and humors, lute strings, melodic modes, and metric modes.[2] In the musician's parlance, often heard are expressions such as *mā fīsh mazāj*, "there is no mood," to describe an artist's musically unconducive state, and *bīqūl bi mazāj*, "he performs" or "sings when creatively inspired." Also closely related is the term *insijām*, which literally means "harmony" or "being in an emotionally agreeable state." It usually denotes both the artist's inspirational condition, and the conducive physical and artistic mood that surrounds his or her performance.

By comparison, the word *basṭ*, which describes the sense of elation generally acquired in musical as well as social events, has a specific mystical meaning. In Sufi writings, basṭ denotes a rapturous experience of "extension," or intensification of spiritual self-consciousness, as opposed to *qabḍ*, namely "constraint," or "compression" of the soul.[3]

Closely related is the concept of *tajallī*, which refers to "mystical revelation," or being in a state of transcendental preparedness.[4] In the ṭarab culture, the concept of *tajallī* is used basically to refer to musicians' temporary sense of ecstatic empowerment and creative preparedness. Saying, for example, that a ṭarab musician is *mutajallī*, or "in a state of revelation," implies that he or she has become elated, has somewhat mysteriously acquired an elevated state of musical consciousness, and has been enabled to perform

1 Among ṭarab musicians, the more formal Arabic words that mean "inspiration" are rather uncommon. For example the word *ilhām*, which is also used by Egyptian Sufis in reference to divine inspiration and the acquisition of extraordinary performance ability (see Waugh 1989: 86–89), is less frequently heard. The same can be said of the word *waḥī* ("revelation" or "inspiration") or the medieval concept of *shaṭḥ*, which describes a certain category of divinely inspired mystical utterances. See Gibb and Kramers 1974: 533 and Ernst 1985: 133.

2 See Farmer 1943: 3–26.

3 See Schimmel 1975: 128–129.

4 See Schimmel 1975: 281 and Nasr 1987: 167.

affectively. In addition, the concept of *tajallī* may refer to the dominant affect that a specific mode appears to exert at a certain time. Musicians may, for example, speak in terms of the "revelation" of maqām Rāst at a specific performance.[5]

Comparably, the concept of salṭanah appears to embrace certain magical and spiritual connotations. It is linguistically related to the Arabic word *sulṭān*, which having emerged in the eleventh century AD as the title of a powerful ruler, is believed to have derived from the Syriac *shultana*, which refers to power. The word "sulṭān" has appeared in several contexts, including the Qurʾān, basically in reference to "moral or magical authority supported by proofs or miracles which afford the right to make a statement of religious import" (Kramers 1987: 543).[6] Today, the same word can be used to describe the irresistible power or absolute command of certain phenomena or urges, for example physical beauty, hunger, sleep, or for that matter, the intoxicating effect of ḥashīsh.[7]

The overpowering–empowering complex

In the musicians' world, the acquisition of musical inspiration entails a certain oppositional duality. More specifically, the concept of salṭanah connotes a) dominating, overcoming, ruling over and b) granting efficacy or mastery. In other words, we can speak of modal ecstasy as being both overpowering and empowering, or somewhat paradoxically as the performer's attainment of artistic authority by succumbing to the ecstatic hegemony of the melodic mode. Such an apparent opposition is perhaps reminiscent of the Sufi notion of attaining a higher level of spirituality through *fanāʾ* or

5 Also sometimes encountered is the verb *injalá*, for example in the expression *injalá al-muṭrib*, which roughly means that the singer has entered into a musically conducive state, or more specifically, that after an appropriate period of musical warm ups his voice has become clear and supple and ready for creating ṭarab. See Mansī 1965: 64.

6 In the *Encyclopedia of Islam* (1987: 545), J.H. Kramers sheds further light upon the concept of "sulṭān." This title was applied to mystic shaykhs, a practice begun with the thirteenth century, particularly in Ottoman-dominated countries. We are told that among the early uses may have been such titles as, *Sulṭān al-ʿUlamāʾ* (the "Sulṭān of Religious Scholars"), connected with Bahāʿ al-Dīn Walad, father of Jalāl al-Dīn Rūmī and *Sulṭān al-ʿĀshiqīn* (the "Sulṭān of Lovers"), given to the major Egyptian Sufi poet Ibn al-Fāriḍ, whose love poems have been set to music by Sufi-trained ṭarab singers. More recently the title has referred to the highly acclaimed artisans or artists, for example the female singer Munīrah al-Mahdiyyah, addressed as *Sulṭānat al-Ṭarab* and the nāy player Amīn al-Buzarī, acknowledged as *Sulṭān al-Nāy*.

7 In his description of the typical ḥashīsh session in Egypt, Ahmad M. Khalifa refers to certain ritualized patterns of behavior and notes that there is a supervisor, usually called *sulṭān*, who has the honor and privilege of having his first "drag" from each new "load" (1975: 202–203).

"mystical annihilation." The ṭarab-related expression *salṭanat al-nagham* or "the domination of the melodic mode" indicates that the mode has imposed its ecstatic authority upon the performing artist, or that the artist has surrendered to the invincible power, or sulṭān, of the melodic mode. However, the equally prevalent expression *salṭanat al-mūtrib*, or "the singer's acquisition of salṭanah" means that such an artist has captured the innate ecstatic feeling of the mode and has been granted extraordinary ability to instill that feeling within the listeners.

The two notions of surrender and empowerment, or of being dominated and becoming dominant, are closely intertwined in statements made by musical critics, connoisseurs, and performers regarding artistic inspiration. In reference to the remarkable moral, personal, and musical attributes of ʿAbduh al-Ḥāmūlī, one biographer writes that the artist:

> . . . was distinguished from the rest of the singers of his time not only by his powerful, resonant voice and his highly enchanting musical creations, but also by the God-bestowed spirit that would take hold of him during his salṭanah in the various modes. Consequently, he would come up with the most amazing and marvelous vocal renditions, thus lifting up the thoughts of his listeners upon the wings of his magical visions so they would imagine that they have ascended to heavenly ranks and seen things they had not seen or dreamt of . . . (Rizq ca. 1936: 45)

Comparable imagery of succumbing to power and becoming empowered appears in one narrative describing a vocal performance by Shaykh Muḥammad al-Maslūb (1793–1928).[8] Presented somewhat poetically by the modern music critic Kamāl al-Najmī, this narrative is based on a first-hand report by an elder Egyptian connoisseur. When al-Maslūb acquired salṭanah during a festive musical evening, "his appetite for singing was stimulated" (1972: 151). When a specific dawr was requested of him, "he was filled with cheerfulness, and exuded munificence (*aryaḥiyyah*) and ecstasy (*ṭarab*), as he released his voice at a high tessitura, thus utterly dazzling the listeners" (Ibid.). In addition to describing the audience's verbal responses, al-Najmī provides a metaphoric image of the artist while in a salṭanah state. What comes to mind here are the two related Sufi notions of annihilation and transcendence, the inspired singer becoming nothing but a voice:

> How beautiful, tender, and amazing Shaykh al-Maslūb was when haunted by salṭanah (*taslṭana*) and taken by ecstasy (*wajd*), thus departing away from being and existing only as a voice that was singing. Love, who can hide it? . . . Love is the divulger of secrets. (Ibid: 152)

[8] Although these dates may be approximate, this singer is said to have lived some 130 years and to have led a very long performing career. See Shafīq and Kāmil n.d.: 8–9.

Sometimes, the domination–empowerment complex is represented through vivid imagery of royalty and political authority. In a book on Shaykh Zakariyyā Aḥmad, the late Amīn Fahmī, himself a qānūn player, music theorist, and educator, offers a description of this late singer and composer on the basis of direct observation:

> When I used to listen to the Shaykh as he sang and acquired salṭanah in his singing, I always imagined that he was an uncrowned king . . . when his body rose, his eyes glimmered, his face quivered, and his hands moved, he took control of his listeners and captured their senses, so they would be overcome by silence, elevated pride, and elation (*nashwah*). They would look up to him with exaltation and reverence, as if they were the subjects of a nation whose name is ṭarab, and this is their king addressing them through tunes from heaven. (Fahmī n.d.: 10)

As shown here, ecstatic surrender and empowerment are manifested in the artist's appearance as well as through his musical delivery. The ecstatically transformed performer gains artistic and physical powers that are mysterious and awe-inspiring. In turn, the listeners experience an elative sense of surrender, a feeling of communitas that, as Fahmī puts it, binds them together as citizens of the ṭarab nation.

The themes of dominating and being dominated are also common in music related conversations. Musicians and connoisseurs explain that without salṭanah, a performer becomes emotionally ineffective or powerless. In other words, his or her performance becomes devoid of spirit and feeling. Referring to early-twentieth-century musicians, the Egyptian qānūn player Muḥammad al-ʿAqqād (Jr.) explained that ecstatic transformation used to make the difference between excelling and failing to impress. As he put it, even Shaykh Yūsūf al-Manyalāwī, despite his exceptional vocal ability and magnificent talent, needed salṭanah to make any musical impact. "If he sang without salṭanah you would not even care to listen to him." According to al-ʿAqqād and others, salṭanah enables the artist to captivate the listeners, and to compel them to listen. It causes the audience members to shake their heads or to utter exclamations of enchantment. Summing up the notion of being overpowered and empowered is al-ʿAqqād's explanation: "when you have salṭanah you are captivated by it and you cannot help it, but having it also makes you invincible like a king."[9]

"Time split from time"

The overpowering–empowering complex also entails transformation of the physical and perceptual faculties of the artist, and by extension the

9 From the interview with Mr. al-ʿAqqād in Los Angeles in 1984.

participating listeners. Musicians who acquire salṭanah develop an altered sense of time, a condition associated with "losing oneself" and becoming totally engulfed by the musical process. This phenomenon has been noted in the performances of a renowned late nineteenth-century artist:

Muḥammad ʿUthmān was a people's artist in the full sense of the word, as his evening performances (*sahrāt*) used to bring together individuals of different classes and ages. When he was captivated by the ecstasy of ṭarab (*nashwat al-ṭarab*) he used to rise carrying his ʿūd with one hand and gesturing with another. He would continue to sing and play while standing among members of the audience, so the listeners would become very enthusiastic and would request him to deliver more and more. The dawn might have broken while he was still in this condition. (Shafīq and Kāmil n.d.: 20)

Implicit in this account is the development of transformed temporal awareness accompanied by added effortlessness and a higher threshold of physical endurance on the part of the performer. Losing sense of time is also mentioned in a modern poetic depiction of a performance by ʿAbd al-Ḥayy Ḥilmī (1857–1912), during which this muṭrib was overtaken by salṭanah:

The sammīʿah did not sense the passage of time . . . The night had set upon heaven and earth. The moon was a shining cup filled with the wine of the beautiful voice. The assembly of merriment was becoming more agreeable and cheerful from one hour to the next. Ṭarab was granting them an uplifting feeling of lightness (*yastakhif-fuhum*) so they would sing after ʿAbd al-Ḥayy as if they were his chorus. Their ecstasy (*nashwatuhum*) made them imagine that their night was split away from time and will never end up in a morning. (al-Najmī 1972: 158)

Here, salṭanah (and ṭarab in general) is portrayed as an altered sense of time, more specifically as "timelessness" or temporal transcendence. The notion of "time splitting from time" appears to imply the existence of two alternate modes of temporal awareness, one pertaining to ecstatic time and the other to nonecstatic time, or time proper.

This view of music making is consistent with the prevalent articulations of modern ṭarab artists. According to al-ʿAqqād "If you have salṭanah, you could easily sing or play from nine o'clock in the evening to nine o'clock in the morning. Time passes and you don't feel it."[10] At ṭarab events, often projected is the feeling that "ecstatic time" is somewhat open-ended, and largely exempt from the barriers that control "ordinary" time. Ṣabāḥ Fakhrī's long performances, including those I have attended, are good illustrations. Similarly, it is customary for ṭarab artists to cheer up an eager crowd through such opening, often perfunctory, remarks as "God willing, we are here till morning." Usually met with highly enthusiastic gestures, such remarks seem

[10] From the same interview as above.

to help initiate a mood of timelessness, and to provide assurance that this mood will be allowed to take its full course.

How salṭanah occurs

The manner in which salṭanah as an overall inspirational condition develops tends to be enigmatic. It is not always clear what causes it to happen, whether it is voluntary or involuntary, who can acquire it and under what circumstances, and whether its primary source lies within or outside the artist or the artistic event. As Sayyid Makkāwī explains, the idea of forcing inspiration to descend (*istinzāl*) upon the musician is truly absurd.[11] However, by and large, ṭarab performers recognize certain preconditions and procedures that pave the way for or induce the salṭanah state. These preconditions and procedures belong to a variety of domains: cultural, personal, contextual, physical, emotional, and musical (see Figure 5.1).[12]

Eastern soul

Musicians stress that for a person to experience salṭanah, or in a broader sense ṭarab, he or she must be fully attuned to a certain pervasive local disposition. In the mid-nineteenth century, al-Shidyāq presented ṭarab as part of the Eastern mental–emotional character.[13] Today, artists identify ṭarab or salṭanah with a somewhat abstract but genuinely felt native ethos, or Geist, in Arabic, *rūḥ*, literally, "soul" or "spirit." Accordingly, the ability to truly fathom the music's emotive dimension presupposes having a deep-rooted sense of "Eastern-ness" or "Arab-ness." Regardless of their ethnic or religious backgrounds the performers and their audiences must be connected to the music's indigenous essence, its local feel. They must possess *rūḥ Sharqiyyah* (Eastern soul) or *nafas Sharqī* (Eastern breath). As the violinist ʿAbbūd ʿAbd al-ʿĀl explains, since every nation or people has its own rūḥ, a performer must absorb (*yatasharrab*) a certain nation's rūḥ in order to feel its music and perform it properly.[14]

11 From the 1994 conversation with Mr. Makkāwī.
12 A modified version of Figure 5.1 appeared in Racy 1991b: 23.
13 Cachia 1973: 45.
14 From a conversation in Los Angeles in the early 1980s.

Genuine artistry

The ability to experience salṭanah also requires what musicians call *aṣālah*, or "genuineness." In order to feel the music, a performer who may already have Eastern soul must be a *fannān aṣīl* literally "genuine" or "thoroughbred artist," someone with authentic musical talent. More specifically, genuineness means innate ability to feel and express the musical idiom, particularly the melodic modes. A genuine artist is someone for whom the performance of ṭarab genres, for example instrumental or vocal improvisations, is "a second nature." Such an artist must be able to extemporize melodic and rhythmic nuances and instrumental fillers, to have a good sense of intonation, to execute proper qaflāt, and to interact heterophonically with other performers in the ensemble. In short, "genuineness" grants the artist special ability to experience salṭanah and ultimately to evoke genuine ṭarab within his or her listeners.

Feeling

Furthermore, a musician must be endowed with *iḥsās*, or "feeling," in other words, emotional responsiveness to the affect of ṭarab music. Having feeling also implies that the performer is capable of creating music that is emotionally expressive. To describe a musician who has feeling, listeners may say: *bīqūl bi-iḥsās* "he performs with feeling," or in the same vein, *ṣawābʿuh ḥilwah*, "he has sweet fingers," as opposed to *ṣawābʿuh mālḥah*, literally "he has salty fingers." Arab musicians usually speak of feeling as an innate musical gift. Although it can momentarily surge or subside, depending, for example, upon the specific performance event and the musical work being performed, the basic ability to feel tends to exist permanently within the artist. As Ṣabāḥ Fakhrī explains: "Feeling is born with musicians when they are born. Those who have musical feeling, those are the ones from whom genius (*ʿābqariyyah*) can come out. Those who have no feeling (*ḥiss*) are just ordinary."[15]

Artists with iḥsās are also known to feel their own performance intensely. For example, we read that when ʿAbduh al-Ḥāmūlī performed, "his ṭarab was no less than that of the person listening to him, and his ability to improvise tunes excelled beyond all levels" (Kāmil 1971: 29).[16] Similarly, the early-twentieth-century composer and singer Shaykh Maḥmūd Ṣubḥ

[15] From the 1990 interview with Mr. Fakhrī.

[16] In this case, Kāmil is quoting the late musical authority Ibrāhīm Shafīq (1896–1968).

(1898–1941) is said to have become so enchanted by his own sung poems that he often chided his listeners for failing to respond with exclamations of approval.[17] Performing with feeling seems particularly apparent when the singing is reinforced by mystical or religious overtones. Reportedly, a lesser-known Syrian singer by the name of Najīb Zayn al-Dīn (1881–1946), who specialized in Sufi songs but also mastered the art of ṭarab singing, often wept "when he was overtaken by ṭarab ecstasy".[18] The same high level of artistic sensitivity in combination with religious piety appears to affect the Lebanese singer Wadīʿ al-Ṣāfī, who explains that when he sings his own Christian songs expressing devotion to God he sometimes breaks into tears in the middle of singing because of the overwhelming nature of the experience.[19]

Umm Kulthūm, who began her career as a performer of religious songs and later became a ṭarab role model, is known to have felt her own music very deeply. Her biographer Niʿmāt Fuʾād wrote that like any of her faithful sammīʿah, Umm Kulthūm responded to her own songs intensely. When she viewed her film, *Widād* with a few friends and heard her own singing in the film, "she wept from ṭarab and joy." We are also told that she often sat alone in her room and listened to her songs on records and tapes as she covered her face with her hands. Whenever she was moved by a certain passage or "musical move" (*ḥarakah*) "she exclaimed as any sammīʿ would: *Yā shaykhah mish kidhah*! roughly "Oh Shaykhah (literally, female of *Shaykh*), isn't it like that!" *Dah gnān*! "That is amazing!" and *Ayh dah*? "What is that?" (Fuʾād 1976: 233). In a similar vein, Aḥmad Rāmī, the renowned poet who wrote a vast number of Umm Kulthūm's song-texts, is reported to have said:

> Umm Kulthūm is enamored by her own voice and has the utmost love for her art to the extent that when she sings a tune and excels in it, her voice causes her to become ecstatic (*taṭrab min ṣawtihā*), and the utterance of "Āh!" emerges from her chest, but very softly so that the audience would not hear it. Shaykh Abū al-ʿUlā [Muḥammad] used to tell me: "This girl has singing in her blood (*bitghannī bi-dammahā*) . . . can you believe it, she says Āh! to herself?" (quoted in Fuʾād 1976: 368)

To sum up, the innate ability to feel the music, or to interact with one's own performance ecstatically, prepares the artist to attain high levels of salṭanah. In some ways, such an ability elevates him or her from the mere role of ṭarab provider to the admirable status of a ṭarab "feeler," or that of an accomplished amateur. Feeling grants the artist the same emotional prerogatives enjoyed by his or her sammīʿ as well as sharpens his or her ability to

17 Bin al-Khaṭīb 1980: 70–71.
18 al-Jundī 1984: 153.
19 From an interview with Mr. al-Ṣāfī in Los Angeles on August 7, 1984.

excel and impress. At the same time, the accomplished musician's own ecstatic sensations are expected to be circumspect. His or her feeling must be directed inwardly for the ultimate purpose of generating ecstasy within others. The ecstatic musician must seek a creative balance between feeling the music and performing it with feeling.

Body and spirit

The acquisition of salṭanah also calls for transient physical and emotional conditions that are directly linked to the performance event. Physically, the musician must be rested, comfortable, and in good health. Salṭanah is unlikely to occur if the artist is too exhausted, too sleepy, or has eaten too much or too little. The half-joking statement often voiced by hired musicians, "no food, no music!" may have real artistic implications after all. In addition to being rested before a performance, a singer may need to pay special attention to his or her diet, selecting the right foods and staying away from those known to hurt the voice. Ṣabāḥ Fakhrī, for example, explains that there are foods that he avoids immediately before the performance and others that he never eats.

Salṭanah also demands being emotionally prepared, in other words being in a proper state of elation. Stressing that emotional comfort is a prerequisite for affective ṭarab making, Ṣabāḥ Fakhrī explains that before a performance, musicians and musical connoisseurs often express such concerns as, "today the muṭrib is in a state of ecstatic preparedness (*mitjallī*); we beg that no one upset him (*yiz'iluh*), or agitate him (*yinarfizuh*)." If the singer is upset the connoisseurs do their utmost to lead him back into a conducive emotional condition, otherwise "the evening is ruined."[20]

Ambiance

In context, the artist becomes inspired through interacting with a musically initiated audience that is eager to listen and to become emotionally involved in the ṭarab experience. The listeners must be endowed with the talent to feel the music and to express what they feel in effective and idiomatically correct ways. A similar role is played by the accompanying musicians, who can also inspire a featured artist and enhance the quality of the performance as a whole. The profound impact of the performance ambiance upon the

[20] From the 1990 interview with Fakhrī.

Syrian singer Ṣabāḥ Fakhrī (b. 1933) performing in Los Angeles in 1990. Photo by Barbara Racy.

performer's creative ability is eloquently described by Ṣabāḥ Fakhrī, who speaks about his own experience:

In order for me to perform best, first I have to be sure that I am physically in good condition and that I am accompanied by good musicians, as well as equipped with a good sound system, one that I have tried out and adjusted in advance. Beyond that, it is the audience that plays the most significant role in bringing the performance to a higher plateau of creativity (*ibdāᶜ*) . . . I like the light in the performance hall to remain on, so that I can see the listeners and interact with them. If they respond, I become inspired to give more. As such, we become reflections of one another. I consider the audience to be me and myself to be the audience.

Of course, the performer has also to be ecstatic (*maṭrūb*). Obviously, to be able to deliver something, you must have it yourself first and then reflect it, as the moon shines by reflecting the light it receives from the sun. In a large measure, the ecstasy emanates from the audience, particularly the sammīᶜah, although the singer must also be endowed with rūḥ and iḥsās, in addition to being in a state of basṭ or tajallī at the time of performing. Indeed, elation causes the talented artist to shine.[21]

[21] From the same 1990 interview with Fakhrī. This quote was included in Racy 1991b: 8.

Biographers attest to the creative role played by audience members before and during the performance event. In several writings, the importance of coaxing the artist musically through verbal pleasantries is well-recognized. At one specific event hosting the early twentieth century Egyptian singer ʿAbd al-Laṭīf al-Bannā (1884–1969), "sweet talk" occurred as a prelude to the performance proper, thus coinciding with drinking, eating, and socializing. It consisted of such compliments as "Indeed, nothing will make us drunk except your voice, Oh! Sī ʿAbduh! [or Master ʿAbduh]," thus complimenting this singer by comparing him to his famous predecessor ʿAbduh al-Ḥāmūlī, and "We have not heard a great master of ṭarab like you, Oh! Sī ʿAbd al-Laṭīf!" (al-Najmī 1970: 146). According to the report, when this singer's companions noticed his ensuing state of insijām, one of them rushed to bring him an ʿūd so he would accompany himself.

Creative listening

During the performance proper, salṭanah within the artist is maintained and reinforced by the creative feedback between the performer and the audience. The organic relationship between the two is illustrated by Fakhrī's statement: "I consider the audience to be me and myself to be the audience." It is also expressed through various metaphors and analogies. One established violin player likens the audience to a sexual partner. In his analogy, sexual arousal (a metaphor for artistic inspiration) in one partner would induce a similar response in the other partner, thus leading to a perpetual cycle of sexual pleasure in both. The famous Lebanese singer Wadīʿ al-Ṣāfī (b. 1921) expresses the same idea but through visual analogy. In his view, the audience and the performer are like two mirrors facing each other. The image, which stands for inspiration, appearing in one mirror is reflected by the other mirror, and in turn the reflection is reflected again back and forth.[22]

As implied by these explanations, the artist's ability to produce ṭarab is boosted by the audience's ecstatic responses. In context, the voiced exclamations, chosen creatively from a rather self-contained repertoire of verbal gestures, express the listeners' own sensations, as well as initiate and maintain the performer–listener feedback process.

The following are among the numerous exclamations that are heard in both live and recorded ṭarab performances. Very common is the expression *Āh*! which can reflect extreme sensations of pain, bewilderment, amazement, and pleasure. Heard on many early recordings, the expression is sometimes repeated as *Āh*! *Āh*! or combined with others such as *Āh yā rūḥī*! literally, "Oh

22 From the same 1984 interview with al-Ṣāfī.

my soul!" It can also be followed by the name of the performer, for example, *Āh yā Umm Kulthūm*! Another frequently heard expression is *Allāh*! literally, "God," a usage that appears to have a long history. During the first half of the nineteenth century Edward Lane wrote: "The natives of Egypt are generally enraptured with the performances of their vocal and instrumental musicians: they applaud with frequent exclamations of 'Allāh!' and 'God approve thee!' 'God preserve thy voice!' and similar expressions" (1860/1973: 354).[23] Very often this expression, which may connote wonderment, admiration, and being overwhelmed by an idea or a feeling, is uttered two or more times in succession, the result sounding like *Allāhallāh*! with emphasis on the long ā vowels. Also when deeply haunted by the salṭanah of the mode, the listeners may intone this or a comparable expression on the exact pitch that the singer had just ended his phrase on. Furthermore, the sammīʿah may utter the common expression *Allāhu akbar*! "God is great!" which opens the call to prayer and in common speech can express a state of being overwhelmed by profound sensations or spiritually moving experiences.

We encounter other gestures that express the listeners' wonderment, but whose religious or spiritual connotations, if existing at all, are less direct. These include *Yā salām*! literally, "Oh peace!" roughly meaning, "How marvelous!" *Yā ḥalawtak*! basically, "How sweet you are!" and *Yā rūḥī*! or "Oh my soul!" In common usage, the soul, which in Sufi tradition has distinct spiritual efficacies, symbolizes things that are extremely dear, such as one's life or one's child. Similarly, on some early recordings the expression *Yā waladī*! literally, "Oh my child!" is heard. Another related exclamation is *Yā ʿaynī*! "Oh my eye!" an expression of endearment that in common parlance expresses the feeling of being impressed for example by a beautiful image.

A further category depicts the artist as an authoritative figure who captivates the listeners and controls their emotions. For example, *Yā sīdī*! literally, "Oh my master!" or *Yā sīdnā*! "Oh our master!" may be addressed to the performer. Sometimes the idea of emotional submission to artistic authority is given further prominence through such expressions as *Aywah*! "Yes!" or *Aywah yā sīdī*! "Yes master!"

Other exclamations beg the artists to continue to perform, or to repeat a certain phrase. Referred to earlier in this century by Kāmil al-Khulaʿī was the prevalent expression *Kamān*! which means "Again!" and usually expresses the audience's interest in hearing a line of poetry or a musical phrase once more. Occasionally this request is followed by the performer's name, for example *Kamān yā Sitt Umm Kulthūm*! "Once more, oh Lady

[23] Interestingly, Edward Lane, whose book first appeared in 1836, noticed that in Egypt the exclamation "Allāh!" was "pronounced in an unusually broad manner, and the last syllable drawled out, thus – '*Allauh*!'" (1860/1973: 354). His observation continues to apply today.

Umm Kulthūm!" or voiced more emphatically as *win-Nabī kamān*! "Again for the Prophet's sake!"

The listeners may also utter titles of respect that address the performers individually and portray them as masters of their trade or as powerful evocateurs of ecstasy. The title *Sī*, short for *Sayyid*, which expresses respect for a person or artist, was commonly used in Egypt, as in the case of Sī ʿAbduh al-Ḥāmūlī. Other social titles of respect such as *Afandī* were also addressed to the singer or the instrumentalist, especially in the early twentieth century. Similarly *Ānisah*, or "Miss," has been applied to young unmarried female singers. Nowadays, the title *Ustādh*, which is used profusely as a reference to a learned man, is also commonly applied.

Other expressions allude to the listeners' own transformed state, in other words to how the musicians are affecting them. Upon hearing a brilliant young ʿūd player at an informal gathering some twenty years ago, an elderly musician referred to the player as *Yā Shaqī*! or "You, Mischievous One!" When hearing a powerful qaflah during an intimate performance in Cairo, one listener said to the late buzuq player ʿAlī al-Dhuhnī: *Ḥarām ʿalayk*! "Be merciful!" or literally, "It is unlawful for you to do this [to us]." At a different point in the same performance one sammīʿ remarked: *Ḥatmawwitna l-yum*? or, "Are you trying to make us die today?"[24] During a performance of taqāsīm that I gave on the buzuq, one highly established qānūn player from Baghdad said to me: *Niḥnā shū ʿāmlīn maʿak*? literally, "What did we do to you?" or to paraphrase, "Have we done anything wrong to you that you are doing this to us?" Depicting music as a form of pleasurable "affliction," such exclamations are indeed complimentary, if not also clever variations on the theme of ecstatic transformation.

Finally, the verbal reactions of the sammīʿah, particularly in intimate musical gatherings, are usually subtle as well as combined with effectively timed and communicated moans, headshakes, and facial expressions. Also, in the large haflāt, individual expressions are often drowned out by loud cheers and whistles or at times yield to an atmosphere of distant formality or even apathy. Nonetheless, the various interactive gestures play a crucial role as salṭanah enhancers. As causes and effects of the transformative musical condition, they feed directly into the ecstatic flow of the performance.

Musical requisites

Under appropriate social, physical, and emotional conditions, the salṭanah state can be induced musically. Listening to or performing music in a given

[24] These gestures were heard on a cassette recording of a performance by al-Dhuhnī for a handful of attentive listeners. The cassette was a courtesy of the late ʿAlī Reda of Egypt.

maqām can generate salṭanah in the form of ecstatic fixation upon that maqām. The use of musical "starters" as such can be described as a sort of musical pollination or sympathetic magic that enables the artist to tune in to the ethos of the maqām being introduced.

Various types of musical preludes may serve as salṭanah initiators. The dūlāb and the taqāsīm, as well as the bashraf and the samāʿī, are among the primary examples. The ability of such genres to capture the true character of the maqām makes them ideally suited for modal stimulation. Whether metric or nonmetric, improvised or precomposed, such tools owe their inspirational effectiveness significantly to the dexterity of the interpreters. According to Muḥammad al-ʿAqqād (Jr.), one of the most valued skills of the early twentieth century accompanists was their extraordinary ability to invoke salṭanah through minimal musical means, for example, through short preludes or even introductions of just a few notes.[25] Such musical devices appeared frequently on early 78-rpm recordings, whose fixed short durations created a dire need for suitably short yet ecstatically potent musical openers.

Before World War I, the inducement of salṭanah musically often proceeded slowly and gradually. Citing an eyewitness report, one author described such a process at a performance by ʿAbduh al-Ḥāmūlī held at the court of Khedive Ismāʿīl. This artist's takht ensemble, including the chorus, sat at one end of the courtyard, as the Khedival family sat at the opposite end. The ensemble began by performing taqāsīm, instrumental ensemble pieces, and muwashshaḥāt while the singer, as well as the royal family, sat and listened. This introductory phase continued:

> . . . until ṭarab had been fully established and the mode had imposed its salṭanah. At that point, carrying his drink, ʿAbduh moved toward the musicians and as he came close to them, he started to sing. Then after joining them and sitting in the middle, the ḥaflah really began. (al-Jundī 1984: 42)

In another source, we read that ʿAbduh al-Ḥāmūlī often asked his qānūn player Muḥammad al-ʿAqqād (Sr.), who was also a singer of sorts, to begin the evening by singing "in order to establish a suitable atmosphere of salṭanah" for the celebrated singer (Kāmil 1971: 31).

Notably, the evocation of modal ecstasy through musical stimulation permeated the structure of the late nineteenth- and early twentieth-century Egyptian waṣlah. In certain ways, the typical linear order of the generic components (as a rule all in the same mode) created and helped maintain a strong modal feeling within the individual accompanists and ultimately in the featured artist, thus enabling him to reach an ecstatic peak toward the end

[25] From the same 1984 interview with al-ʿAqqād.

of the performance. Usually an opening taqsīm, most often on the ʿūd, established an initial phase of modal ecstasy for the ensemble members. In turn, the modally inspired instrumentalists performed a prelude, normally a dūlāb or a samāʿī with taqāsīm solos on such instruments as the nāy and the violin, either following the samāʿī composition or in between its inner sections.[26] This introductory instrumental segment, which gave added emphasis to the maqām of the waṣlah, initiated further salṭanah within the chorus and the muṭrib, as well as within the instrumentalists themselves. Then together, the singer and his chorus performed a short muwashshaḥ heterophonically, with the muṭrib singing intermittently, thus "warming up" for the rest of the performance and intensifying his own salṭanah further. After that came a short preparatory qānūn taqsīm that in turn led to the qānūn-accompanied nonmetric improvisatory layālī-and-mawwāl by the featured vocalist. In turn, the layālī and mawwāl enabled the vocalist to create ṭarab and also to condition his voice even further, thus achieving the level of modal ecstasy required for executing the dawr, which constituted a climactic, and in certain ways, the most complex phase of the waṣlah. Sometimes a qaṣīdah, which was typically improvised, appeared at the end of the third and last waṣlah of the evening, when the salṭanah of the muṭrib, the takht accompanists, and the listeners was at its highest level.[27]

In later decades, salṭanah "starters" have included modern compositions, or fragments of compositions that musicians have considered ecstatically loaded. According to Muḥammad al-ʿAqqād (Jr.), musicians of his generation often used the opening theme from one instrumental composition by ʿAbd al-Wahhāb titled "*Shaghal*," as a salṭanah starter in Bayyātī. They played it first and then repeated it in alternation with taqāsīm by different ensemble members.[28]

Such musical triggers can also be incidental or unexpected. One might be walking down the street and faintly hear someone humming a tune in maqām Ḥijāz or a radio broadcasting a song in maqām Ṣabá, and almost unconsciously find oneself improvising or composing in those modes. Comparable

26 The insertion of taqāsīm passages between the main sections of the samāʿī, which is an Ottoman-based genre, has been described as an Arab or Egyptian practice. Examples of such interpolations can be heard on some relatively late Egyptian recordings, for example those appearing after World War II and featuring the celebrated ṭarab singer Ṣāliḥ ʿAbd al-Ḥay. See Racy 1980.

27 Apparently, the structure of the Egyptian waṣlah was flexible and had changed in time. The typical generic content described above is based on several historical accounts (for example Mansī 1965/1966: 62–64), as well as reports by elderly Cairo musicians and more recent recorded examples. Basically, no complete recordings of waṣlāt have come to us from the early recording era. It is also known that for early radio broadcasts, primarily after 1934, the waṣlah, which had already been declining, had to be more standardized and limited to half an hour in length. For more information on the history, structure, and ecstatic design of the waṣlah see Racy 1980 and 1983b.

28 From the 1984 conversation with al-ʿAqqād.

suggestion may result from listening to someone tuning the qānūn to a specific mode or from listening to a drone on a musical instrument or even from unconsciously hearing the hum of a machine or a florescent light. Melodic ostinati can also be quite stimulating. Usually incorporating the tonic and a few lower notes of a specific mode, an accompanying melodic–metric pattern can both initiate a feeling of salṭanah in that mode and reinforce that feeling throughout the performance that may ensue.

Certain timbres and sonorities can be similarly conducive. For example, the sound of a good ṭarab instrument is known to have a tremendous inspirational impact upon the performer.[29] Also, reverberation, or "ambiance," created acoustically in a resonant performance-hall, or electronically at a recording studio, or through a public address sound-system, may produce magical sensations within ṭarab musicians. By prolonging the resonance of the notes, the resulting echo effect tends to inspire melodic phrases that are slow-paced and succinctly structured. Furthermore, in performance such phrases tend to overlap and perhaps blend harmonically with one another, thus creating an effect that is distinctly ecstatic.

Lower registers are also considered particularly suited for salṭanah. In one of al-Sunbāṭī's ʿūd recordings the shifting of the customary tessitura of the mode several notes lower is said to have boosted the music's level of salṭanah. Meanwhile, the late Egyptian ʿūd player and composer ʿAlī Reda preferred to lower the tuning (*dūzān*) of his instrument because the resulting effect was ecstatically more evocative.[30] Within certain limits, such lowering seems to render the tone "sweeter" and the ornaments more expressive and easier to articulate. Furthermore, reduced string tension, which appears to enhance certain overtone effects, encourages performing at a leisurely and more ecstatic pace. Along similar lines, Muḥammad al-ʿAqqād (Jr.) stressed that salṭanah is compatible with playing slowly, adding that it is almost impossible to achieve salṭanah through music that is extremely fast.[31] Last but not least, good intonation, which in turn produces desirable resonance, is a prerequisite for ecstatic performing. As Simon Shaheen explains, in order to play with salṭanah, it is imperative that the instrument be tuned impeccably.

It is also noted that when such instruments as the ʿūd or violin are used, the modes tend to produce salṭanah more readily when played on certain

[29] For example, the resonance of ʿūds made by the famous (now deceased) Syrian craftsmen of the Naḥḥāt family is sometimes noted for its delectable effect. Similarly, the Egyptian composer and ʿūd player, Riyāḍ al-Sunbāṭī, is said to have advised one of his students not to fix a subtle buzz on the student's ʿūd, because that particular effect added an enchanting dimension to the sound. This report about al-Sunbāṭī comes from a conversation with ʿAlī Reda in the middle 1980s.

[30] The information comes from the conversation mentioned above.

[31] From the 1984 conversation with al-ʿAqqād.

tonal steps. It is felt that when a suitable "key" is chosen, the acquisition of salṭanah is facilitated by the elevated level of technical fluency and the added sympathetic resonance of certain strings. Conversely, less salṭanah might result if the mode were to be played on a tonic that leads to awkward fingering or to diminished sympathetic resonance. Also, the intensity of the ecstasy tends to vary from one maqām to another. As musicians explain, it is easier to create salṭanah in common maqāmāt such as Bayyātī, Rāst, Ḥijāz, and Ṣabá in part because these modes have progressions that are particularly familiar, expansive, and deeply ingrained in the minds of the listeners and performers. As indicated in the preceding chapter, also recognized is the domineering ecstatic qualities of Sīkāh-Huzām, Ṣabá, Ḥijāz and other modes that are closely related to them. Similarly, the ecstatically potent Sīkāh Gharīb often becomes so deeply entrenched that a subsequent departure to another maqām would seem extremely trying both technically and emotionally.

The feeling of creative ecstasy tends to be cumulative. After long performances, artists usually experience sharpened musical ability accompanied by an intensified inspirational surge. Such a cumulative effect may be felt even when a variety of modes or genres had already been presented. In the early twentieth century, Kāmil al-Khulaʿī bemoaned that during evening performances, distinguished guests and officials left early, before the third, and final, waṣlah, was presented. He therefore advised that musicians and their hosts begin the performances early in the evening so that the musicians reach their full inspirational peak when the eminent audience members were still present.[32] In a similar vein, the notion of cumulative musical ecstasy is alluded to by a modern Egyptian music critic and biographer in a book on ṭarab singers and listeners, specifically in a chapter titled, "ʿIndamā Yatasalṭan al-Mughannī" or "When the Singer Acquires Salṭanah." Particularly highlighted is a Ṣāliḥ ʿAbd al-Ḥayy performance held at a tent during the 1930s, an event that featured a number of waṣlāt and illustrated the artist's progressive ecstatic transformation. Notwithstanding the satirical overtones and the hyperbolic language, the writing accounts for the manifestly displayed build up of salṭanah on the part of the singer and the audience members. For example, we read that when this artist sang the dawr at the end of a later waṣlah, "he used to end it as the tempest would end its work, forcefully plucking the listeners out of their seats, causing them to throw their fezes and turbans off their heads, to tear off their clothes, and to release their vocal chords, thus letting out a scream of ecstasy (*wajd*) and ṭarab as the artist reached his highest summit of salṭanah" (al-Najmī 1970: 140).[33]

[32] Al-Khulaʿī ca. 1904: 90.

[33] In this chapter al-Najmī states that his description is based on the report of an eyewitness with whom he had spoken.

Contemporary musicians describe their own cumulative ecstasies in comparable terms. One ʿūd player who has worked in nightclubs for several years explains that quite often he experiences salṭanah in its most potent form after having played for several hours. "When I finish my job at the club I leave with thousands of tunes ringing in my head. When I pick up my ʿūd to play for a few friends after work I am able to readily achieve good salṭanah in the maqāmāt I choose to play in."[34] Incidentally, the sammīʿah cherish the intimate, usually spontaneous, late-night performances that musicians are coaxed to give immediately after an evening public performance. In such gatherings musicians are said to play the "real stuff."

Finally, the time required for the full fruition of the salṭanah state tends to vary from one artist to another. Generally, ṭarab musicians are known to undergo extended periods of social, physical, emotional, and musical conditioning in order to become profoundly ecstatic. However, some appear to deliver ecstatically with little or no preparation. Exemplifying the latter category was ʿAbd al-Ḥayy Ḥilmī, the celebrated pre-World War I vocalist and recording artist. As one biographer puts it:

> All singers begin with preludes and proceed slowly and gradually in their delivery of ṭarab (*iṭrāb*) until their voices become smooth, the instrumental playing becomes more adjusted, and the listeners' feeling is established. Then the listeners would receive ṭarab bit by bit until its effect has come to a full culmination. All except ʿAbd al-Ḥayy Ḥilmī, who was himself made of ṭarab. Every ounce in him makes you ecstatic and enchants you (*tuṭribuka*). Thus, when he starts with the first breath, he initiates in you a sense of enchantment and ecstasy without any introduction or prelude . . . (al-Jundī 1984: 62–63)

Among today's musicians some are similarly noted for their exceptional readiness to perform ecstatically. They seem to respond quickly to salṭanah-generating devices or even to require little or no musical preparation before performing. For example, the celebrated singer Wadīʿ al-Ṣāfī, known for his outstanding vocal improvisations, remarked that other artists, including the late Muḥammad ʿAbd al-Wahhāb of Egypt, have noted his uncommon readiness to deliver ecstatically, "without even a moment of hesitation."[35]

Cosmological factors

Modal ecstasy may also elude, or occur independently of, the various conventional inducers. As ʿAbd al-Ḥamīd al-Tannārī, an established violinist

[34] From a conversation with the musician in Seattle, Washington around 1979.
[35] From the 1984 interview with Mr. al-Ṣāfī.

from Aleppo observes, at times musicians try all night to instill the salṭanah of a certain mode in the muṭrib or within themselves to no avail, despite the existence of seeming ideal physical, human, and musical conditions. However, at other times, the salṭanah of a specific mode occurs quite readily and, furthermore, its dominion seems to preempt all attempts to create salṭanah in any other mode. The Syrian violinist even recalls that on certain days maqām Bayyātī, for example, has sounded extremely good and convincing "although the ʿūd we were using at the time was broken and hard to tune, so bad you wouldn't even want to touch it." On other days, an instrument that may have been of excellent quality seemed to defy all attempts to be tuned properly or to sound pleasing in a certain maqām.[36]

Unpredictable as such, the development of salṭanah is sometimes attributed to forces that exist outside the control of the artists themselves. Occasionally brought up is the old connection between modal ecstasy and the domain of *falak*, or astral world. The particular configurations of such entities as the zodiacs or stars on certain days, or at different times of the day would determine the propriety of the maqām at the time of performing. As some reports indicate, the earlier astral–musical correlations remained current until a few generations ago.[37] Some elder musicians recall that early twentieth-century performers were cognizant and in some cases observant of the modal–temporal connections. According to one report, such renowned Aleppo musicians and composers as Shaykh ʿAlī al-Darwīsh and ʿUmar al-Baṭsh knew how to assign the maqāmāt to cosmologically appropriate performance times, and thus to tap into the salṭanah potentials of each of the maqāmāt.[38] In comparable ways, writers allude to the practice of performing the call-to-prayer to modes that fit certain days or times of the day. In one book on the Islamic call-to-prayer and its practitioners, we read that toward the beginning of the twentieth century, adhān performers at the Ḥusaynī Mosque in Cairo observed a special order:

> The mode of Saturday was ʿUshshāq, that of Sunday was Ḥijāz. But the mode of Monday was Sīkāh if that day was the first Monday of the month, Bayyātī if it were the second Monday, Ḥijāz if it were the third Monday, and Shūrī on [or with] Jahārkāh if it were the fourth or fifth Monday. Furthermore, the mode of Tuesday was Sīkāh, that of Wednesday was Jahārkāh, that of Thursday was Rāst, and that of Friday was Bayyātī. (al-Saʿīd 1970a: 113)

The cosmological exigencies of music making are also described in practical musical terms, especially when speaking about "the old days." Referring

[36] From the 1990 conversation with Mr. al-Tannārī.

[37] For a survey of post-medieval Arabic treatises relating music to the astral world, see Shiloah 1979.

[38] This was indicated by al-Tannārī, who knew some of these musicians personally.

to cosmological manuals and treatises kept by some early-twentieth-century scholars and musical patrons such as the Syrian Fakhrī al-Bārūdī, Muḥammad al-ʿAqqād (Jr.), explains that there are seven stars, each corresponding to one of the notes of the scale of Rāst. Al-Tannārī cites the belief that the planets correspond to seven primary maqāmāt, each of which is based on a different step along a fundamental seven-note scale namely that of the Rāst mode. We become prone to salṭanah in the maqām corresponding to the star influencing us at the time of performing, even without our direct consciousness of that star's influence. As al-Tannārī illustrates, "we often try to 'open a mode' (*niftaḥ naghmah*), without much success, but there are times when our attempts succeed with little or no effort."[39] Of interest here is the concept of "opening," which is also used to describe the unveiling of the occult or the receiving or telling of a fortune. When musicians open a mode, or when a mode becomes accessible to them, a state of tajallī, or modal revelation, is known to set in. As explained by al-ʿAqqād, "If you happen to perform the mode of the star which is revealing itself at the time of performing you get salṭanah twenty times stronger."[40] Along similar lines, Ṣabāḥ Fakhrī indicated that "the predecessors" (*al-aqdamīn*) believed that the "mother modes" were seven and that each day of the week was cosmologically suited for one specific mode, "for example today, Thursday must be for this mode, Saturday for that mode, and so on."[41]

Meanwhile, al-ʿAqqād, who maintained that the modal–temporal observance gave his grandfather and others who worked with famous singers such as ʿAbduh al-Ḥāmūlī better access to modal ecstasy, described a specific cosmologically based strategy that those early artists had followed. Thus, a certain form of "cosmic scanning," or modal trial and error was conducted. The singer began the performance event by listening to his accompanists perform for an extended period of time, as they wandered over various maqāmāt in order to find out which maqām seemed to "reveal itself," in other words which star was casting its influence at that time. Also, sometimes musicians would tune the qānūn initially to maqām Ḥijāz because the extended scale of this mode supposedly embraced the essences, or nuclei of all the basic modes.[42] They played in a somewhat impromptu manner across the Ḥijāz scale until one modal configuration proved ecstatically operative at that moment. Such a configuration became the mode of the waṣlah that followed. Somewhat comparably, al-Tannārī of Aleppo recalls a

[39] From the same 1990 conversation.

[40] This quote is from the 1984 interview with al-ʿAqqād.

[41] From the 1990 interview with Mr. Fakhrī.

[42] This is probably in reference to the various intervallic clusters that make up the scale. In maqām theory, such clusters, usually in the form of tetrachords that encapsulate certain modal essences, can serve as the foundations for other full-fledged modes. See for example al-Ḥilū 1961: 80–86. Also refer to Chapter 4, Note 47.

more recent practice of deliberately playing in different modes “until the right mode gets to stick” (*ḥatta al-naghmah tiʿlaq*).[43]

In today’s practice, the astral paradigm has clearly lost its appeal. For one thing, genres that emphasize modal consistency, improvisatory spontaneity, and the instantaneous initiation of ecstasy have become less central. Similarly noteworthy is the increased diversification in the listeners’ tastes, not to mention also the waning of cosmological thinking altogether and the advent of Western musical values, compositional techniques, and educational approaches. Ṣabāḥ Fakhrī states that his generation abandoned the cosmological rules of modal selection not out of artistic incompetence or inability to perform with modal consistency:

> I can, for example, sing one whole night from early evening till morning of the following day, adwār, qaṣā’id, mawāwīl, and qudūd, all in maqām Rāst. However, I changed the [cosmological] practice because I am not an astronomer (*ʿālim falak*) to know about the hours and the heavenly courses (*madārij*) and to watch for the hour of fortune, the hour of misfortune (*al-sāʿah al-naḥsah*), and so on in choosing the right mode.[44]

Fakhrī mentions that in order to decide on an initial maqām for the performance, the ensemble members sometimes try to find out what mode the qānūn player is tuned to and ask him to run a few themes in that mode. If that mode, for example Rāst, is found ecstatically compelling (*naghmah musalṭinah*), it would be taken up and the repertoire is selected accordingly. And sometimes after starting to sing in any given mode, Fakhrī may conduct his own modal scanning as he visits various modes briefly in order to sense which one is truly domineering (*musayṭirah*) and therefore suitable for singing at the moment. However, the Syrian singer describes his approach as a compromise between accepting whatever mode appears to command salṭanah, for whatever reason, at the time of performing, and fulfilling the need to change modes throughout the performance in order to create variety and assure the continued attention of today’s ḥaflah-goers:

> I give the audience a bouquet of different flowers. In the garden, I take the listener from one flower to another in order for him not to become bored, because humans have a propensity toward boredom. God created for them the four seasons, the day and the night, the different colors and foods. Therefore, I bring to them a variety of musical styles.[45]

43 From the 1990 conversation with al-Tannārī.

44 From the 1990 interview with Mr. Fakhrī.

45 In this statement, from the 1990 interview, the concept of “style
alwān, the plural of *lawn*, which literally means “color,” but als
stylistic “flavor.” For more information on this usage see Racy 1

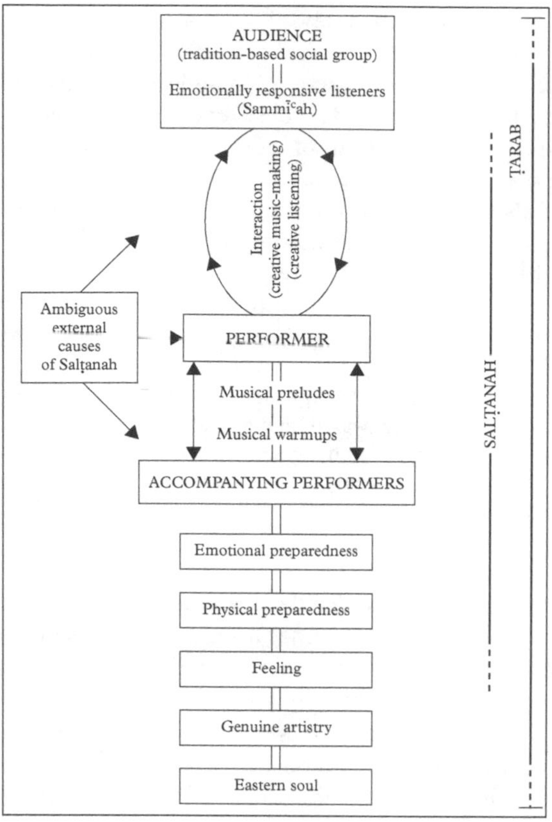

Figure 5.1 An Ecstasy Model

Music with salṭanah

Although strongly felt, the musical manifestations of salṭanah are difficult to pinpoint or articulate. In most cases, they are implicit in the performers' musical parlance. Often used is the term "*fīhā salṭanah*" or "it has salṭanah" to describe an ecstatically imbued musical work or rendition. Furthermore, such manifestations are indirectly acknowledged when describing how such parameters as tonicity, phrasing, cadencing, and modulation are approached. Consequently, the study of salṭanah as music seems to call for a comparative methodology, one that seeks to collate individual musical renditions that are known to vary in their levels of ecstatic efficacy. Yet even then, the approach requires selecting performances that diverge stylistically and emotionally from a shared aesthetic base. Furthermore, the chosen renditions must be contextualized, or more specifically, examined in light of their individual performance settings, as well as in terms of the relationship between the music's emotive quality as felt by the performers or the listeners and the detailed musical structure as such. In essence, the analyst needs to probe inwardly into the realm of perception and outwardly into the musical syntax. Naturally, such an endeavor favors the use of actual musical performances, particularly those that can be closely examined and intimately felt.

With this in mind, I look at my own performances. Specifically, I provide my own critical assessment of three taqāsīm on the nāy all in the same maqām, namely Ṣabá, but performed during the last twenty years or so on three different occasions.[46] One performance was presented before a United States west-coast audience consisting largely of non-Arabs. At the time, the listeners seemed attentive but also predominantly formal and reserved. During the performance, I sensed slight intonational variances within the ensemble I was playing with. Furthermore, for accompaniment, the ensemble provided a drone which, rendered primarily on plucked instruments, seemed a bit too disjunct and obtrusive. For various reasons, my performance seemed to have little or no salṭanah. My rendition displayed correct intervals and an acceptable overall modal structure. However, with few intervening pauses, the melodic phrases were rather undifferentiated, and the overall compositional trajectory seemed highly amorphous. Moreover, there was only cursory emphasis upon the main tonal centers of maqām Ṣabá, and just as important, the qaflāt tended to be perfunctory or at times nonexistent.

The second of these performances appeared basically as a short, few-minute interlude within a much longer performance by an ensemble of about a half-dozen instrumentalists and a featured singer for a less attentive, largely Arab, audience in the United States. The heterogeneous ḥaflah attendants included a few sammīʿah whose ranks were overshadowed by a talking, socializing, eating, and drinking majority. The performance was marked by high levels of sound amplification. Here, I felt that my improvisation was of an average ecstatic quality. I remember performing with considerable agility and precision, in part due to the high levels of preparedness acquired through hours of performing prior to my solo. At the same time, the music displayed a rather ordinary quality. The melodic progression was typical and the qaflāt tended to be elaborate but also highly standardized. The music seemed to move by its own inertia rather than through the instantaneous emotional input of the listeners and fellow musicians. Although I presented a few staple accidental notes and modulatory hints all characteristic of Ṣabá, the taqsīm appeared to unfold at an exceptionally fast pace as it quickly moved toward the higher pitches and finally rested upon the tonic.

[46] These analyses are guided by sound recordings selected from various cassette tapes of my own performances. The first performance took place around 1980, the second in the early 1980s and the third in the middle 1980s. A comparable analysis of these examples appeared in Racy 1991b: 19–21.

The third performance I deemed highly ecstatic, as well as technically excellent. This nāy taqsīm in Ṣabá was performed in Beirut at a musical jalsah attended by a group of young ṭarab fans and some highly established artists who included conservatory teachers and instrumentalists employed by the Lebanese radio station. Preceded by polite but insistent cajoling on the part of the listeners, most of whom knew me personally, my solo occurred after about two hours of sporadic group performing, a period during which food and drinks were consumed and intimate socializing had already taken place. Reflecting the muḥāsabah of several well-seasoned artists and the lively input of young ṭarab aficionados, the taqsīm demonstrated distinctive stylistic properties. Structurally, it consisted of discretely formed vignettes, modal or thematic units that were separated by carefully planned and timed pauses. Maintaining an overall moderate tempo and unhurried melodic movement, the performance established the mode Ṣabá both succinctly and emphatically. Accidental notes, although noticed and applauded by the listeners, were used sparingly so as to ensure the tonal and intervallic consistencies required for maintaining the Ṣabá feeling. The modulations, specifically to ʿAjam ʿUshayrān, which rests on the third step below, and then to Kurd on the original tonic, were typical occurrences in a Ṣabá taqsīm, but their appearances seemed to come as positive surprises to the listeners. Meanwhile, the qaflāt were unequivocal, but often took the form of subtle hints and innuendoes. Finally, the individual thematic units, the musical micro-events, and the various digressions were all reflective of the emotional input of the ecstatically motivated, and in some cases analytically minded, listeners.

To close, the choices of the study examples and the modalities of analysis are unavoidably subjective. Similarly, the correlations we may establish between context, ecstasy, and musical structure are highly interpretive. Actually, salṭanah may come to fruition with or without the presence of an audience and furthermore, the relationship between the musical substance and the ecstatic content is far from simple or straightforward.

Salṭanah spoilers

The salṭanah state is essentially ephemeral and quite vulnerable. It can end gradually after having taken its natural course throughout a musical piece or an evening performance. At the same time, numerous adverse conditions – social, emotional, or musical – can either prevent salṭanah from developing or wash it away after it has already been established. Excessive fatigue, hunger, illness, or drunkenness are likely to block the path of salṭanah. Emotional stress can have a similar effect. Musicians cite the negative impact of such occurrences as a family dispute, a car accident, or tension among musicians, for example just before performing at a nightclub. They may also blame the lack of salṭanah on a faulty sound system, the absence of sammīʿah, or the existence of a few "unharmonious" persons at a small jalsah. Lack of audience participation or the display of gestures that are excessive, affectatious, or musically out of place can cause the creative state to gradually die out or can simply make it impossible to establish. Similarly, nonidiomatically worded exclamations, which tend to betray lack of initiation on the part of the listener, may fail to inspire the performer. A featured artist may explain his or her failure to perform well through such statements as "there is no atmosphere" (*mā fīsh jaww*).

Music-related spoilers are numerous. Excessive tuning and retuning in the middle of a performance may disturb an already established feeling of modal ecstasy and may require the performing artist to develop the initial ecstatic energy of the mode all over again, an endeavor that does not always succeed. Similarly, as Simon Shaheen explains, a wrong note or a string going slightly out of tune during a ʿūd taqsīm could wipe out an intense feeling of salṭanah. Inhospitable grounds for modal ecstasy include: exaggerated use of accidentals; inadequate emphasis on the basic notes of the maqām; abrupt shifts to other maqāmāt; extreme repetitiveness or sluggishness in the unfolding of the mode; bad intonation, for example resulting from not having a sufficient number of tuning levers on the qānūn; excessive percussiveness; and rigid adherence to the metric accents. Also, sudden tonal transposing is known to be extremely jarring. Sometimes, stemming from the need to find a comfortable tessitura for the vocalist, tonal shifting often means that salṭanah has to be re-established on the new pitch level. This process is particularly problematic when the shift is made from one tonic to another that is less compatible with it, as often happens to one that is adjacent to it.

Such adverse circumstances are frequently encountered at recording sessions. The technical demands of recording, the stark recording settings, the limited durations of the records, and the pressure to deliver music quickly to satisfy the industry's commercial objectives can all impede the development and maintenance of modal ecstasy. In response, early recording artists appear to have used various salṭanah inducing strategies. Muḥammad al-ʿAqqād (Jr.), who recorded with major ṭarab artists, recalls the inhibiting atmosphere of the studio and the musicians' attempts to inspire the leading recording artists, particularly during the 1940s:

> At the studio ʿAbd al-Wahhāb or Ṣāliḥ ʿAbd al-Ḥayy would tell us: "for the Prophet's sake start saying [performing] something in the maqām [of the performance]". So, you would hear us, me on the qānūn, the leading violinist, and the nāy player, all "noodling" on our instruments playing small snippets in the maqām until the singer has acquired salṭanah.[47]

[47] From the 1984 interview with al-ʿAqqād.

In some ways, the modern studio can generate a powerful sense of salṭanah within the recording artist through various instantaneously created effects and sonorities, including appropriate types of drones, echoes, and timbres. However, having to record a performance piecemeal, or to re-record a composition or parts of a composition several times in a row is likely to diminish or even obliterate a sense of modal ecstasy that had been developed through gradual physical, emotional, and musical conditioning. In a way, recording many "takes" of an improvisation and expecting such an improvisation to remain ecstatic is like telling a certain joke several times in succession and expecting that joke to sound funny each time. Al-ʿAqqād in fact recounted that ʿAbd al-Wahhāb re-recorded one small section of his song "*Yā Wabūr Qullī*" some 125 times, because during the original take, although he had been in a state of salṭanah, his voice had inadvertently produced an effect that he disliked. The singer finally settled with the first rendition because in the others he had become tired and had lost the fresh energy manifested in the first trial.[48] This and similar incidents continue to illustrate the tensions between feeling and technical perfection, the desire to record with salṭanah and the media's call for artistic expediency.

Finally, the role of salṭanah as a creative dynamic has been curtailed by recent musical developments, including the predominance of precomposed and fully rehearsed works, the increased use of notation, and the prevalence of such standard studio techniques as multi-track overdubbing and the recording of individual musical components separately. Similarly limiting has been the overriding tendency to think of the maqāmāt as mere scales and to treat them as such, rather than to recognize them as emotive–tonal–intervalic complexes. Meanwhile, the confluence of Eastern and Western orientations in today's musical pedagogy, as well as the common cynicism toward traditional performance mannerisms, may have contributed to the rise of a joke involving a student in a solfège class at a major Arab conservatory. At the time of examination, when the teacher asked the student to sight-read a melody in a specific maqām, the student replied "I am sorry, today I have no salṭanah."[49] Nonetheless, both as a concept and experiential state, salṭanah retains a central position in ṭarab artistry. Of primary concern to the musicians and the listening initiates, it provides the psychological and aesthetic base for affective ṭarab making.

[48] Conceivably the number of repeats is exaggerated, although the dilemma described here is very real.

[49] George Sawa points out that this is a real incident that took place at a conservatory in Alexandria. When the student told her that he had no salṭanah, the teacher replied, "Then sing without salṭanah!" (From a conversation with Dr. Sawa).

6 Lyrics

Song lyrics add to the overall ṭarab experience a powerful ecstatic dimension. Among ṭarab musicians, text writers, composers, and listeners, the lyrics are generally referred to as *nuṣūṣ*, or "texts" (singular, *naṣṣ*), or sometimes as *shiʿr*, namely "poetry." They are also known simply as *kalām*, literally "speech," or "words," or more specifically as *kalām al-aghānī*, namely "song-speech" or "song-words." Accordingly, "song-speech" is differentiated from both the formal classical poetry and from everyday speech. Identified with the *muʾallif*, or "lyricist," who writes, or as the jargon goes "makes" (*yaʿmal*) the words, the lyrics constitute a verbal genre with distinctive stylistic features, aesthetic properties, and emotional efficacies.

Background

Ṭarab lyrics may address a variety of topics – social, political, religious, philosophical, and so on. However, the predominant and most ecstatically-oriented texts are amorous. In Arab literary history, secular love has provided the basis for a major poetical genre known as *ghazal*, or "love poetry," and as Lois A. Giffen (1971) demonstrates, has inspired a considerable body of related theoretical writing and ādāb codes. Pre-Islamic and medieval classical poetry, for example from the Umayyad and ʿAbbāsid periods, contribute to the modern lyrical expression both linguistically and thematically. However, the expressive modalities of the lyrics seem to derive most directly from the Sufi-based poetry that flourished during and after the thirteenth century. In some ways, the ṭarab texts illustrate the mutual historical and artistic cross-overs between the mystical and the secular worlds. Furthermore, modern studies suggest that these texts are Arabic variants of a broadly shared Near-Eastern idiom.[1] Rooted in the literary and spiritual cultures of Moorish Spain, North Africa, Egypt, and the East-Mediterranean world, the

1 See the literary discussions in Nicholson 1921, Schimmel 1975, Ḥusayn 1964, and Andrews 1985.

ṭarab lyrics exhibit striking similarities to earlier Perso-Ottoman ghazal texts. In his study of Ottoman ghazal poetry, Walter Andrews (1985) presents a variety of typical thematic motifs and political and spiritual worldviews that are also prevalent in the Arabic lyrics. Moreover, as extant Arabic sources, for example the nineteenth century anthology of Shihāb al-Dīn of Egypt and other more recent collections indicate,[2] the textual practice exhibits a high level of historical continuity. Indeed, the overall style and thematic orientation of the lyrics are among the most stable facets of the ṭarab expression.

At the same time, ṭarab lyrics can be viewed as a self-contained repertoire with its own literary and historical integrity and internal variety. The modern texts incorporate poems in classical Arabic, for example those written by medieval Sufi poets such as Ibn al-Nabīh al-Maṣrī (d. 1222) and Ibn al-Fāriḍ (ca. 1181–1235), both of whom lived in Egypt. Furthermore, the material includes a large number of poems in vernacularized classical Arabic. Among these are the muwashshaḥāt texts, which are usually interspersed with colloquialisms, except for a few classical texts by earlier poets such as Ibn ʿAbd Rabbihi (860-940), Ibn Sanāʾ al-Mulk (1155–1211) and Lisān al-Dīn al-Khaṭīb (1313–1374), and other modern texts modeled after them. In addition, the lyrics embrace a vast number of colloquial texts that tilt toward classicism in terms of vocabulary and patterns of pronunciation. Stylized as such, this textual orientation can be found in major vocal genres such as the Egyptian dawr and ughniyah, or modern ṭarab song. The currently used texts have both contemporary and premodern authors, and particularly in the case of the muwashshaḥāt, the authorship is often unknown. Incidentally, many of the anonymous muwashshaḥāt texts have appeared in earlier anthologies, such as the one compiled by Shihāb al-Dīn, who was a lyricist himself. A vast number of song texts have been composed by well-known twentieth-century poets, Aḥmad Shawqī, Aḥmad Rāmī, and others.

The amorous content

As love poems, ṭarab lyrics share certain traits. Generally speaking, they are highly stylized or stereotypical, thus presenting the amorous theme through

[2] Since the early twentieth century, particularly with the proliferation of phonograph recording and the rise of a mass musical public, numerous such anthologies have appeared. Many refer directly to the disc recordings from which the songs were taken. Among the earlier sources are: al-Khulaʿī ca. 1904; ʿĀshūr, collector, AH 1340; al-Būlāqī, collector, 1927; and ʿAṭiyyah, collector, n.d. The last one specialized in women's songs and carried the title *Maghānī al-Jins al-Laṭīf*, namely "Songs (or roughly, Enticing Singing) of the Gentle Sex." In more recent decades, dozens of such anthologies have been published especially in Syria and Egypt, for example those containing muwashshaḥāt and adwār texts, and others featuring texts sung by famous ṭarab artists, Umm Kulthūm, ʿAbd al-Wahhāb, and others.

standardized expressions, images, and allusions. Furthermore, the poet as a rule speaks in the lover's voice as he communicates about his love experience or describes the beloved and the surrounding love-related setting. In turn, the beloved, who in Sufi poetry can be seen as a metaphor for the Divine, is almost always spoken of in the generic masculine, or in essence genderless, form. Exceptions exist when the beloved is addressed in a similarly neutral or abstract feminine form. In either case, however, the texts may be sung interchangeably by male or female singers. Comparably, other related figures, including the lover, who in Sufi tradition stands for the seeker of Divine experience, are usually in the masculine form. Thus, presenting the amorous subject matter in general or symbolic terms, the texts are not to be understood literally. In the following discussions, references to the various poetical figures maintain the generic masculine form unless otherwise indicated by the lyrics.

In terms of variety, the literary material embraces at least two overlapping major stylistic components: 1) the muwashshaḥ-based orientation, which exhibits distinct thematic links with the overall Ottoman ghazal tradition and is typical of Syria, especially Aleppo, although to a certain extent can be found in Cairo and other neighboring cities; and 2) the Egyptian-based orientation, which is quite extensive and influential throughout the Arab world. The two orientations are discussed below.

Love, nature, festivity, and intoxication

The first orientation, particularly the texts of the muwashshaḥāt and to a large extent the related qudūd genre, projects an unmistakable ambiance, one that is dominated by colorful images and a certain joie de vivre. Here, the texts give ample attention to the lover and the beloved, but also make frequent mention of the festive gatherings of close companions who may include the beloved and others who have fallen in love. Similarly, wine-related expressions, which in Sufi poetry serve as metaphors for mystical transformation, tend to prevail. The drinking setting may be depicted as a *ḥān*, "tavern" or "wine house." Allusions are made to the *sāqī*, or the "wine server," and in some cases, the beloved may be depicted as the wine provider who serves the *nudmān*, or "drinking partners." Also typical are such expressions as *kās*, or *ka'ṣ*, "cup," *aqdāḥ*, "drinking utensils," *saqānī*, "he gave me (wine) to drink," and *imlālī*, "fill (the cup) for me." Intoxication appears as an adjunct to the amorous condition. Allusions to musical entertainments, and the ṭarab experience are also common.

Preoccupation with idyllic landscape is also quite obvious. In fact, the lover's assembly is often portrayed as a party in a lush garden, or *rawḍ*.

References are made to shady trees and flowers, for example *ward*, or "roses." Portrayals of the beloved's beauty are linked to nature. The poet-lover represents the beloved's figure or bodily stature (*qawām*), or more specifically, his eyes, cheeks, hair, waist, and so on through a standard stock of natural images. The beloved is most often depicted as a gazelle (*ghazāl, ḍabī, rīm*). His gracefully bending figure may be likened to a twig (*ghuṣn*) or a small willow branch (*ghuṣayn al-bān*), or his rosy cheeks may be compared to roses.

Finally, the texts describe the tribulations of the lover or lovers. They usually describe the process of falling in love as a drastic transformation that results, for example, when the beloved's eyes cast their potent arrows upon the potential lover. Typical expressions are: *ṣādanī*, "he hunted me;" *ramānī bi sahmi hawāhu*, "he hit me with the arrow of his love;" and *sabānī*, "he captivated me" or "I was smitten by him." Meanwhile, the lover may speak of the scheming cynics and their attempts to turn the beloved away from him, and express his own wish to win the beloved's attention. He may also refer to the pains of unfulfilled desire and describe his perpetual yearning to be united (*waṣl or wiṣāl*) with the beloved.

The following are representative examples, mostly from very well-known songs. Providing my own approximate translations and transliterations, I generally list the two hemistiches of each poetry line (or in some cases three or more rhymed phrases) in sequence, with semicolons separating them. The texts, or in some cases excerpts, are transcribed in their "bare" poetical forms, that is without the tarannumāt that are added specifically in the muwashshaḥāt renditions. These examples are mainly intended to depict the subject matter and do not necessarily account for the musical–poetical structures. Here too as in the original sources, the translated texts represent both the beloved and the lover almost always in the generic masculine gender. Furthermore, in order to illustrate the formulaic nature of the texts, I somewhat arbitrarily single out and italicize those expressions that are highly standardized and seem to reoccur quite frequently throughout the entire repertoire. The same approach concerning the italicization and the use of gender is applied to other textual illustrations throughout this chapter.

The following excerpt from a text that appeared in Shihāb al-Dīn's nineteenth-century anthology (ca. 1840/ca. 1892: 87) incorporates an assortment of concepts, images, and verbal forms all typical of the muwashshaḥ genre. Using a tripartite phrasing and rhyming scheme within each line, this excerpt includes stock expressions that refer to the beloved's beauty, and his symbolic role as a wine server:

Zāranī bāhī l-muḥayyā; Yatahādá bil-*jamāl*; Bahjatu n-nuḍḥḍḥār.
The one with charming looks visited me; Moving gracefully with *beauty*; Delight to the eyes of the onlookers.

Wa-*jalá ka'>s* al-*muḥayyā*; Wa-*raná* yaḥkī l-*ghazāl*; Wa-ʿalaynā jār.
He *purified* the *cup* of his *appearance*; And *gazed* resembling a *gazelle*; And treated us unjustly.

In the text of a well-known muwashshaḥ we find frequent reference to the lover's longing for the beloved, who is constantly referred to as a gazelle. Also alluded to is the bad influence of the cynics or spoilers. The following is the opening couplet of a five-couplet poem:[3]

Yā *ghazālī* kayfa *ʿannī abʿadūk*; Shattatū shamlī wa-*hajrī* ʿawwadūk.
Oh, my *gazelle* how *they distanced you from me*; They caused our separation and made you accustomed to *abandoning me*.

Baʿd *widdī* ṭūl *ṣaddī* ʿallamūk; Laytahum ya *munyatī* lam yaʿrifūk.
After *my affection* they taught you *to turn away from me*; I wish, oh, *my desire* (*belove*d), they did not know you.

Meanwhile, the theme of wine is prevalent in a text that speaks about intoxication and the camaraderie of partakers, or lovers:[4]

Imlālī l-aqdāḥa ṣirfan; W-*asqinīhā liṣ-ṣabāḥ*.
Fill up the cups for me with pure wine; And *let me drink it 'til morning*.

Shurbuhā tīhan wa ʿujban; Nūruhā *kal-fajri lāḥ*.
Drinking it is haughtiness and wonderment; Its light s*hone like the rising sun*.

Āhi min *khamrin* qadīmah; *Shurbuhā yubrī s-saqīma*.
Oh, what an aged *wine*; *Drinking it heals the sick* (*or lovesick*).

Ṭāliʿī fīhā saʿīd
My fortune in it is happy.

Kullu man qad *hāma tīhan*; Huwa *nadīmī līs-ṣabāḥ*.
Whoever *wanders proudly*; will be *my drinking companion 'til morning*.

The themes of wine, the seductive beauty of the beloved, and the lover's own condition, particularly given the admonition or blame of the cynics, all appear in another muwashshaḥ text set to music by the Egyptian composer Muḥammad ʿUthmān:[5]

Malá l-kāsāt wi-*saqānī; Nāḥīla l-khaṣri* wa-l-*qaddi*.
He *filled the cups* and *gave me a drink*; *The one with a thin waist and figure*.

[3] From al-Ḥilū 1965: 135.
[4] From al-Ḥilū 1965: 84.
[5] From al-Ḥilū 1965: 31.

Ḥayāt ir-*rūḥ* fī lafḍḥuh; *Sabānī laḥḍḥ*uhu l-hindī.
The *Soul becomes alive* when he speaks; His *glance*, like a mighty sword, has *captivated* me.[6]

Mulīmī lā tasal ʿannī; Wa khallīnī ʿală *ʿahdī*.
Oh, *you who blame me* leave me alone; And let me honor *my pledge*.

Direct mention of music and musical ecstasy appears in a typical setting of drinking and ṭarab making. The beloved, depicted as a wine provider, also entertains musically and thus causes the lover and his companions to become enchanted, as well as intoxicated. This picture is conveyed in an excerpt from a very well-known text set to music by Shaykh Sayyid Darwīsh:[7]

Yā *shādī* l-alḥān; Asmiʿnā; Rannata l-ʿīdān.
Oh, *chanter* of tunes; Allow us to hear; The resonance of the lutes.

W-*aṭrib* man fil-*ḥān*; W-aḥsibnā; Min ḍumni n-*nudmān*.
Entertain (render ecstatic) those at the *tavern*; And consider us; Among the *drinking companions*.

The thematic similarities between the muwashshaḥāt and the more vernacular qudūd can be illustrated by two opening couplets of a very popular qadd:[8]

Qadduka l-mayyās, yā ʿumrī; Yā *ghuṣayn al-bān* kal-yusrī.
Your bending figure, oh my beloved; It is a *small willow-twig*, like a ben tree.

Inta *aḥlā* n-nās fī naḍḥarī; Jalla man sawwāk yā *badrī*.
You are the *most beautiful* in my view; Exalted be the One who created you, oh my *full moon*.

Anā wi-*ḥabībī* fī *jnaynah*; Wil-*ward(i)* mkhayyim ʿalaynā.
My beloved and I are in a *garden*; And the *roses* are casting their shadow over us.

Rūḥ yā *ʿadhūl* mi ḥawalaynā; *Ḥayyart* il-ʿālam *yā ʿumrī*.
Oh, *cynic blamer* go away from us; *You confounded* everybody, *oh, my beloved*.

Direct allusions to the garden, the flowers, the nightingale, and the beloved appear in another very well known qadd, whose opening couplet is presented below:[9]

6 The word *hindī* (which also means "Indian") is a medieval reference to the sword or a type of sword, also referred to as *muhannad*, *hunduwānī*, and *sayf hindī*. See Lane 1863/1984, vol. 2: 2904.
7 From al-Ḥilū 1965: 41.
8 From Maḥfūḍḥ 1964: 393.
9 From Maḥfūḍḥ 1963: 292.

Il-*bulbul* nāghá ʿalá *ghuṣn il-full*; Ah yā shaqīqa n-nuʿmāni.
The *nightingale* sang tenderly upon the *Arabian-Jasmine twig*; Oh, red anemone.

Qaṣdī *alāqī maḥbūbī*; Bayn il-*yasmīn* wir-*rīḥāni*.
My aim is to *meet my beloved*; Amidst the *jasmine* and the *sweet basil*.

Love, pathos, and awaited reunion

The orientation represented by the Egyptian texts exhibits certain typical stylistic and semantic features. Here, we encounter a) portrayal of the lover's own feelings vis-à-vis the beloved and the world, b) distinct pathos, particularly in connection with unrequited love, c) an underlying amorous scenario constructed through a variety of renditions and interpretations, d) reverence toward the beloved and overtones of political and religious authority and jurisprudence, particularly in texts written during and prior to the early twentieth century, and e) a tendency to incorporate clever innuendoes, double meanings, and witty play on words.

These texts present a number of players, the most central being: 1) the beloved, primarily addressed in the masculine gender (although in this particular orientation, the feminine gender does appear occasionally); 2) the lover, or potential lover, represented by the poet; and 3) the lover's own society. These players may be directly represented or at least implied by the various love-related vignettes and motif, which are reassembled in countless variations and sequential orders. In its abstracted form, the amorous scenario usually embraces the following elements:

Description of the beloved

References to the beloved and his attributes tend to set the stage for the love experience. The beloved may be addressed in the singular form, as *al-maḥbūb*, or *al-ḥabīb* (the beloved) or in the plural form as *al-aḥibbah*, or *al-aḥbāb* (the beloved ones). Furthermore, he may be given such endearing attributes as *al-asmar* (the dark one, or brunette) or *khill* (lover, or close companion), and depicted as someone with perfect qualities (*kāmil il-awṣāf*) and irresistible beauty. He may be referred to as *al-ḥilū*, or *al-jamīl* (both meaning the beautiful one), or praised as *farīd il-maḥāsin* (the one with unique beauty), or *malīk il-ḥusn* (the king of beauty), or described through grand expressions such as *sulṭān jamālak* (the royalty, or power of your beauty). Such beauty metaphors as the *badr*, or *badr al-tim* (both meaning full moon) may also be used. Similarly encountered are descriptions of the beloved's personal traits, for example *ṭabʿuh d-dalāl* (coquettishness is in his nature). The beloved may also be given honorific titles such as *Sīdī* (My Master).

The depictions may also be more specific, particularly when the physical traits of the beloved are addressed. The texts speak about *malīḥ il-qawām* (the one with a beautiful figure), or *ghuṣnun yatamāyal* (a gracefully bending twig or branch), or *ghuṣn il-bān* (willow twig). They may also focus upon more detailed morphologies. The concept of *ward al-khudūd* (the roses of the cheeks) alluding to the beautiful redness in the beloved's cheeks, is often coupled with references to key physical features such as *al-ḥājib* (the eyebrow), *al-jafn* (the eyelid), *rimsh il-ʿuyūn* (the eyelashes), and *ash-shafāyif* (the lips). However, particular attention is given to the beloved's eye or eyes, sometimes described as *il-ʿuyūn is-sūd* (the black eyes).

At this stage, the scenario presents the potential lover as an innocent bystander subjected to a force that is both bewildering and irresistible, namely the beloved's physical appearance, usually described in beauty related terms. In essence, beauty is the agent that sets the love drama in motion.

Falling in love

The beloved's beauty transforms an ordinary person into a lover, thus marking the first step within the unfolding love story. The "beautiful one" is also transformed conceptually in the mind of the lover into the "beloved one." The amorous sentiment itself is represented by a variety of general concepts such as *hawá*, *ʿishq*, *ḥubb*, *gharām*, *hiyām*, all of which can be translated as "love," or more accurately perhaps, as "infatuation." Meanwhile, the lover refers to himself as *mughram*, *mutayyam*, *walhān*, and *ṣabb*, which all mean "love stricken," or "lovesick."

The process of falling in love is described by the lover. An initial encounter is usually cited, for example *lammā shuftuh* (when I saw him), or *lammā qābiltuh* (when I met him). The encounter, which usually occurs unintentionally as an act of fate, renders the susceptible lover totally captivated, as indicated by the expressions *shaghalnī* (he preoccupied me), *fatannī* (he charmed me), *sabānī* (he captivated me), and *shabaknī* (he entangled me). References to falling in love may also be less direct for example, *lammā nkawayt bin-nār* (when I was seared by fire) in reference to the fire of love, or *lammā btalayt* (when I was afflicted).

The most important love agent, however, is the eye (or *ʿayn*) of the beloved, whose looks (*liḥāḍḥ*) become the Cupid's arrows that hunt the lover. Thus, the lover describes how he fell in love through such statements as *ramānī bi sahm il-ʿayn* (he hit me with the arrow of his eye), *aṣl il-gharām naḍḥrah* (the cause of love is a gaze), the latter being the title of a famous late nineteenth century dawr, and *laḥḍḥuh asarnā* (his look captivated us). In this last phrase, the lover uses the plural "us," a typical feature that, in addition to referring to the lover himself, embraces all lovers as a "species" of individuals with a common fate, or perhaps a shared sense of camaraderie. Lovers may be categorically referred to as *ahl il-hawá*, or "people of love," the title of a song by Umm Kulthūm.

Other agents are also involved, among the most important being the soul. The lover expresses his amorous condition through such expressions as *ʿishiqt(i) rūḥak* (I fell in love with your soul), and *malak rūḥī* (he captured, or possessed, my soul). A further element is the lover's heart (*fuʾād*, or *qalb*), which initially responds to the love stimulus (the beloved's beauty) and causes the soul, a sublime entity, to succumb to the amorous state. Thus, the lover may admonish his heart and speaks of it as a reckless player that has brought about afflictions upon the lover, as well as upon itself. Expressions such as *yā fuʾādī* (Oh, my heart) and *il- fuʾād ḥabbak* (my heart fell in love with you) are quite prevalent.

After describing how love was initiated, the lover reflects briefly upon his own condition and accepts love as his unavoidable destiny. Now fully transformed, he has to settle with his new role and fortune, as he refers to the experience as *naṣībī* (my lot, or luck), and *qismitī wayya l-ḥabīb* (my fate with the beloved). He may even speak of inner symptoms indicative of being in love, for example, becoming highly obsessed or jealous toward the beloved, as illustrated by the phrase *aghār ʿalayk* (I become jealous or protective toward you).

The beloved's behavior

Already love stricken, the lover describes the beloved's conduct and mindset. The beloved is shown to be oblivious or even totally unaware of the condition of his lover. He remains *mirtāḥ il-bāl* (with his mind at ease) and sleeps through the night without worries. The beloved's apparent lack of interest may also be due to his forgetfulness. The lover may juxtapose the two opposed conditions of *nisītnī* (you forgot me) and *aftikrak* (I remember you), or *bafakkar bīk* (I think of you). The beloved, whose persona may conjure certain political and juridical authority can also be shown as being unattainable or essentially outside the lover's immediate realm of experience. Therefore, his character is marked by *tīh*, "vanity," or "haughtiness" and *dalāl*, namely coquettishness and pampering typical of aristocratic or affluent life style.

In some instances, the beloved may also be inconsiderate or harsh. He may be viewed as a *ḏḥālim* (tormentor) and his treatment may be referred to as *ḏḥulm il-ḥabīb* (the cruelty of the beloved). Moreover, the beloved may be admonished for turning away and making himself inaccessible. His behavior is described through such concepts as *ṣadd* (rejection) and *hijrān* (going away). It is also implied in such expressions as *tikāyidnī layh?* (why do you cause me trouble?), *tikhāṣimnī* (you become angry with me), *ʿannī yimīl* (he turns away from me), *tuhjurnī* (you desert me), and *tighīb ʿan ʿaynī* (you disappear from my sight, or my eye does not see you anymore). The beloved may also renege on the *waʿd* (promise, or love oath) or make false *mawaʿīd* (pledges or appointments), thus augmenting the lover's agony.

The lover's condition

Particularly emphasized is the lover's distress which results from having fallen in love, as well as from the beloved's perceived harshness or lack of attention. Accordingly, the lover's condition is marked by two related types of stress, emotional–physical and social, which are both described through various connotative phrases and idioms.

References to emotional and by extension physical stress focus on the lover's restlessness and deteriorating health, as in the words *alam* (pain), *ʿadhābī* (my suffering), *shaqāyā* (my misery), and *kuthr il-asiyya* (the excess of harsh treatment). Pointing directly to the bodily condition are the phrases *ḥubbak yidhawwibnī* (your love makes me dissipate, or makes me melt away), *jismī naḥal* (my body has become thin), and *ana l-ʿalīl w-inta d-dawā* (I am the sick one and you are the medicine).

Metaphoric allusions are also made for example when speaking of *ʿadhāb il-qalb* (the suffering of the heart) or using such expressions as *jarḥī* (my wound), *yijarraḥnī* (he wounds me), and *yidāwī l-jirāḥ* (he heals the wounds). Also common in this context are the analogies of fire and burning: *ḥubbak kāwīnī* (I am seared by your love) and *nār ḥubbak* (the fire of your love). The lover may even describe actual symptoms of stress such as *anīnī* (my moaning), *nawhī* (my wailing), and *bukāyā* (my crying).

Further expressions imply psychological transformation. Examples are: *wajd* (intense longing); *hiyām*, which refers to infatuation but has the connotation of wandering aimlessly; *junūnī* (my going insane), or *ḥubbak yijanninnī* (your love is making me crazy); *shajan*, which denotes a certain form of melancholy; and *waḥshah* (loneliness), or as the title of a famous dawr goes, *yā m-anta waḥishnī*! (how much I miss you! or feel lonesome without you!). The lover may also represent his own experience through the imagery of a bewildered nightingale, or *bulbul ḥayrān*, the title of a 1930 song by ʿAbd al-Wahhāb.

One of the most prevalent themes of emotional–physical stress pertains to the lover's sleeplessness. Thus, while others, including the beloved himself, succumb innocently and blissfully to sleep, the lover complains about spending long sleepless nights, with no companion except the night itself. The notion of love-related sleeplessness is implicit in common phrases such as *ḥarram ʿalayya n-nawm* (he made it impossible for me to sleep), *yā ṭūl saharī*! (how long I stay up at night!), *sahrān liwaḥdī* (I stay up alone at night), which is the title of a song by Umm Kulthūm, and *laylī ṭal* (my night has become very long). One song by Farīd al-Aṭrash starts with: *saʾalnī l-layl, bi-tishar layh*? (the night asked me, why do you stay up?). The sleepless lover may also find solace in the moon, which in Arabic has a masculine gender, possesses connotations of beauty, and may become a reminder of the beloved.

Social stress is depicted through expressions that describe the lover's relationship with his own society, usually characterized as being unsympathetic and at times outright cruel. The people surrounding the lover may admonish him for falling in love or for submitting to the pitiable condition he is in. Consequently, such concepts as *lawm* (harsh criticism), and *lāʾim* (one who criticizes) are widely encountered. The act of *lawm* is usually committed by the *ʿadhūl* or *ʿādhil*, namely the cynic or blamer who attempts to separate between the lover and the beloved. Often used is the plural form, *ʿawādhil* (cynics).

Envy is also portrayed. The lover's envious peers show malice toward him and wish to thwart his efforts to fulfill his amorous dreams. The concept of envy (*ḥasad*) is voiced in such expressions as *ʿayn al-ḥasūd* (the eye of the envious person, or the evil eye), and *ḥasadūnī wi-bāyin fī ʿaynayhum* (they were envious of me and it showed in their eyes), being the title of a 1928 song by Muḥammad ʿAbd al-Wahhāb.

Society may harbor a sentiment that is even more pernicious, namely *shamātah*, which does not have a close English equivalent, but can be explained as rejoicing at, or deriving satisfaction from, someone else's misfortune.[10] The passive-aggressive cynics delight in seeing the lover suffer and deem his suffering well deserved. The lover may reprove these cynics through such expressions as *layh tishmatū fiyyā?* (why do you gain satisfaction from my suffering?). He may also rebuke his beloved for deserting him and unwittingly perhaps, subjecting him to shamātah from others. In one song by the Lebanese singer Wadīʿ al-Ṣāfī, we hear the expression: *shammattū fīnā l-qarāyib w-il-ḥabāyib yā ghāyibīn* (you who have deserted us have caused our relatives and dear ones to show shamātah toward us).

The lover may attempt to avoid societal disparagement. Expressions such as *adārī* and *akhabbī*, both meaning "I exercise caution" or "try to hide" are used, but often with the realization that love cannot be concealed. Love is "written on the forehead" (*maktūb ʿalá l-jibīn*) or as the title of an old qaṣīdah text sung by Umm Kulthūm goes: *aṣ-ṣabbu tafḍaḥuhu ʿuyūnuh* (the lover's eyes expose him), keeping in mind that the word *tafḍaḥ* also means "to scandalize" or "to make notoriously open." In the same sense however,

10 The concept of *shamātah* may have a close parallel in the German expression *Die Schadenfreude*, which similarly refers to joy about somebody's misfortune.

love cannot be hidden away even from the beloved himself, as in one song by Muḥammad ʿAbd al-Wahhāb the lover says: *wi law darayt ʿannak ḥubbī tifḍaḥnī ʿaynī bi hawāyā* (if I were to hide my love from you, my eye would divulge my love). Significantly, the eye, which instigates love in the first place, makes the love condition almost impossible to conceal.

Aftermath

The scenario tends to end with reflexive statements pertaining to love, the beloved, and the lover himself. Almost invariably, the texts express a sense of unrequited love and unfulfilled hopes, but also project an ongoing quest. The lover attempts to engage the beloved through pleas or even admonition (*ʿitāb*). He may also beg for his affection (*widd*, or *widād*). Wishing to unite with him, he may use such expressions as *atmannā qurbak* (I desire being close to you), *jud bi-l-wiṣāl* (make a generous offer to reunite), *wāfīnī* (be forthcoming, or come to me), and *ʿudlī thānī* (come back again to me). Similarly, the lover may solicit the sympathy of the beloved. He may ask for his *ʿaṭf* (compassion) and call upon him to have mercy upon the lover's heart (*irḥam fuʾādī*) or, ironically, may ask the beloved himself to give the lover some consolation, as illustrated by the expression *tiwāsīnī* (you console me).

The lover may also humble himself before the beloved and portray himself as being worthy of pity. He may exclaim *tadhallal li man tahwá* (make yourself meek toward the one you love), or as the title of one of Umm Kulthūm's early songs goes: *lī ladhdhatun fī dhillatī wa khuḍūʿī* (I derive pleasure from my meekness and submission).[11] He may also wish to complain about the beloved to the beloved himself. In effect, he appeals to the beloved's own sense of justice and compassion, although he may also speak of him in ambivalent terms as both the ultimate goal, or *munāyā* (my desire), and the perpetrator. Commonly used are such expressions as *ashtikīlak min ḥubbī*, (I complain to you about my love). In this case, the beloved may be portrayed as a judge and implored: *uḥkum bil-ʿadl* (make a just verdict). The lover may also allude to a separate figure in the love drama, namely *qāḍī l-gharām* (the judge of love), who is called upon to arbitrate and bring justice to the lover.

Meanwhile, the lover attempts to transcend the painful reality. He may live in perpetual hope, as illustrated by the phrase *afḍal amannī al-nafs* (I continue to give hope to my soul), or live with the memory of the beloved, as implied by the title of one of Umm Kulthūm's songs, *izzay ansāk*! (how could I ever forget you!). He may also encounter the beloved through signs

[11] The submission theme is encountered mostly in early song lyrics and in some Sufi poems. Although essentially symbolic, it has irked some modern-minded Arab critics, who have deemed it too excessive, if not extremely self-deprecating and even masochistic.

and hints, and establish communication with him on a more symbolic or "spiritual" level, rather than through physical contact. The lyrics speak of seeing the beloved's *ṭayf* (namely, image, vision, or phantom) as, for example, indicated by a phrase in one of ʿAbd al-Wahhāb's songs, *anā zarnī ṭayfak bi-manāmī* (I was visited by your image in my dream). The lover's dream (*manām*) becomes an important medium through which the lover establishes contact with the beloved. The lover may also communicate directly with the image or the shadow (*khayāl*) of the beloved, as implied by the expression *anājī ṭayfak* (I converse intimately with your image).

Finally, the lover may rationalize the entire affair by describing it as unavoidable destiny. He may attribute it to human weakness and state that love is irresistible because God created within us eyes to see beauty. The lover may take an oath to love no one except the beloved. In some cases, he may also hope, or make an oath, not to fall in love again, or beg his heart not to bring upon him such an ordeal again. He may voice his oath in such a statement as *yiḥram ʿalayya l-ʿishq* (let there be no falling in love for me again).

To illustrate the expressive and semantic features of this orientation, we may first look at an excerpt from a premodern qaṣīdah by Ibn al-Nabīh al-Maṣrī. This text was set to music and recorded by Shaykh Abū al-ʿUlā Muḥammad in the early twentieth century, and sung and recorded by Umm Kulthūm in the 1920s.[12] Here, the poet speaks about devotion, his heart, and the sweet pain inflicted by the beloved:

Afdīhi in ḥafiḍha l-*hawá* aw ḍayyaʿa; *Malaka l-fuʾāda* fa mā ʿasá an aṣnaʿa?
I sacrifice myself for him, whether he keeps our *love* or loses it; *He captivated my heart*, what shall I do?

Man lam yadhuq *ḍhulma l-ḥabībi* ka-ḍhalmihi; *Ḥulwan* fa-qad jahila l-*maḥabbata* wa-ddaʿá.
Whoever has not tasted a *beloved's tyranny* like his; *Sweet* [tyranny], he would be ignorant about *love* and pretentious.

Comparable imagery appears in muwashshaḥ texts that have been written or rewritten by Egyptian lyricists, or have been particularly favored by Egyptian composers. Such texts appear to integrate both the standard expressions of the muwashshaḥ genre and the pathos, emotional introspection, and references to power and authority typical of the Egyptian textual orientation. The following example by an unknown writer was set to music by the early twentieth-century Egyptian composer Shaykh Sayyid Darwish.[13] It ends with the lover describing his love metaphorically as a state of mad infatuation and begging for justice, compassion, and forgiveness:

12 From al-Maṣrī and Kāmil, collectors n.d: 39.
13 From al-Ḥilū 1965: 48.

Ṣuḥtu *wajdan*, ya *nadāmá*; *Wāṣilūnī* w-*arḥamūnī*.
I cried out of *ecstatic yearning* oh, *(drinking) companions*; *Come back to me* and *have compassion for me*.

Innī *ṣabbun* fī *hawākum*; Sāla *dam'ī* min *'uyūnī*.
I am *smitten* by *your love*; *Tears* poured out of *my eyes*.

Dhubtu min *shawqī gharāman*; F-*anṣifūnī* w-*arḥamūnī*.
I melted away because of my *amorous yearning*; *Let there be fairness* and *compassion toward me*.

In *junintu* al-yawma fīkum; F-*a'dhurūnī* fī *junūnī*.
If I *became mad* about you today; *Forgive me* for *my madness*.

Similar amorous motifs are exhibited by the Egyptian mawwāl. Having a folk counterpart that comments on various local issues, this poetical genre has been used by medieval and post-medieval poets, including Sufis.[14] The following example belongs to a mawwāl type called *a'raj*, or "lame," a structure known to have been developed and cultivated specifically by Egyptian poets.[15] In terms of punning (or sometimes just rhyming), this type has five textual lines that follow an AAABA scheme. Its nickname, "lame" comes from the fourth line ending with a word that deviates from the homonym (or rhyme scheme) shared by the other lines. The following mawwāl was sung and recorded before World War I on a Gramophone disc by Shakyk Yūsuf al-Manyalāwī:[16]

Yā *ahl il-gharām* i'limūnā 'an *jarāyiḥkum*.
Oh, *people of love*, inform us about *your wounds* (*or afflictions*).

Dayman *asārá l-gharām* 'ammā jará yiḥkum.
Those captivated by love always speak about what happened.

Wid-*dam' fawq il-khudūd* lamā *jará* yiḥkum.
When *tears pour over* (the lover's) *cheeks* they govern.

Wadī *amīr il-jamāl* ṣāḥib *qawām* 'ādil.
And here is the *prince of beauty* whose *stature* is straight (just).

Min ba'd 'arḍ iḍ-*ḍanā* wi-llī jará, *yiḥkum*.
After I present the case of my *weariness* and all that has happened, let him *judge*.

14 See discussions in Ḥusayn 1964.
15 See Wāṣif 1956: 37.
16 From al-Būlāqī, collector 1927: 154.

The above famous text incorporates numerous standard ṭarab themes, as it talks about "the people of love," and presents symbolic love symptoms such as "tears pouring over the cheeks," not to mention also casting the beloved in the role of judge, or disinterested arbitrator. However, this piece also displays striking literary ingenuity not only in the use of homonyms, but also in the "double talk" that runs particularly through the last two lines. In the expression *amīr al-jamāl* (the prince of beauty), the word for "prince" glorifies the beloved's beauty, but also carries the implications of supreme political or moral authority. Furthermore, the phrase *ṣaḥib qawām ʿādil* in reference to the beloved means he has a straight or upright figure, yet the word *ʿādil*, or "straight," also means "fair" or "just" in the legal sense. Also cleverly used is the closing expression *yiḥkum*, which means both "to rule over" or "govern" and "to judge."

The following text of a very well-known late nineteenth-century dawr composed by Muḥammad ʿUthmān can also be studied for its representational, as well as creatively conceived, content.[17] It speaks of the initial cause of falling in love and the fate of the lover:

Aṣl il-*gharām naḍhrah*; Yā *shabkitī* m il-ʿayn.
The cause of *love* is his *gaze*; Oh, how I was *entrapped* by his *eye*.

Wil-*waʿd(i)* da yijrī; Wi-kān lī *ghāyib* fayn.
And this *promise* flies away; Where has he *been, so far away* from me?

Yallī *kawayt il-fuʾād irḥam*; Asbāb *ḍanāyā* l-*ʿayn*.
Oh, the one who *seared* my *heart have mercy*; The cause of my *suffering* is his *eye*.

W-il-*waʿd(i)* da kān yijrī; Wi-kān lī *ghāyib* fayn?
And this *promise* has been flying away; Where has he *been, so far away* from me?

In another well-known dawr text written by Ismāʿīl Ṣabrī and set to music by Muḥammad ʿUthmān,[18] the poet praises the beauty of the beloved, describes the hazards of falling in love, and admonishes his heart for bringing upon itself the troubles of love. Of structural interest is the single unrhymed phrase added at the very end:

Qaddak amīr il-*aghṣān*; Min ghayr mukābir.
Your figure is the prince (the most beautiful) of *branches*; Without a contender.

Wi-*ward(i) khaddak sulṭān*; ʿAlá l-*azāhir*.
The *rose of your cheek* is a *sulṭān*; Ruling over the *flowers*.

[17] From Shafīq, collector 1963: 9.
[18] From Shafīq, collector 1963: 89.

Wil-*ḥubb(i)* kulluh *ashjān*; Yā *qalb(i)* ḥādhir.
And *love* is full of *sorrow*; Oh, my *heart* beware.

Da *ṣ-ṣadd(i)* wayya l-*hijrān*; Jazā l-mukhāṭir.
Such *turning away* and *separation*; Is the punishment for the risk taker.

Yā *qalb(i)* a dinta *ḥabbayt*; Wi-riji'ʿt(i) *tindam.*
Oh, my *heart*, here you have *fallen in love*; And you began *to regret it.*

Wi-ṣabaḥt(i) *tishkī* mā ra'ayt; Lak ḥadd(i) *yirḥam.*
And you started to *complain*, but found; No one who *has sympathy* for you.

Ṣaddaqt(i) qawlī wi-laqayt; *Dhull* il-*mutayyam.*
You believed (confirmed) what I said and experienced; The *humiliation* of the *love-smitten.*

Yā mā naṣaḥtak.
Oh, how many times I have advised (warned) you!

In the above example the use of authority symbols such as *sulṭān* and *amīr* is typical. Such symbols are brought to an even greater focus in the lyrics of another well-known dawr. Set to music by ʿAbduh al-Ḥāmūlī, the nineteenth-century text was written by Shaykh ʿAbd al-Raḥmān Qurāʿah, at one time a *muftī*, namely, "religious judge."[19]

Allāh yiṣūn dawlit *ḥusnak*; ʿAlá d-dawām min iz-zawāl.
May God protect (preserve) the authority (rulership) of *your beauty*; Forever from perishing.

W-yiṣūn *fu'ādī* min nablak; Maḍī l-ḥusām min ghayr qitāl.
And protect *my heart* from your arrows; Sharp sword without combat.

Ashkī limīn ghayrak *ḥubbak*? Anā l-*ʿalīl* w-inta *ṭ-ṭabīb.*
To whom but you can *I complain* about *loving you*? I am the *sick one* and you are the *doctor.*

Ismaḥ wi-*dāwīnī* bi-*qurbak*; W-aṣnaʿ jamīl iyyāk *aṭīb.*
Oblige and *cure me* by *being near me*; Do a good deed and *I will be healed.*

Another dawr text written by Aḥmad ʿĀshūr and set to music by Ibrāhīm al-Qabbānī[20] focuses upon the fateful transformation from being blissfully ignorant about love to becoming love-stricken and joining the camaraderie of other lovers:

[19] From Shafīq, collector n.d.: 117.
[20] From Shafīq, collector 1963: 101.

Min qabl(i) mā *ahwá l-jamāl*; Kunt *alūm* il-*ʿāshiqīn*.
Before *I became enamored by his beauty*; I used to *criticize lovers*.

W-ankur wujūd l-*maḥabbah*; W(i)-ḥin *raʾayt* hadhā l-*ghazāl*.
And deny the existence of *love*; But when I *saw* this *gazelle*.

Ṣabaḥt(i) dimn *il-mughramīn*; Aʿdhur jamīʿ il-*aḥibbah*.
I became one of *the lovers*; Excusing all *those in love*.

Yā qalbī mālak *wil-hawá*; Ma kunt(i) khāliṣ fī *naʿīm*.
Oh, my heart, leave *love* aside; (Before, falling in love), you were settled in a state of *luxury*.

Wi kunt(i) qāʿid mistirīḥ; Il-*ʿishq(i)* da *mā-lūsh dawā*.
And you were comfortably rested; *Love has no cure*.

Yiṣbaḥ *il-mughram saqīm*; Wi-yutrak il-*ʿāshiq jarīḥ*.
The *lover* becomes *ill*; And the *infatuated* is left *wounded*.

The lover may also chastise the beloved and ponder giving up love or even befriending someone else to make the beloved jealous. Concluding with such a rebellious twist is a dawr text set to music and sung by Shaykh Sayyid Darwish who was known for his innovative musical works. The following are the opening three lines: [21]

Anā *ʿishiqt* wi shuft(i) ghayrī kithīr *ʿishiq*; ʿUmrī mā shuft il-*murr* illa fī *hawak*.
I *have loved* and seen many others *love*; I have never seen *bitterness* except in *your love*.

Wi-kam *ṣabart* mā kansh(i) fī yūm nittifiq; Maʿ inn(i) *qalbī* kān *asīr yiṭlub riḍāk*.
And how *patient I have been*, but at no time did we reconcile; Although *my heart* was a *captive asking for your good graces*.

Khunt il-widād min ghayr mīʿād, in kān ʿanād; Balāsh *tighīr* lammā tishufnī maʿ siwāk.
You betrayed the affection without notice, if it is stubbornness; Don't *become jealous* when you see me with someone else.

The following selected examples from Umm Kulthūm's songs illustrate the typical features of the textual idiom, as well as the inclusion of novel poetical structures, thematic variations, and twists within the general amorous scenario.[22]

21 From Ḥammād 1970: 162.
22 For a detailed presentation of the various thematic and structural innovations and the individual stylistic traits of Umm Kulthūm's major lyricists, see Danielson's dissertation (1991b) and book (1997).

In a *mūnūlūj* (or "monologue," a dramatically conceived, through-composed song genre), recorded around 1926,[23] the lover presents a narrative-like scenario according to which the beloved's image visits him and asks him to revive his love rather than succumb to despair. Written by Aḥmad Rāmī and set to music by Muḥammad al-Qaṣabjī (1892–1966), a pioneering composer who worked closely with Umm Kulthūm, the text constructs the love drama indirectly through personal reflections, pleas to the beloved, and messages conveyed by the image itself. The following excerpt consists of the opening four lines:

Zarnī ṭayfak fī manāmī; Jaddid il-ʿahd(i) llī rāḥ.
Your image visited me in my dream; It renewed (your) *bygone pledge* (of love).

Inta *ṭawwilt(i) khiṣāmī*; W(i)-huwwa jāh bil-*wajd(i) bāḥ*.
You had a *quarrel* with me *for too long*; But (your image) came and *divulged* (your) *yearning*.

Qallī, *ṣāyin* lak *widādak*; W-inta *ghāyib* ʿan *ʿaynayhā*.
(The image) said to me, (She, the beloved) is *honoring* your *affection*; While you are *away* from her *eyes*.

Bass(i) layh *tiqsī fuʾādak*; W-il-*widād* bāyin ʿalayhā?
But why are you *so hard on your heart*; When her *affection* is apparent?

In another Umm Kulthūm song, a dawr recorded around 1930, we encounter a somewhat novel thematic orientation as the text speaks of a happy reunion after a long period of separation.[24] Written by Aḥmad Rāmī and set to music by Dāwūd Ḥusnī, the text refers to the beloved's decision to come to the lover and end the latter's long and painful wait. Notably, the title uses the ambivalent expression *sharraf* (from *sharaf*, or honor), which can be translated as "he honored with his presence," or "has honored us by coming." Because this is a highly formalized expression used for royalty or officials, it can be understood as a token of respect for the beloved, but can also mildly chide the conceited beloved, as for example the phrase "His majesty has come" may be said sarcastically or in jest. In any case, the general tone of the poem centers on *ʿitāb*, or "admonition" directed at the beloved, who makes a happy but long overdue return. This excerpt below consists of the first two lines, then the last line followed by a closing single hemistich:

Sharraf *ḥabīb l-qalb* baʿd *il-ghiyāb*; Wi-kan *ṭawīl*.
My *heart's beloved* showed up after *being away*; Which was *long*.

[23] From al-Maṣrī and Kāmil, collectors, n.d.: 83.
[24] From al-Maṣrī and Kāmil, collectors, n.d.: 151

Wi-baʿd(i) *ṭūl il-hajr*, *yiḥlá* l-*ʿitāb*; Wayyā l-*khalīl*.
After a *long separation*, voicing *admonition becomes enjoyable*; With the *intimate one*.

Qaṭaft il-*ward min khadduh*; Shiribt il-*ḥilū* min shahduh.
I picked the *roses from his cheek*; I savored his *sweet* honey.

Wi-*dhāq ḥalāwt il-waṣl qalbī l-ʿalīl*.
And *my lovesick heart tasted the sweetness of reunion*.

In another well-known Umm Kulthūm song titled *Arūḥ li-Mīn*? (to whom do I go?) recorded at the Cairo Radio station in 1957, the love theme takes the form of an inquiry.[25] In the text, written by ʿAbd al-Munʿim al-Sibāʿī and set to music by Riyāḍ al-Sunbāṭī, the opening stanza has a melody that descends from the area of the upper tonic of the maqām (Rāst) down toward the tonic. The music appears to express the sense of questioning conveyed by the text, which echoes the familiar theme of finding no one to provide sympathy toward the lover except the beloved himself. The stanza goes as follows:

Arūḥ li-mīn w-aqūl; Yā mīn *yinṣifnī minnak*?
To whom do I go and say; Who will *bring me justice for what you did*?

Ma huww anta *farḥī* w-inta; *Jarḥī*, wi-kulluh minnak.
Since it is you who are *my joy* and; *My wound*, and it is all coming from you.

Arūḥ li-mīn?
To whom do I go?

Finally, in one of Umm Kulthūm's songs with text by ʿAbd al-Wahhāb Muḥammad and music by Riyāḍ al-Sunbāṭī, the love scenario exhibits a reversal of roles.[26] The lover depicts the beloved as having become love afflicted himself. Titled *Ḥasībak liz-Zaman* (I will leave you for time, or let time exact justice from you), the text presents considerable variety in the lengths of the lines and the metric and rhyming configurations. The opening section excerpted below describes the lover as being somewhat rebellious as he tries to make the beloved himself experience the torments of love:

Ḥ-*asībak* liz-zaman; Lā *ʿitāb* walā *shajan*.
I will *leave you*, let time judge you; Without *admonition* or *painful feelings*.

Tiqāsī min-*nadam*; Wi-tiʿraf il-*alam*.
You will *suffer* from *regret*; And will get to know *pain*.

[25] From al-Maṣrī and Kāmil, collectors, n.d.: 315.
[26] From al-Maṣrī and Kāmil collectors, n.d.: 313.

Tishkī, mish *ḥas'al* ʿalayk; *Tibkī*, mish *ḥarḥam ʿaynayk.*
You will *complain*, but I will not *pay attention to* (care for) you; You will *cry*, but I will not *have mercy for your eyes.*

Yallī *mā raḥamtish ʿaynayh*; Lammā kān *qalbī* fī īdayk.
You, the one who *did not have mercy* for (my heart's) *eyes*; When *my heart* was in your hands.

Dārit il-ayyām ʿalayk.
The days have turned against you.

Many of the elements presented thus far also appear in the texts that Muḥammad ʿAbd al-Wahhāb sang throughout his career, roughly from the mid-1920s to the mid-1980s. The songs of this artist, who composed his own music, often departed from the traditional ṭarab model both musically and textually and incorporated various novel images and forms of expression.[27] Nevertheless, the traditional lyrical themes remain prevalent in his love songs. In one early *ṭaqṭūqah* (a strophic song-type usually of a popular quality) by ʿAbd al-Wahhāb, the text speaks of the image of the beloved visiting in a dream, and also describes the lover's vain attempt to hide his love from the beloved in order to prevent him from becoming too conceited or unapproachable.[28] The following excerpt consists of the opening two-line refrain and the first of the three main verses:

Khāyif aqūl illī fī *qalbī*; Titqal wi tiʿānid wayyāyā.
I am afraid to say what is in *my heart*; For you might act hard to get and become disagreeable with me.

Wi-law *darayt* ʿannak *ḥubbī*; Tifḍaḥnī *ʿaynī* fī *hawāyā.*
But if I *hide my love* for you; *My eye* would (scandalously) divulge *my love.*

Anā *zarnī ṭayfak fī manāmī*; Qabl(i) ma-*ḥibbak.*
Your image visited me in my dream; Before *I fell in love with you.*

Ṭammaʿnī bil-*waṣl(i)* w-*fātnī*; W-anā *mashghūl* bak.
It enticed me with *union* and *left me*; When I was *preoccupied* with you.

ʿĀyiz *aʿātbuh* lakin *khāyif*; Yirūḥ yiqūl innī *baḥibbak.*
I would like to *admonish it*, but *I am afraid*; That it will go and say that *I love you.*

Wi-law *darayt* ʿannak *ḥubbī*; Tifḍaḥnī *ʿaynī* fī *hawāyā.*
But if I *hide my love* for you; *My eye* would (scandalously) divulge *my love.*

[27] For historical discussions on the various innovations in the texts sung by ʿAbd al-Wahhāb, see Saḥḥāb V. 1987: 141–220 and Azzam 1990.
[28] From ʿAbd al-Majīd 1970: 269.

In ʿAbd al-Wahhāb's film-song lyrics, such themes are retained, although to some extent they are tied to the overall film plots. This is the case, for example, in the 1938 film *Yaḥyā al-Ḥubb* (Long Live Love, usually translated as *Vive L'Amour*), featuring ʿAbd al-Wahhāb (as Fatḥī) and the renowned ṭarab singer and actress Laylá Murād (as Nadia). Although the film story has a happy ending marked by reunion, the themes of pathos, loneliness, societal cruelty, lovesickness, and the lovers' yearning to be together, dominate most of the film's songs and sung dialogues. According to the plot, Fatḥī, a bookkeeper at a bank in Cairo, also a talented singer and, as later revealed, the son of a wealthy landowner, falls in love with the bank owner's only daughter, Nadia, who is musically inclined herself and at the time engaged to an entomologist. At one point, the love affair is momentarily troubled by a sudden misconception, a twist common in Egyptian film plots. Nadia thinks erroneously that Fatḥī has turned away from her after she sees him display affection toward another woman, whom she thinks is Fatḥī's lover, but in reality turns out to be his sister. In the lyrics, by Aḥmad Rāmī, the beloved is referred to both in the masculine gender, particularly when reference is made to love in general, and in the feminine gender, when Fatḥī seems to address Nadia directly. The following is an excerpt from a sung dialogue that ends with the two lovers courageously deciding to make their love known:[29]

FATḤĪ: *Ṭāl intiḍhārī liwaḥdī*; Wil-*buʿd(i) ʿannak alīm.*
My *waiting alone has been long*; *Separation from you is painful.*

W(i)-fiḍilt(i) min *kuthr(i) wajdī*; *Asʾal ʿalayk* in-*nasīm.*
Because of my *intense yearning*; I kept *asking* the *breeze about you.*

Adī l-*qamar* shāhid ʿalayyā; Isʾalīh ʿan *ṭūl ʿadhābī.*
Here, the *moon* is my witness; Ask it about *my long suffering.*

Ḥayrān afakkar fī llī biyyā; Min *dhunūnī* w-īḍṭirābī.
I am puzzled thinking of what is within me; Because of my *anguish* and agitation.

Aqūl *li-rūḥī*, ayh jará? Yā hal tará!
I say to *my soul*, what happened? I wonder!

Ma tkallimīnī *yā nūr ʿaynī*; Wi-ḥyāt *hawānā* ruddī ʿalayyā.
Why don't you speak to me, *oh, light of my eye*; For *our love*'s sake answer me.

[29] From *Vive L'Amour* (n.d.), an Arabic pamphlet that advertised the film in the United States and included a brief description of the plot along with some lyrics and sung dialogues. A more detailed synopsis of the plot is provided by Shūshah, n.d.: 68–79.

NADIA: Mish ʿārfah aqullak ayh; Baʿd *illī shuftuh* fī *gharāmī*.
I don't know what to tell you; After *what I encountered* in *my love*.

Kān il-*ʿadhāb* dah layh; Mā bayn shukūkī wi-awhāmī?
What was this *suffering* for; Between my suspicions and my illusions?

Min yawm ma *hawayt*; W-anā baghālib ḍamīrī.
Since the day *I fell in love*; I have been battling my conscience.

W(i)-*yā raytnī* mā jayt; Wi-qidirt aktum shuʿūrī.
And *I wish* that I hadn't come; And that I was able to hide my feelings.

FATḤĪ: layh *innadam*? huwwa *qalbī*; *Nākir ʿuhūd* il-*widād*?
Why this *regret*? Is *my heart*; *Reneging* on the *pledges* of *compassion*?

Qūlīlī ayh bass(i) dhanbī; Lammā *nawayti l-buʿād*?
Tell me what I did wrong; When *you decided to go away*?

Taʿālī bayn aḥḍānī; Da l-*ḥubb*(*i*) huwwa l-jānī.
Come, let me embrace you; It is *love* that should be blamed.

Qūlīlī *khayfah* ayh?
Tell me what are you *afraid of*?

NADIA: *Khayfah kalām in-nās yifarraq shamlinā.*
I am afraid that *people's gossip* will *drive us apart*.

Khadaʿt(i) ahlī wi-*riḍayt luqānā*; W-layh *nikhabbī* ʿanhum *hawānā*?
I deceived my family and *accepted our being together*; And why should we *hide our love* from them?

Finally, in one well-known ughniyah, or as sometimes introduced, "operett," titled *ar-Rābīʿ*, or "Spring," sung by Farīd al-Aṭrash, the text treats the four seasons as metaphors for the different phases of the love experience. Thus, we encounter a progression, or perhaps a regression, starting with *spring*, during which love is surrounded by the trappings of natural landscape, then *summer*, which leads to separation, lovesickness, and suffering, as the flowers wilt and the nightingale turns his singing into wailing. *Autumn* is depicted as a time of pain and despair, followed by *winter*, which is associated with long nights and complaints about loneliness and the tribulations of love. The text ends with hope that the cycle will unfold again and that the beloved's image will emerge with the return of spring. Written by the late Egyptian lyricist Maʾmūn al-Shinnāwī, the poem also combines the imagery of gardens and roses with an idyllic portrayal of the Nile river, its gentle waves "singing" with the gentle breeze. The opening two lines, sung in a somewhat cheery waltz-like meter, act as a refrain that reappears toward the very end. The following are only the first nine lines of a relatively long text of some twenty-eight lines:[30]

Adī r-rabīʿ ʿād min tānī; Wil-*badr*(*i*) *hallit anwāruh.*
Here, spring has come back again; And the *full moon is casting its light.*

Wi-*fayn ḥabībī* illi *ramānī*; Min *jannit*(*i*) l-*ḥubb*(*i*) l-*nāruh.*
And *where is my beloved* who threw me; Out of the *paradise* of *love* into *his fire.*

Ayyām riḍāh ya *zamānī*; Hāthā wi-khūdh *ʿumrī.*
Oh, time, the *days* when I was in *his good grace*; Bring them back to me and take *my life* (what is most precious to me).

Willī *rāʿaytuh ramānī*; *Fātnī* wi-*shaghal fikrī.*
And the one I used to *treat with care flung* (*his arrows*) *at me* (*or discarded me*); *He left me* and *preoccupied my mind.*

Kān in-*nasīm ghinwah*; In-Nīl yighannīhā.
The *breeze* was a *song*; That the Nile used to sing.

Wi-mayyituh l-ḥilwah; Tifḍal tiʿīd fīhā.
And its sweet (beautiful) water; Would sing it again and again.

Wi-mawjuh l-hādī kān ʿūduh; Wi-*nūr* il-*badr*(*i*) awtāruh.
And its gentle waves used to be its lute; And the *light* of the *full moon* its strings.

Yilāghī l-*ward*(*i*) wi-*khudūduh*; *Yināǧī* l-*layl* wi-asrāruh.
It chats tenderly with the *roses* and (the beloved's) *cheeks*; It *converses intimately* with the *night* and its secrets.

Wi-anghāmuh bi-*tiskirnā*; *Anā wi-huwwa*, mā fīsh ghayrnā.
And its tunes *make us drunk*; *He and I* alone.

Lyrics as a worldview

How relevant are the ṭarab lyrics to contemporary Arab life? Do they reflect the actual experiences of the poets, singers, and listeners? What makes them appealing to the modern ṭarab public? On a certain level, these texts do evoke the cultural and spiritual "ecology" (Andrews 1985) of the Near East.

30 This transcription of the text is derived from a live recording of the song: *Farīd al-Aṭrash; Amīr al-Ṭarab, Ughniyat al-Rabīʿ* (47-minute cassette recording); Golden Series, Stereo T C-MCCO 128, made in Greece.

For one thing, they seem intimately linked to the intellectual backgrounds of those who create them. Maʾmūn al-Shinnāwī (b. 1955), a young Egyptian poet and lyricist and son of a renowned twentieth-century lyricist whose name is also Maʾmūn al-Shinnāwī (d. 1994) describes such rootedness in the context of his own family. Having lived in the United States since the early 1980s, he explains that although he himself did not study the classical poetical meters, one of his grandfathers was the teacher of *ʿarūḍ* (Arabic prosody) at al-Azhar, Cairo's major religious university, whereas his other grandfather was al-Azhar's head Shaykh. Furthermore, his late uncle Kāmil al-Shinnāwī (1908–1965) and his father, who memorized the Qurʾān at the age of seven, both assimilated the principles of literary eloquence (*balāghah*) and the poeticisms embodied by the Qurʾanic text perfectly well. Having entered the arena of journalism for some time, they also emerged as illustrious ṭarab lyricists.[31]

Furthermore, ṭarab lyrics make sense on a variety of levels and thus have been used to serve different social and political ends. To illustrate, Sufi-derived love poems that speak of higher authority and embrace both secular and mystical connotations, or aspects of "this world" and "that world" (Andrews 1985: 69–84) have been used by ṭarab singers for praising political figures. For example, Shayk Yūsuf al-Manyalāwī is known to have sung such a poem by Ibn al-Fāriḍ before Sulṭān ʿAbd al-Ḥamīd I in Istanbul, thus earning an honorific medallion from the appreciative Ottoman ruler.[32]

Similarly, puns, double entendres, and word substitutions contribute to the literary appeal of texts, but can also serve as tools for voicing protest. During the early years of the twentieth century, ʿAbd al-Ḥayy Ḥilmī, recorded an old qaṣīdah in which the tormented lover addresses the beloved woman by saying that he wishes to complain about her to "the judge of love." The text closes with a request that the judge "defend my rights and bring me justice against you." However, Ḥilmī, who had legal grievances against Gramophone Company Ltd., which was recording him at the time, turned the above theme to criticism of the company. While recording, he ended the above closing phrase with the added exclamation *Yā, Sharikah!* which meant "Oh, Company!" an innuendo that apparently went unnoticed by the Company's recording staff, who in all likelihood

[31] From an interview I had with Mr. Al-Shinnāwī (Jr.) in Los Angeles on February 16, 1987.

[32] In this case, too, some modern critics have complained that such texts, inherited from earlier, especially Ottoman, epochs have served the purpose of *tazalluf* (excessive or undignified flattery) toward the rulers. The reference to al-Manyalāwī is from Rizq ca. 1936: 119–120. The qaṣīdah mentioned begins with the text *Tih dalālan fa-anta Ahlun li-dhāka*; *Wa taḥakkam fal-ḥusnu qad Aʿṭaka*, roughly, "Be coquettishly proud, since you are worthy of that; And exercise absolute authority, since beauty has empowered you to do that."

were European and did not speak Arabic.[33]

More importantly perhaps, the love lyrics tend to resonate with the amorous experiences of the listeners. Given the generic mode of depiction and the ambivalent gender of the key poetical figures, the lyrics are versatile enough to fit a variety of actual amorous situations. It is said that individuals hear their own love stories in Umm Kulthūm's song lyrics.[34] Notably, in recent decades some of the traditional images and literary devices have become less current. Examples include the type of punning that existed in mawwāl texts, such older juridical concepts as *qāḍī al-gharām*, "the judge of love," and the various poetical symbols of authority. Similarly, new images and modes of expression have been introduced into the conventional amorous mold.

However, as a literary art form, ṭarab poetry remains highly formalized and appears out of sync with both the modern parlance and the ordinary daily flow. Through characteristic wit, the Egyptian music critic Kamāl al-Najmī points out the irony in depicting the beloved as being thin like a willow twig (*ghuṣn al-bān*), an image that seems incompatible with the premium on the rotund female figure, particularly in local aristocratic circles.[35] Along similar lines, when I asked one lyricist to help me define *al-bān* (a term that he used in his own poetry and that, as I found out later, meant willow), he answered with a coy smile, "I have never seen it in my entire life." His reaction seemed to imply that not being able to define such a term precisely should not diminish its value as a poetical device. The same might be said of the nightingale and the gazelle, obviously far from familiar sights in the modern Arab metropolis.

To conclude, the study of ṭarab lyrics reveals two seemingly opposed tendencies. On the one hand, the texts appear quaint and removed from the immediate life experiences of the poets, singers, and listeners. On the other hand, they seem to enjoy a phenomenal degree of currency and emotional appeal. Lyricists continue to produce texts that are quite formulaic and replete with standard references to rose gardens, eyes that captivate, lonely lovers, false hopes, and so on. In this light we may simply ask: why do the various conventional expressions and amorous motifs persist and what role

33 The title of this qaṣīdah was, *Alā fī Sabīl(i) l-Lāhi mā Ḥalla bī minkī*. I have obtained a tape copy of the recording with the added exclamation from ʿAbd al-ʿAzīz al-ʿAnānī, an early-disc collector in Cairo. The content was part of the repertoire analyzed in my doctoral dissertation. See Racy 1977: 220–326.

34 This notion was expressed in the documentary film: "Umm Kulthūm: A Voice Like Egypt" produced and directed by Michal Goldman and narrated by Omar Sharif (1996).

35 In a book chapter titled, *Qadduka l-Mayyās*, or "Your bending figure," al-Najmī (1970: 122–125), similarly reflects upon the theme of *qāḍī l-gharām* (judge of love). Accordingly, the legal mediation of this poetical figure was needed particularly when the lovers had no direct communication with one another. This theme we are told was gradually abandoned after the early decades of the twentieth century (Ibid.: 117–121).

do they play in the modern ṭarab experience? In the following discussions I posit that ṭarab texts are emotionally effective not despite, but because of their tendency to generalize, abstract, and stereotype. I also argue that in today's essentially secular domain of ṭarab the ideology of love constitutes a primary agent of ecstatic evocation.

Lyrics and ecstasy

As emotional tools, ṭarab lyrics operate in at least three related ways: direct evocation; auditory-semantic appeal; and symbolic suggestion.

Direct evocation

Emotional transformation stems directly from the emotionally loaded expressions that pervade the lyrical idiom. For one thing, the emotions conveyed by these expressions enjoy a distinct sense of familiarity: "loneliness, togetherness, sadness, joy, pain, pleasure, love, and hate are all derived ultimately from the universal and fundamental experience of unity followed by separation" (Andrews 1985: 113). Moreover, the expressed emotions can operate autonomously, as well as make sense within their immediate literary contexts. Their transcendental quality has been observed in the case of Ottoman ghazal poetry:

> Although the intellectual context of concepts such as loneliness, pain, separation, longing, madness, distraction, and grief may change according to the various applicable patterns of interpretation, the emotional content of the vocabulary remains quite stable. That is, loneliness or feelings of separation or alienation may have as their motivation estrangement from God, or from the temporal authority, or from a less abstract or abstracted loved one, but the emotion itself is the same in all cases and must be assumed to be meaningful on empirical grounds. (Andrews 1985: 111)

Muwashshaḥ lyrics, for example, may evoke elative or communal feelings that transcend contextual specificity. Similarly, the Egyptian-based lyrical repertoire may intimate the experiences of emotional introspection, surrender to overpowering sensations, pain and pleasure, separation and hope, and so on beyond their immediate poetical settings.

Meanwhile, the overall style of presentation enhances the effectiveness of the emotive material. The evocative expressions essentially enjoy distinct prominence. Rather than existing as mere adjuncts to explicit narrative plots, they serve as the very building blocks that give the amorous design its overall dramatic shape. In other words, the familiar scenarios are somewhat pointilistically sketched out in terms of relatively discrete emotive "pigments" represented by the poet's sentimental pleas, recapitulations, and introspections.

Furthermore, the emotional impact gains poignancy through the personal mode of speaking. Here, the poet sees the world from his own perspective as he reincarnates the personality of the lover, who in turn feels and expresses his own and sometimes his peers' amorous condition. Thus, in a sense, the singer-poet presents emotions as felt experiences and "plays" them out rather than merely communicates about them. Notably, the message he conveys is highly individualized, but also entails a significant dimension of universality. The poet is able to speak not only in terms of "I," but also of "us" as a special love-afflicted group, and even further, of "us" as human beings, who are created with certain amorous or aesthetic predilections and vulnerabilities.

In addition, the lyrical idiom gains emotive effectiveness from being linguistically special. For one thing, ṭarab lyrics tend to shy away from excessively complicated literary structures, as well as from open-ended verbal artistry. They seek to avoid extremely unpredictable, varied, and unfamiliar modes of expression, which are more typical of the highly individualized "artistic" creations of the classical poets. At the same time, the lyrics depart from the excessively familiar, or for that matter the ordinary modalities of everyday speech. The ṭarab texts can be said to avoid either of these two extremes and perhaps to combine suitable elements from both of them. In comparable terms, Clifford Geertz has interpreted the popular sung poetry of Morocco as having a "betwixt and between quality," or as being "half ritual song, half plain talk" (1985: 114). More specifically, ". . . in speech terms, or more exactly speech-act terms, poetry lies in between the divine imperatives of the Quran and the rhetorical thrust and counterthrust of everyday life, and it is that which gives it its uncertain status and strange force" (Ibid.: 117).

Such intermediary status grants ṭarab poetry a distinctive character or perhaps a certain ritualistic quality and ultimately defines it as a specialized language of emotions. It is shown that the texts' peculiar literary profile contributes significantly to their powerful appeal. Reportedly, Aḥmad Rāmī defended the stylized song-text style that he and other major lyricists had favored by arguing that the conventional classical poetry does not always succeed in arousing the profound emotions expected of ṭarab lyrics. He is known to have said to the classical poet and lyricist Aḥmad Shawqī: "Your ghazals do not burn."[36] Similarly, he is noted for having utilized a verbal repertoire that is highly stylized but also quite familiar to the ṭarab ear. As

[36] In other words, Shawqī's ghazals, or classical love-poems, do not cause burning. This statement was quoted in Fu'ād 1973: 72.

biographer Niʿmāt Fuʾād (1973) points out, although in his early classical poetry Rāmī had used highly romantic and imaginatively conceived figures of speech, his song lyrics were dominated by a standardized stock of some 181 emotionally suggestive expressions, which can be regrouped in various thematic configurations and "recycled" from one poem to another. These include such terms as: *anīn*, "moaning;" *asá* "sadness;" *amal*, "hope;" *aṣūn*, "I protect" or "honor;" *bukāʾ*, "crying;" *jufūn*, "eyelids;" *ḥubb*, "love;" *ḥanān*, "compassion;" *damʿ*, "tears;" *dalāl*, "coquetry;" *sahar*, "staying up at night;" *shawq*, "longing;" *shakwah*, "complaint;" *ṣadd*, "turning away;" *ḍaná*, "weariness;" *ṭayf*, "image;" *ʿadhāb*, "suffering;" *ʿuyūn*, "eyes;" *ʿitāb*, "admonition;" *ʿadhūl*, "one who criticizes or spoils;" *lawʿah*, "distress;" *mīʿād*, "date" or "appointment;" *nawḥ*, "wailing;" *wajd*, "yearning;" *wiṣāl*, "reunion;" *zahr*, "flowers;" and others.[37]

Auditory–semantic appeal

Further transformation results from the auditory–semantic impact of individual words or word clusters. Embracing a combination of sound and sense, such impact is largely abstract and transcends the literal meaning of the verbal form that conveys it. It is experienced as a sonic–emotive flavor, an ethos that is felt rather than something that is merely conceived or visualized. The poetical significance of such an effect is noted by linguist and anthropologist Paul Friedrich. Arguing that poetry's affective tools are embedded in ordinary language, which he describes as "an infinitude of used or potential poems waiting to be molded into new realities by the individual" (1986: 35), Friedrich presents both "myth" (in its broader conceptual sense) and "music" as the primary poles of poetical imagination. The latter applies, for example, "when mellifluous sound is fused with harmonious content – or when cacophony is hitched to themes of conflict" (1979: 455).

In Arab culture, sonic-semantic presence is frequently discussed by religious and literary scholars. It is stressed, for example, that the Qurʾān embraces a distinct auditory–conceptual dimension, a verbal message that impresses in terms of both the sense it conveys and the sonic effect it embraces.[38] In a book entitled *Mūsīqá al-Shiʿr* (The Music of Poetry), Ibrāhīm Anīs goes to great length to explain the *jirs*, namely "resonance" or "sound effect," of the various Arabic consonants and their combinations

[37] Fuʾād 1973: 92–96.

[38] Some authors also speak of the Qurʾanic text as having its own powerful form of musicality (see, for example, al-Saʿīd 1970b: 65–73) or as "representing not only the eloquence of the Arabic language, but also the language's own music, or taṭrīb, and all the resounding *jirs* (resonance) it contains, with the art of reciting providing the additional effect of the Eastern maqāmāt," (Fuʾād 1976: 154).

in the form of syllables and words. For example, he states that letters and letter combinations that demand exceptional muscular effort to pronounce or that produce an explosive effect are considered "unmusical." On the other hand, certain letters project a smooth, or "musical" quality and would be most appropriate in the ghazal genre. We are told that some classical poets achieve a desirable effect through using both types of letters in creative configurations, a sort of workmanship that has counterparts in Beethoven's symphonies and in the complex medieval classical poems of al-Buḥturī. We similarly read that certain poets create a lighter musical effect through emphasis on utterances that are tender (*raqīqah*) and serene (*hādi'ah*), a treatment likened to light music, for example Strauss's waltzes, "which people of all ranks are enchanted by," and exemplified by the modern ghazal poetry of Aḥmad Shawqī (Anīs n.d.: 22–36). Anīs's discussions of poetical affect extend to the choice and application of the classical poetical meters, the rhyme endings, and the proper ways of reciting poems.

In ṭarab lyrics, evocation appears to favor particular sound and sense combinations. In nationalistic texts, for example, a line in classical poetry from a song by Umm Kulthūm, one that preaches self-reliance and taking initiative in life, is described as being "devoid of any ecstatic potentials (*taṭrīb*) and *tanghīm* (musical intoning)" (Fu'ād 1976: 417). Love lyrics, on the other hand, are meant to display sonic-semantic effects that suit their emotive nature. Love-related expressions, or for that matter the entire amorous idiom, must be both tender and emotionally inspiring. And similarly, the most ecstatic texts are usually those that display loose, almost prosodic flow rather than adhere to rigid metric or accentual patterns. In this regard, Rāmī was lauded for his use of tender expressions, as well as for his blending of different classical meters or metric designs within single poems, thus enticing the musical composers to create comparably varied and highly enchanting tunes. More specifically, he is said to have highlighted vowelled syllables and elongated sounds, thus making it easier for the singer to produce ṭarab.[39]

Finally, key expressions, for example those used by various lyricists to begin individual poems and that in turn become the titles of the entire songs, are usually chosen for their appealing sonic-semantic ambiance. Such familiar titles as *Yā Nasīm aṣ-Ṣabá* (Oh, Easterly Breeze), *Bulbul Ḥayrān* (Bewildered Nightingale), *Sahrān li-Waḥdī* (I Stay up at Night Alone) and *ar-Rabī'* (Spring) tend to project into their respective songs effects that are highly tantalizing and ecstatically inviting.[40]

[39] See Fu'ād 1973: 139–141.

[40] These are all titles of actual songs that have been performed respectively by Shaykh 'Alī Maḥmūd, Muḥammad 'Abd al-Wahhāb, Umm Kulthūm, and Farīd al-Aṭrash.

Symbolic suggestion

Ṭarab lyrics also transform the listener through their suggestive powers. They do so because their subject matter can be imagined, visualized, and felt. In a comparable vein, it is shown that in Balinese trance rituals, dramatic depictions tend to become livable occurrences, or "presences" (Geertz 1973: 118), and that in South America, a shaman's myth that is recounted in order to cure or alleviate pain may serve as a medium through which "inexpressible, psychic states can be immediately expressed" (Lévi-Strauss 1979: 323–324). Song lyrics are said to allow the listeners both to reflect rationally and to feel the music more intensely. In the case of Sri Lankan songs of exorcism, we read that ". . . while the verses of the songs may hold the patient in a reflective attitude, they also can deepen the direct experiential possibility of the music as a whole" (Kepferer 1983: 189). Comparably, mystical texts have been interpreted as accessible metaphors for other-worldly experiences. The Egyptian munshid makes the participants' mystical yearning real, as he combines notions of separation from and union with the Divine with emotionally expressive descriptions of love. Thus, "the spiritual domain becomes existential in the same manner as the lost love" (Waugh 1989: 131).

Similarly, through various love related images, allusions, and portrayals ṭarab texts create a special mind set, one that ṭarab artists and listeners refer to as *jaww*, literally, "mood," "ambiance," or "atmosphere." It is often said that good words put you in the right mood for ṭarab. In the following discussions, I illustrate some of the possible ways in which the texts establish such a mood. More specifically, I propose that as sung out emotions, the ṭarab lyrics emulate, and ultimately stimulate the transformative musical experience.

The party as a musical event

In ṭarab texts, particularly those of the muwashshaḥāt, the garden-party and the wine-drinking assembly are both reminiscent of the typical ṭarab event. To begin with, the festive implications of these two themes can be readily applied to the ṭarab performance, which traditionally occurs in connection with a celebrative occasion or may simply produce its own elative environment. Similarly suggestive is the collectivism implied by these poetical themes. The muwashshaḥ for example, is often sung by a chorus, or at times by a chorus and a leading soloist. In Syria, the muwashshaḥāt may accompany specially choreographed group-dances generically known as *raqs al-samāḥ*, an added component that contributes further to the collective orientation of the musical performance.

Moreover, the mood of the poetical festive event resembles that of the ṭarab performance. Noteworthy is the parallel between the poet-lover's wish to drink wine or to remain with his drinking companions until morning and the muṭrib's promise that the musical performance will last until morning. Likewise, the behaviors associated with the amorous assembly have close counterparts at the musical event: drinking, eating, and displaying strong emotional and physical reactions (for example uttering impassioned exclamations and becoming haunted by the "beauty" of the music, or of the musicians themselves). For that matter, the tavern can be viewed as a metaphor for the small musical gathering. Also, the garden may appropriately stand for the larger, more public musical performance, which often takes place in a city park, an enclosed picnic area, or a large outdoor café.

In a broader sense, the lyrical party complex and the musical event are similar in their tendency to create boundaries that separate the participants from other more ordinary domains. Both "carve out" particular social, spatial, and temporal zones. In the realm of poetry, such carving is created through the use of extraordinary images and allusions: lush vegetation, gazelles, flowers, beautiful wine-servers, and so on, that distinguish the festive context from the more mundane city-scape. In the domain of music, the carving is similarly imposed by such venues as the jalsah and ḥaflah, and even the nightclub and hotel ballroom. Moreover, the Egyptian *khaymah*, the multi-sided tent which is temporarily erected in desirable places to house musical and other festive events, may be the closest analogue to the poetical party complex. Brightly colored and adorned with abstract floral and geometrical designs, the tent structure seems to fit well with the poetry's frequent mention of rose gardens and other idyllic surroundings, as well as with the participants' momentary sense of togetherness.

Thus, in suggestive ways, the texts evoke the basic performance setting and by extension, the mood and the behavioral antics connected with it. Associated with such transformative experiences as rejoicing and becoming enchanted by the entertaining musicians, the lyrical party-theme can be seen as a catalyst for the overall ecstatic process.

The love scenario as a musical experience

The amorous drama outlined by the love texts entails transformative dynamics comparable to those characterizing the ṭarab experience. The love scenario primarily represents a process of change, or perhaps a rite of passage through which a potential lover is converted into a true lover. In similar ways, the ṭarab listener transits momentarily from the realm of ordinary or reserved behavior into a state of impassioned indulgence or surrender to overwhelming emotions. Key lyrical agents, such as the beloved's eyes triggering the amorous state, can be compared to musically potent stimuli, for example those that induce salṭanah in sensitive and emotionally prepared ṭarab musicians. The love scenario can be interpreted as a commentary on the music-related shift from one mode of consciousness into another.

Lovers as music lovers

In the same vein, the various players within the love scenario can be compared to the main participants in the ṭarab event. In the lyrics, the lovers, or broadly speaking, the camaraderie of individuals who are either in love or who are fully sympathetic to the plight of lovers, are all suggestive of the individuals who partake in the ṭarab process. In a narrower sense, of course, the lover is analogous to the sammīʿ, since both enjoy distinctive emotional sensitivities, both are exposed to overpowering stimuli, both display genuine reactions, and both become emotionally transformed. Perhaps also, like a good lover (or a good Sufi) who accepts his fate humbly as he continues to hope for reunion, a good sammīʿ expresses his emotions quietly while being drawn to the music. Similarly, the distinction in the love drama between the lovers as an in-group and the outside world, or in a more negative sense, the world of cynics who blame, admonish, and wish bad things upon the lovers, is paralleled in the ṭarab context by the distinction between those who savor the music and the dilettantes or even those whom the ṭarab culture deems musically intolerant, insensitive, or disruptive. Indeed, both concepts of "lovers" and "music lovers," as two somewhat distinct and emotionally or spiritually elevated categories, imply a measure of elitism, as well as a sense that both groups verge on the socially and emotionally bizarre or excessive.

Love as musical ecstasy

The phenomenon of love as presented in the song lyrics, as well as in Sufi love-poetry, is intimately connected to the notion of ecstasy. For one thing, the two together have been treated as part of an aesthetic-spiritual complex. We find this in two mystically charged lines of poetry that Shihāb al-Dīn included in an essay that introduced his anthology and discussed the power of music:

> If I did not drink wine and was not ecstatically inclined (*ṭarūban*), and if I did not fall in love with the beautiful ones and become deeply infatuated, then I would be no different from a stone, even if it were the material from which precious jewels are made. (ca. 1840/ca. 1892: 5)

Moreover, the lover and the ecstasy seeker tend to walk similar paths. To some extent, they are both marginalized and depicted as social outcasts whose obsessive behaviors deviate from the social norms of their communities. Both experience *sahar*, or "staying up at night," thus the concept of sleep becomes antithetical to both love and the pursuit of musical ecstasy.

Love and ecstasy also tend to have comparable emotional structures. Apart from sharing certain mystical or transcendental overtones, they embrace comparable sentimental components. In Sufi ghazal texts, love is usually presented as a combination of hope and despair, happiness and sadness, union and separation, pleasure and pain, or in mystical terms, "expansion" and "contraction." Speaking of mystical love aroused by samāʿ, al-Ghazālī wrote:

> The listening of lovers (*samāʿ al-ʿushshāq*) is for inducing yearning, instigating love, and amusing the soul. If it is about seeing the beloved, then the purpose would be to confirm pleasure, and if it is about separation, then the aim would be to provoke constant yearning. Then, if it involves pain, it would embody a kind of pleasure when hope for reunion is added to it. (n.d.: 246)

Such blending of complementary or even oppositional emotions extends to the ṭarab texts. The notion of love as a combination of elation and suffering or of pleasure and pain appears in thousands of song lyrics and is often highlighted by the song titles. The bitter-sweet nature of love is illustrated in such typical phrases as: "Because of the thorns of the roses, I love roses;" "In love there is my misery and in love there is my survival;" "I find pleasure in my humility and submission;" "I remember the one who forgets me;" "I used to enjoy my complaint;" "He is my Inferno and my Paradise;" and "Oh nightingale, your wailing has enchanted me." The lyrics also use direct juxtapositions: "tears and smiles," "my joy and my wound," and so on. Similarly prevalent is the notion of *shajū* which can be roughly explained as "enchanting melancholy," a complex emotion experienced, for example, by the distraught lover when hearing deeply moving sounds, such as the singing, or rather the wailing (*nawḥ*), of the nightingale.[41]

In actual musical contexts the ecstatic experience entails oppositional dynamics not dissimilar to those associated with love. For one thing, the emotional polarities explained by al-Ghazālī resemble the patterns of

[41] In a major nineteenth-century lexicon, we read that the related verb *shajā* or *ashjá* means to grieve someone or to cause "him to mourn or lament, or to be sorrowful or sad or unhappy." It also means to cause someone "to be mirthful, and excited," and according to one interpretation, to cause him to experience ṭarab, namely "lightness arising from joy or grief" (Lane, Vol. 2 1877/1984: 1510). In a contemporary dictionary comparable definitions are provided. For example, the noun *shajan* is defined as "anxiety, worry, sorrow, grief, sadness, melancholy, blues, heartache," whereas the adjective *shajiyy* is defined essentially as something that evokes the above feelings, but also that is: "moving, touching, pathetic, affecting, emotional, sentimental, impassioning, soul-stirring;" and that is "melodious, tuneful, soft, tender." (al-Baʿalbakī 1992: 662).

musical yearning and anticipated fulfillment that dominate the interactive ṭarab process. Somewhat demonstrably, these polarities are displayed by the listeners: smiling; crying; facial gestures of pain and joy; and verbal exclamations that express feelings of being elated, as well as being overwhelmed, or in a mystical sense, annihilated. Similarly, the behavioral indicators of ecstasy within a genuine sammīʿ tend to resemble a confluence of enchantment and melancholy and to project impressions of both fulfillment and anticipation.

Meanwhile, many song lyrics speak explicitly of *wajd*, which in Sufi contexts connotes yearning or experiencing a profound mystical state. One modern Sufi scholar explains wajd as follows: "Sometimes it seems to come from the pain of separation, at other times from a burning love and ardor for God, but usually it is experienced with the pain of separation" (Nurbakhsh 1978: 50). Comparably, in Arabic dictionaries the root *wajada* is equated with such related meanings as "to adore" or "love dearly," and "to grieve for someone."[42] In the ṭarab lyrics, the concept of wajd, which refers to intense amorous longing and carries strong ecstatic overtones, is readily suggestive of the ṭarab condition. The lover's declaration of his wajd, for example in the well-known muwashshaḥ text that opens with *ṣuḥtu wajdan yā nadāmá* (I cried out with ecstatic yearning, oh, drinking companions!), reminds us of the actual pleas of the impassioned sammīʿ. It also brings to attention the various emotionally loaded exclamations which give a voice to the listeners' ecstatic elation and their wish to become musically satiated.

More significantly perhaps, song lyrics use the word "ṭarab" quite frequently. Here, although like intoxication, ṭarab may serve as a metaphor for the amorous condition of the lover or the company of lovers; it turns our attention directly toward musical ecstasy. As typically illustrated in the muwashshaḥāt texts, ṭarab is associated with musical performances either by entertainers at the festive party or by the beloved himself, although most often the distinction between the beloved and the entertainer, or for that matter the wine server, is quite blurred. Such an association is made in the muwashshaḥ entitled, *Yā Shādī l-Alḥān* (Oh, chanter, or enchanting singer, of tunes). It also appears in a muwashshaḥ titled, *Ṭif yā Durrī bil-Qanānī* (roughly, Oh, my precious one go around with the wine bottles) and set to music by the Syrian composer ʿUmar al-Baṭsh. In this case, as the wine server is begged to serve the wine, the "close companion" (*ṣāḥ*), apparently an indirect reference to the beloved, is asked to stand up and sing in maqām Bayyātī and to cause the drinking companions (*nudmān*) to become ecstatic

[42] Obviously, explaining *wajada*, "to experience mystical yearning" in terms of longing and adoration makes more sense than the often encountered explanation, "to find" (cited for instance in Rouget 1985: 258). Yearning and related meanings are included in the definitions offered by Lane 1863/1984: Vol. 2: 2924–2925 and al- Baʿalbakī 1992: 1223.

(*aṭrib*). Notably, the close companion is addressed with great adulation: "You are my soul and my life; for me you are the master (*sīd)* of those who are beautiful. Rise and never be concerned about a gazing outsider (*raqīb*) or one who blames. Be forthcoming, oh, my gazelle, without apology or speech."[43]

The sweet tormentor as musical performer

The position of the beloved vis-à-vis the lover seems to parallel the general relationship between the musician, especially the ṭarab singer and the listener. More specifically, the musical performer, who reincarnates the lover-poet, interacts with the audience in a manner that reminds us of the beloved's "sweet afflictions" upon the lover. Unlike the ṭarab singer, the beloved is almost always absent or disinterested and is experienced mostly in the form of dreams, visions, images, shadows, and memories. However, the beloved can be compared to the ecstatically empowered ṭarab artist who manipulates his admirers' emotions. As lovers become helplessly drawn to the personage of the beloved, the diehard listeners, often called *ʿushshāq al-ṭarab*, or "ṭarab lovers," find themselves uncontrollably attracted to the muṭrib. Similarly, as the lover pleads with the beloved to be forthcoming, considerate, and accessible, the impassioned listeners beg the muṭrib to satisfy their ecstatic cravings. As the beloved generates feelings of restlessness and hope, the performing musician creatively plays out the two opposite poles of momentary musical deprivation (for example, by introducing delayed or inconclusive cadences) and musical fulfillment (for instance, through using powerful qaflāt or proceeding from a passage of modal uncertainty to a point of modal resolution). As the beloved enjoys the role of an endearing manipulator who toys with the lover's emotions and makes the lover rejoice or cry, the muṭrib similarly acts as a musical teaser who produces within his captive listeners successive moments of enticement and anticipation.

To conclude, the textual material complements and reinforces the musical idiom through an ecstatically suggestive repertoire of themes, images, concepts, and scenarios. Intended to be sung, the texts achieve their full suggestive potentials when they are effectively set to music. Furthermore, the variations, subtle digressions, and dramatic twists, all executed within a framework of stylistic and thematic consistency, give the literary idiom further appeal, freshness, and consequently suggestive impetus. In this manner, literary variants can be compared to the "expected" musical surprises that add ecstatic life to musical compositions and improvisations.

43 This and the previous muwashshaḥ example are listed in al-Darwīsh, collector, 1955: 64 and 143 respectively.

A lyricist's profile

The creation of affective lyrics requires talent and specific literary skills. It also calls for certain personal attributes, above all, emotional sensitivity and good musical sense. These various qualities have been attributed, for example, to the celebrated Egyptian poet and lyricist Aḥmad Rāmī (1892–1981). Biographer and critic Niʿmāt Fuʾād presents an analysis of Rāmī's artistry in light of his personality, individual interests, and life experiences. Rāmī was born in an area of Cairo where a number of musicians lived. As a baby, we are told, he was very responsive to music, which comforted him and caused him to stop crying. "He was a little child with a true ecstatic inclination (*ṭarūb*), as if nature knew that one of the agencies of ṭarab is a poet" (Fuʾād 1973: 6). At a very young age, Rāmī accompanied his father, who was Khedive ʿAbbās Ḥilmīʾs' doctor, on a two year sojourn to the Aegean island of Thasos, where the child was exposed to Turkish and Greek languages and cultures. Upon returning to Egypt and attending a Cairo school, he lived in an environment where religious anthems and chants were commonly heard, a context that suited his ecstatic nature (*ṭabīʿatihi al-ṭarūb*). During his early youth, his poetical interest was supposedly triggered by reading a book that he found in his paternal aunt's library and contained old Arabic ghazals. The book was entitled *Musāmarat al-Ḥabīb Fī al-Ghazal wa-al-Nasīb* (roughly, Companionship with the Beloved; On Love Poetry and Odes of Courtship). Soon Rāmī came to know major poets of his time, such as Aḥmad Shawqī, Khalīl Miṭrān, and Ḥāfiḍḥ Ibrāhīm. He also frequented performances at the Club of Eastern Music, where he was able to develop further intimacy with the music and to share his poetry with others during the intermissions between musical waṣlāt. Realizing that Rāmī was a genuine music lover, some of the famous musicians asked him to come with them to their own performances.[44]

In 1923, he was sent by the Egyptian government to study in France. After his return in 1924, he worked for many years at *Dār al-Kutub*, Egypt's National Library, and continued to pursue his literary career, which led to the publication of three collections (or *dawāwīn*, singular *dīwān*) of classical Arabic poetry. With knowledge of French, English, Persian, and some Turkish, he also researched the *Rubāʿiyyāt* of ʿUmar al-Khayyām, and based on renditions in European translations and in the original Persian, he produced his own translation of this work in classical Arabic poetry. Given the title *Shāʿir al-Shabāb*, "the Poet of Youth," he was introduced to Umm Kulthūm early in her singing career, in 1924. Deeply enamored by her talent

[44] Fuʾād 1973: 12–13.

and personality, he became one of her major lyricists.[45] Composing over three hundred song-texts, the majority in *zajal*, or colloquial Egyptian poetry, Rāmī also provided lyrics for thirty musical films and for numerous established singers. Working at the government radio station as a song-text referee, and at different times advising Umm Kulthūm on her selection of song texts, Rāmī was widely emulated as a lyricist.

Rāmī's personal traits, which tend to remind us of the lover's profile in ṭarab poetry, were perfectly suited for his role as a ṭarab lyricist. First of all, he was endowed with *ḥiss*, or "feeling." He was tender and sensitive, and through his proper education and poetical experience, he was able to translate his tenderness and sensitivity into emotionally moving poems. Indeed, feeling is recognized as a primary requisite for poetical creativity. As explained by Ma'mūn al-Shinnāwi (Jr.): "It is not enough to know the rules; first, you must have feeling, which is the most important thing for a poet to have. It is the basis of poetical talent."[46]

Second, Rāmī was able to experience pathos very intensely. His deep sense of *alam*, or "pain" was supposedly developed because Rāmī's own life was surrounded by tragedy, although pathos may have also typified the broader artistic or social milieu in which the poet lived. We are told that during his student years, Rāmī, who had already suffered from his own illness and witnessed the sickness and death of his father and, later on, the deaths of his brother and daughter, frequented lament sessions on Thursdays "in order to listen and weep till the late afternoon" (Fu'ād 1973: 13). It is similarly noted that Rāmī utilized pain in order to create moving poetry, "like an insightful scientist who derives gold from the soils of the mine" (Ibid.: 23,24). In one public interview cited by Fu'ād, Rāmī explained that tragic events in his life had a significant influence upon his poetry, adding that his melancholy was usually connected with love of nature, as in expressing the sadness of a farewell through reference to the sunset. Rāmī is quoted as saying:

> It makes me quite happy when I read my poetry and see those listening to me cry. A smile is a simple thing, but tears are a difficult matter, indeed. In crying I find the greatest pleasure. I always love to cry. (Fu'ād 1973: 109)

Third, as an individual, Rāmī was, paradoxically perhaps, quite jovial, a quality to a certain extent embraced by the term *ṭarūb*, or "being ecstatically inclined." To some, his lively spirit, love for good company, and warmly expressed emotions seemed puzzling in view of the *nuwāḥ*, or "lamentation"

45 See Danielson 1991b: 106. It may be noteworthy that Umm Kulthūm did not like Rāmī personally despite his obsession with her art and the strong professional connection between the two. This was alluded to in the documentary film mentioned in Note 34 above.

46 From the same interview of February 16, 1987.

Egyptian lyricist Aḥmad Rāmī (1892–1981), front row, fourth from right, at a performance by Umm Kulthūm. Photo courtesy of Dār al-Ṣayyād.

prevalent in his song texts. One commentator, Muḥammad ʿAbd al-Majīd Ḥilmī, reflects upon the apparent contradiction in Rāmī's personal and artistic complexions as follows:

> . . . a young man who is ecstatically inclined (*ṭarūb*) and playful (*laʿūb*), you never see him but laughing, kidding, and exhibiting a delightful spirit. [Yet] you find nothing in his poetry except wailing and morbid gloom . . . Some people say that Rāmī is a skilled craftsman (*ṣannāʿ*) who elicits crying from laughter and portrays pain out of the substance of ecstasy (*ṭarab*) and joy! . . . (quoted in Fuʾād 1973: 111)[47]

Highlighting the pleasure–pain or happiness–sadness duality in Rāmī's personality, this assessment attests to the complex relationship between the lyricist and his literary product.

[47] Along similar lines, one critic finds it striking that Rāmī's poetry was impervious to Western literary influence despite the poet's direct exposure to Western culture (quoted in Fuʾād 1973: 110–111). Incidentally, Rāmī's "romantic" style is said to differ from the styles of other lyricists, such as Byram al-Tūnisī, who is described as being more of a visual artist than a deprived lover, or Ṣalāḥ Jāhīn, whose texts reflect his special interest in folk life and the countryside. See Fuʾād 1973: 132–137.

Fourth, Rāmī possessed musical sensitivity, an attribute implicit in the concept of "ṭarūb." Indeed, Rāmī's musicality was eloquently expressed by the epithet "sammīʿ" that various musicians gave him. We read that: "Aḥmad listens to singing with ecstatic fervor (*shaṭḥ*) and absorption (*istighrāq*); He is knowledgeable of the craft and shows mastery whenever he sings" (Fuʾād 1973: 12). Reportedly, when once asked what profession he would have preferred to his own, Rāmī replied that had he not been a poet he would have loved to have been a singer.[48] Notably, Rāmī's reputation as a sammīʿ extended beyond Egypt. Iraqi musicians and music aficionados provide a vivid description of his exceptional musical enthusiasm. During a performance of Iraqi maqām given by the celebrated Muḥammad al-Qubbanjī, the Egyptian poet became so ecstatic that he threw his jacket up into the air.[49]

Rāmī's musical sensitivity had a direct influence upon the ways in which he created his lyrics. We are told he never composed poetry except when he heard music. Further, he did not compose his poems by writing them down, but rather by intoning them musically. "Perhaps that was the secret behind the tenderness and fluidity of his texts" (Fuʾād 1973: 13). Rāmī was particularly inspired by vocal music. He reported being deeply moved by florid melismatic singing (*al-ṣawt al-murajjaʿ*), even when the sung passages were without actual words and were incidental to the basic composition, adding that "such passages very often compel me to sing and to produce poetry" (Fuʾād 1973: 108).

The fifth and probably most significant component was love (*ḥubb*), understood in its encompassing and even abstract or mystical sense. In Rāmī's life, love was a prime mover, a quintessence that permeated his diverse poetical genres and culminated in his love lyrics. As Fuʾād writes, Rāmī's ghazals, generally devoid of wine-related themes, deal with love not in sensuous or physical terms, but rather through images of yearning, deprivation, and reunion. We are told that even elegies would be cast in the form of love, expressed in specific terms toward the deceased.[50]

Finally, the sentiment of love was translated into love for the music. Rāmī is said to have been deeply moved by the performances of various singers, especially Umm Kulthūm. His classical poems written as tributes to ʿAbd al-Wahhāb, Ṣāliḥ ʿAbd al-Ḥayy, and others spoke of his own fondness for the ecstatic music created by these artists. The same can be said of his poems eulogizing such artists as Sayyid Darwīsh, Abū al-ʿUlā Muḥammad, and Maḥmūd Ṣubḥ.[51]

48 Ibid 1973: 97.
49 I have heard this report from a number of individuals in Baghdad during the 1980s.
50 Fuʾād 1973: 97–98.
51 Ibid. 54–55.

Poetical creativity

The composition of ṭarab lyrics is usually prompted by the poet's *infiʿālāt*, or "inner emotional tribulations," which in turn result from a variety of physical, emotional, and artistic stimuli. In an interview, Rāmī stated that indeed he was interested in being original and innovative, but first of all his poems had to please him personally and to reflect his own deeply felt emotions.[52] In practical terms, the process of composing lyrics can be either introspective or reactive, slow and gradual or impulsive and sudden. In this regard, Rāmī described two coexisting and complementary compositional approaches. The first applies when a text takes a long time to emerge. That is, when a qaṣīdah stays, or "ferments" (*takhtamir*), in the poet's mind for years before it acquires its final form. Rāmī noted that the idea of one song text that Umm Kulthūm sang had remained within him for seven years before it developed into a complete poem. However, he explained further that intense emotional experiences caused by unexpected or extraordinarily moving occurrences usually inspire the full fruition of such a poem. For example, the urge to fully complete the song text, *Raqq il-Ḥabīb* (The Beloved Became Tender), occurred when the poet felt certain joy and was worried about departing from this world before experiencing that joy most intensively. Rāmī added that incidental triggers as such do not interfere directly with the main substance, or spoil the unity of the "fermenting" qaṣīdah type, but usually affect it somewhat marginally, for example by introducing a streak of sadness into an essentially happy poem.[53]

The second approach to poetical creativity is more instantaneous. In this case, the triggering circumstances exert a direct influence upon the poetry. However, here, as well as in the first approach, the final content tends to develop organically through a certain progressive flow, "from ideas leading to ideas, and concepts leading to concepts" (Fuʾād 1973: 105). It is also accomplished through a creative thought process, rather than by following a specific formula for assembling words, "otherwise we would be carpenters and blacksmiths" (Ibid.: 105). Incidentally, Rāmī pointed out that since he most often encapsulated his central idea in the opening lines of the poem, he often found it extremely difficult or even impossible to expand the poem beyond that initial point. Meanwhile, the loose or highly interpretive relationship between the song texts and the triggers that lead to their creation is attested to by Maʾmūn al-Shinnāwī (Jr.), who explains that the stimuli that inspire him to compose poetry do not necessarily become the literal topics of the composed texts. Such triggers can be specific occurrences that the poet

[52] Ibid. 109.
[53] Ibid. 102–105.

learns about, for example, the illness of a friend, or intense feelings such as missing one's family or homeland. In one of his love poems, al-Shinnāwī indicates that his depictions of the beloved were inspired by nostalgia for his country, Egypt.

Poets may feel a mysterious urge to compose poetry. Generally implied by the concept of *ʿafawiyyah*, or "spontaneity" and sensed mostly in connection with the instantaneous compositional mode, their inspirational state is usually free of preconceived poetical thoughts. As Rāmī put it:

> In any case, we are people of spontaneous thoughts (*abnāʾ khawāṭir*). This is probably most obvious in the qaṣāʾid that are created at the spur of the moment and are not preceded by a fermenting idea. In these poems I would feel propelled to create poetry, but I would not have a specific idea to base the poetry on . . . (quoted in Fuʾād 1973: 105)[54]

Similarly, the urge to compose is known to produce poems that are superior both artistically and emotionally. Maʾmūn al-Shinnāwī (Jr.), for example, stresses that his most cherished poems are those that emerge spontaneously or even unexpectedly. He states that ideally he would not sit down to write his poems, but rather poetry lines come to him naturally. The best poetry appears uninvited. It imposes itself and takes hold of the poet and compels him to write it down. As al-Shinnāwī further explains:

> I prefer that the text comes out without preparation and if something is wrong with it then I would fix it. When someone asks me to sit down and write a song text for him, I feel that I am doing mere paper work or just setting letters together (*raṣṣ ḥurūf*). Whatever comes out without anybody asking me for it is much stronger because it stems from my own feeling. Poems that I am asked to compose I usually forget, but those that come out of me spontaneously stay in my mind and I can recite them for you anytime. I have seven or eight such favorite song-lyrics that I can always recite.[55]

Along comparable lines, poets speak of contexts or practices they find most conducive to spontaneous creativity. Rāmī mentioned that when he composed, he intoned his poems musically in a dark place and never wrote them down until they were ready. He even referred to some of his idiosyncratic compositional habits, for example, stating that a rectangular piece of paper and a specific pen had to be used at the time of composing. Moreover, he had to be alone in his special room, which he described as being pervaded by a melancholic atmosphere, adding that the best time to compose was the nightfall, "when I feel awake and everyone else is asleep" (Fuʾād 1973: 106).

Rāmī also followed specific procedures for inducing poetical inspiration.

[54] The information on Rāmī's poetical creativity comes from Fuʾād 1973.

[55] This and the preceding statements by al-Shinnāwī are from the interview of February 16, 1987.

As he described them, such procedures are comparable to the musical stimuli that instill salṭanah within the ṭarab musicians, or even to the efficacious verbal reiterations that are used in the Sufi dhikr. Accordingly, sometimes he felt like composing poetry but found himself uninspired to do so. Therefore he went into seclusion and kept repeating certain poetry lines by a specific poet or lines from a poem he had composed himself. That enabled him, as he put it, "to make himself (or his soul) compassionately tender (*yuḥannin nafsahu*)" (Ibid: 108) and finally to attain the desired inspirational state. We further read that as soon as he began to compose a poem, he felt compelled to finish it by the end of the composing session.

Texts, composers, performers, and listeners

Once the text is completed, it usually enters the domain of the musical composer or improviser. Here, too, the text must be felt emotionally. For example, a composer may select an amorous text that inspires him and creates within him powerful *aḥāsīs* (feelings) or *infiʿālāt* (inner emotional tribulations). He might favor texts that suit his compositional style or perhaps ones that are witty or readily engaging, provided they possess the potentials for ecstatic evocation and are truly singable.

The composer's treatment of the lyrics can be observed in the case of Riyāḍ al-Sunbāṭī. It is said that if poetry had its own hidden music this Egyptian ṭarab composer was able to render that music in terms of actual musical compositions. And similarly, al-Sunbāṭī was praised for his extra-ordinary ability to translate feelings and sentiments into music.[56] Speaking of his own creativity, al-Sunbāṭī regarded poetry as the ideal outlet for his musical ideas. He was quoted as saying, ". . . tunes erupt and wander within me in search of an enormous release, which is found in poetry" (al-Ṭawīl n.d.: 50). Setting to music poems by Rāmī, Shawqī, and other major poets, al-Sunbāṭī also explained that poetry provided him with the emotional impetus required for composing music. As we read in one biographical study:

> For that reason I focus upon it [the poem] before I construct my tune. However, if the composer creates the tune first, then searches for words (*kalimāt*) or poetry to fit his tune, that would be a misguided operation from beginning to end. It is imperative for the composer to live the words and their meaning first, so he would sense the feelings (*aḥāsīs*) that had gone through the poet's soul. After that, he would cast his tune flexibly according to the emotional tribulations (*infiʿālāt*) evoked within him by the words. The composer must live the meaning first, otherwise the tune will become contrived and unnatural. (quoted in al-Sharīf 1988: 375)

[56] See al-Ṭawīl n.d.: 47.

Al-Sunbāṭī referred to his own internalization of the feelings of the poet Ibrāhīm Nājī and his own experiencing of the meanings of the poet's qaṣīdah, *al-Aṭlāl*, which he set to music and which Umm Kulthūm sang.[57]

The lyrics likewise must be felt by the performers. An affective ṭarab singer is said to "feel the words" and subsequently to express his or her feeling in performance. Vocalists are known to favor texts that engage them emotionally and render their performances ecstatically moving. Umm Kulthūm, who has reportedly stressed that song is first and foremost the words, has frequently commented on how deeply moved she was when she sang Byram al-Tūnisī's *Shams al-Aṣīl*. This text described the sun's rays, just prior to sunset, imparting a golden color upon the palm trees. We are told she never sang a text unless she was moved by it.[58] Similarly, Umm Kulthūm, Muḥammad ʿAbd al-Wahhāb, and others are known to have played an active role in selecting the texts they sang and to have influenced the lyricists, at times convincing them to replace certain words that seemed harsh or not conducive to singing.[59]

In performance, singers who feel the words express their feeling in a variety of ways. They may dress up the lyrics with vocables and melismas, vary the timbre and intensity of their voices, introduce effective pauses and ornaments, and reinforce the textual content through hand and facial gestures. The late-nineteenth-century celebrity ʿAbduh al-Ḥāmūlī is known for having acted out the words most expressively. Accordingly, "if the content was grand he would render his voice grand, if it was tender he would make his voice tender, and if it embraced question-and-answer, you would hear his voice questioning and answering" (Mansī 1965: 165). Umm Kulthūm is said to have interpreted the meanings and the sound effects through masterful *ikhrāj*, or "production" and *tajsīd*, namely, "embodiment" or "actualization." In one case, a musical critic who voiced bitter criticism of a tune that ʿAbd al-Wahhāb had composed for Umm Kulthūm stated that her impressive diction and hand and facial gestures, as well as her varied vocal nuances covered up the technical faults of that tune.[60]

Rendered in this way, the lyrics are ultimately "relived" by the audience. Especially among the textually minded listeners, sung poems may operate as primary rousers of the ṭarab condition. In a televised interview Muḥammad al-Qubbanjī, the late performer of Iraqi maqām, an art form that gives tremendous emphasis to sung classical poetry, remembered a performance he had given in Egypt in connection with the Cairo Congress of Arab Music in 1932. As he recounted, in one of the songs the audience responded with

[57] Al-Ṭawīl n.d.: 53.
[58] Danielson 1991b: 383–384 based on Fuʾād 1976.
[59] In the case of ʿAbd al-Wahhāb, for example, see Azzam 1990: 244–246 and 317–320.
[60] These comments on Umm Kulthūm, including the reference to the above critic appear in Fuʾād 1976: 419.

overwhelming enthusiasm, adding that one notable figure in the audience displayed a sudden surge of excitement atypical of his otherwise reserved demeanor. Afterwards, the celebrated Egyptian poet Aḥmad Shawqī, who obviously had the lyrics in mind, asked the Iraqi singer: "What poem did you sing to make that gentleman lose his composure?"[61] Often, the singer's own textually induced ecstasy is projected onto his audience. Conversely, his textual delivery gains emotional efficacy through the inspirational input of the responsive listeners.

That being said, the textual component does not always occupy center stage. In some cases, the texts serve as pretexts for the composers' and performers' musical creations, which often acquire structures of their own, a phenomenon that Pierre Boulez has explained in terms of highly compact "textual time" yielding to more elongated "musical time."[62] Indeed, many ṭarab listeners do not pay much attention to the words or have special fondness, if not outright preference for instrumental music. Certainly, a large number of ecstatically potent vocal performances either use texts minimally or are totally textless. Such phenomena notwithstanding, lyrical evocation remains central to the ṭarab culture and its overall ecstatic foundation.

61 From a video cassette on which the Iraqi artist performs and speaks about his own music. The video was purchased in Dubai in June, 1988.

62 From a panel with Boulez and others at Royce Hall, the University of California at Los Angeles in winter, 1989.

7 Ṭarab in perspective

When Villoteau described a musical event he witnessed in Egypt, he made implicit reference to a particular cultural setting, a typical performance tradition, an emotional experience, and a musical expression. Similarly, the "jam sessions" in Beirut with two young musicians, a violinist and his brother, an ʿūd player, embraced these complementary realms. When the musicians' father requested that we play taqāsīm, we obliged, thus providing him with aesthetic gratification, and in some ways, gaining better grounding in the musical tradition. Those events entailed artistic inculcation or, in a sense, cultural negotiation, collective music making, ecstatic evocation, and the utilization of a certain musical text. In the following discussions these and other related aspects of the ṭarab phenomenon are viewed in their broader social and expressive contexts and reinterpreted against related theories and comparable world models.

Ṭarab as culture

As shown in this study, the domain of ṭarab has been an integral part of the local culture. Especially before the 1980s, the traditional musician's world has maintained an overall relationship of resonance with its broader societal base. By and large, the musicians' attitudes, their work patterns, and the ways in which they learn their skills have been reflexive of broader social, economic, and political structures. A case in point has been the physical separation of the sexes in contexts of performing and listening to music, particularly before World War I. More recently, ṭarab artistry has been viewed as part of the local cultural heritage, or at times of the national image. Celebrated singers such as Umm Kulthūm have been venerated as emblems of pan-Arabism. In turn, the ṭarab milieu has adapted to the overriding forces of change. The artists' careers have become closely linked to the economic networks, technological media, and modes of mass consumption that have pervaded modern Arab life. Ṭarab singing stars have taken advantage of such highly effective venues as the musical film, the government-sponsored radio station, and the modern recording studio.

However, also demonstrated is a significant variance between the ṭarab culture and Arab culture in general. Capable of cutting through ethnic, religious, political, and national boundaries, the world of ṭarab has operated by conventions that depart from, and sometimes challenge, established norms. For one thing, it has centered around a professional trade that society has traditionally viewed with ambivalence and whose members have generally enjoyed a relatively modest socio-economic status. In a broader theoretical sense, this domain may not fit I. M. Lewis' profile of a "marginal cult" partly because of its mainstream appeal and centralized realm of activity.[1] Nevertheless, it has existed as a specialized subculture, thereby distinguishing itself through a unique set of skills, a body of theoretical and practical knowledge, a jargon, and a relatively high level of public visibility.

Furthermore, musical artistry has provided a rather unique path toward upward social mobility, public recognition, and at times stardom. While musical amateurism has enabled middle and upper class artists to bypass a musically unsympathetic climate propagated by class consciousness and religious conservatism, the ṭarab profession has offered a channel for female artists to enter the public musical arena and at least since the early twentieth century to work closely with male counterparts. In one respect, the musical profession has negatively stigmatized female entertainers and, as Karin van Nieuwkerk explains, prompted them to "neutralize and redefine the femininity of their bodies" (1995: 178). In another respect, the music has enabled them to cross significant gender-related boundaries. As Ellen Koskoff writes: "Music performance can and often does play an important role in inter-gender relations, for the inequalities or asymmetries perceived in such relations may be protested, mediated, reversed, transformed, or confirmed through various social/musical strategies, through ritual behavior, disguise, secret language, or social 'deceptions' involving music" (1987: 10). In the ṭarab culture, the female entertainers' ability to traverse social and sexual boundaries has been made possible by both the popularity of female artistry and the distinctiveness of music as an aesthetic experience.

Throughout history, ṭarab music has been a prime vehicle for communicating emotions. In the Near East, the expressivity of poetry as a literary genre and in some cases the idealized–mystical overtones of sung love poems have provided a safe outlet for emotions that otherwise may seem excessive or antisocial. Through the conventional lyrical idiom such emotions are "kept within bounds and released only in acceptable forms and at appropriate times" (Andrews 1985: 116). At the same time, sung poetry has granted certain members of society a distinct emotional–ecstatic voice, sometimes amidst antithetical codes of morality. As shown in the case of one

[1] See Lewis 1971/1989.

patriarchal Arab tribal group, women's sung poetry operates as a "discourse of opposition to the system and of defiance of those who represent it: it is antistructure just as it is antimorality" (Abu-Lughod 1986: 250–251). Comparably, ṭarab has provided male and female singers and their audiences an effective as well as a socially sanctioned system for exteriorizing intimate feelings.

In short, the ṭarab culture has flourished not because it has emulated other cultural domains or conversely because it has differed from them, but because it has done both. Essentially, ṭarab's social milieu and professional modus operandi have complemented other moral and intellectual facets of Arab life. As Jacques Berque has argued, historically the ṭarab culture, and by extension ṭarab music, has been cherished as well as critiqued because it has fulfilled specialized, yet quintessential, emotional and psychological needs.[2]

Ṭarab as process

In this study, the ṭarab performance has been portrayed as a cultural microcosm. Generally illustrated have been the congruities between ṭarab events and the broader societal norms, economic relationships, behavioral codes, and political hierarchies. At a typical ḥaflah, the deferential seating arrangement, the listeners' varying levels of discretion in displaying their emotions, and the musicians' sense of obligation toward the requests of their patrons, all speak of the intimate relationship between the musical process and the social system at large.

However, the ṭarab performance exhibits varied, or at times contradictory, traits that give it a character of its own. For one thing, the typical music-making event may assume a ritual-like structure or mood, but may also share with many rituals a certain casualness or informality. Ḥaflah events in particular may remind us of public rituals which are said to resemble "busy intersections" (Rosaldo 1984: 190). By comparison, the more private gatherings tend to correspond to what I would call "secluded alleys." Sometimes, this latter image applies almost literally, since such gatherings are often carried out within separate venues, for example in a temporarily erected, ornate, cloth tent, which I have earlier interpreted as a metaphor for the social and emotional autonomy of the ṭarab process.

Furthermore, like rituals in general, ṭarab performances tend to entail a certain linear flow or sense of directionality. Some jalsah events are shown to incorporate an entry phase of social, mental, and physical conditioning,

2 See Berque 1964: 211–236.

one that establishes a conducive ambiance leading to the musical performance proper. Encompassing a certain sequence of musical and extramusical microevents, the performance proper may, in turn, lead to an exit phase that ends the performance as a whole and eases the participants back into their ordinary modes of behavior. In this regard, the tripartite model generally applied to initiation rituals tends to fit the ṭarab performance, both socially and experientially. The phases of separation, transition, and incorporation are somewhat comparable to the entry, maintenance, and exit phases of the more structured jalsah. However, in this case, the rite-of-passage interpretation has its own shortcomings. To begin with, the participants, usually members of a group that is already musically initiated, undergo the experience not so much in order to transit from one social–spiritual status into another, but rather to savor the "transitory" phase per se. More specifically, they experience a "liminoid state" (Turner 1977: 43) during which they are gratified by the music's momentary ecstatic effect.

Also, as in many types of rituals, the structure of the ṭarab performance can assume countless variations and departures. Perhaps here, as in other highly transformative processes, for example those with culinary, sexual, or intoxicative associations, the total effect depends largely upon the presentational or production-related components. Traditionally, ḥaflah, jalsah, and cabaret performances are not routine executions of fixed repertoires. Unlike certain world performance-contexts in which the musical or dramatic material is carefully reenacted, as well as revered for its inviolable historic, spiritual, and in some cases mythical authority, the ṭarab performance leaves ample room for contextually inspired and spontaneously generated interpretations. The singer, for example, may determine the length of the performance, the musical genres to be included, and the amount of improvising, all of which are dependent upon the listeners' input and the performance ambiance as a whole. Such flexibility makes the performative process practically synonymous with the musical experience itself. In a sense, the performance is the music.

As a somewhat ritualized occurrence, the ṭarab performance also has a transformative orientation. Events such as the jalsah or ḥaflah can be therapeutic or cathartic, thus enabling individuals or groups of individuals momentarily to shed their quotidian concerns and to be "their own emotional selves." The effectiveness of the performances may stem from such factors as the physical proximity among the participants, the physical self-containment of the performance setting, the collectiveness of the aesthetic experience, and the lax attitude toward time. Especially in nightclubs, such factors may also include the various visual stimuli, for example special lighting, colors, sexually suggestive images, and for some listeners perhaps the high levels of sound amplification. Added to these is of course the musical sound itself and the transformative effects of the amorous song-lyrics. Thus, the ṭarab event becomes potent as an experiential complex, or as a sensory–visual "feast."

At the same time, the ṭarab performance can operate primarily as a musical event, as an act with a central aesthetic purpose. Unlike many ritual occurrences, ṭarab gatherings tend to be musically driven. The various etiquettes, preparatory conversations, physical gestures, exclamations, and exchanges of jokes all seem to operate in ways that enhance as well as socialize the ecstatic stream. In some ways differing from conventional ritual symbols, which are said to be multivocal and to represent opposing sensory and ideological poles,[3] these mini-performances appear to work in synchrony, and to contribute to the overall ecstatic experience along directionally compatible paths.

The ṭarab experience can, and often does, exist outside the boundaries of ritual. Some of the most prevalent and quite memorable musical occurrences are nonstereotypical and dissociated from strict performative norms. Thus, the ṭarab process, which can be both "efficacious" and "entertaining," is able to stand on its own by virtue of its irreducible musical core.[4] Ṭarab music is often enjoyed privately, for example by an artist performing only for himself. As shown earlier, when a performer makes music alone he may "play" his own sammīʿ and experience an internal feedback process that is both creative and ecstatically conducive.

In short, the performance process is special because it can both emulate and transcend established social patterns and conventions. Like a modal improvisation, the ṭarab event is flexible as well as internally coherent. For that reason, the musicians can truly be said to perform the performance. Similarly, the urge to make music or to succumb to its ecstatic effect can be highly spontaneous, natural, and intuitive. In this respect, the musical process is different from other life experiences, yet comparable to how we experience life itself.

Ṭarab as ecstasy

The relationship between the ṭarab emotion and Arab society in general tends to be elusive, partly because the two domains seem rather incomparable. At least on the surface, however, we can observe aspects of coherence between the notion of ecstatic transformation and some of the dominant worldviews. Despite the traditional religious aversion to music as

3 These and other related attributes of ritual symbols were presented by Victor Turner (1985: 56).

4 The words in quotes are from Richard Schechner's work on performance (1976: 196–222).

a professional domain, the ṭarab experience is generally deemed desirable, if not indispensable. Ṭarab sensations have been associated with an established craft of music-making and channeled and propagated through culturally sanctioned performance events, codes of musical behavior, listening related mannerisms, and performance strategies. Over the centuries the experience of musical ecstasy has been assigned an unmistakable niche in social and even spiritual life, as witnessed for example by the various ecstatic Sufi practices as well as by the elaborate definitions of "ṭarab" in early Arabic dictionaries.

Further aspects of coherence are symbolic. As mentioned earlier, the ability to feel the music has been associated with a certain locally based form of cultural–emotional attuning, generally referred to as "Eastern soul." Such an ability has been equated with "genuine artistry," a trademark of the effective ṭarab musician. Along these lines, in Egyptian and east-Mediterranean Arab cities, the titles of "muṭrib" and "muṭribah" have been enjoyed by the skilled and highly esteemed male and female mainstream singers.[5]

At the same time, significant variance has existed between these two broad domains. As shown earlier, the ṭarab emotion, particularly when highly exhibitive, may be deemed socially inappropriate. Also, when associated with secular entertainment, ṭarab ecstasy can project obvious festive connotations and would be avoided in solemn contexts, for example at times of grief or official mourning. Thus, ṭarab music is tolerated, or highly appreciated, as long as it does not violate certain social decorum.

Such an uneasy relationship between musical ecstasy and its social base should make us particularly cautious about the depictions of certain cultures as being inherently ecstatic, characterizations that are typically included in what I have referred to as "profile theories" of musical ecstasy. Although often advanced under the banner of cultural relativism, theories about the exceptional ecstatic proclivities of specific ethnic, racial, or geographic entities tend to stem from gross comparisons rather than from close observations of internal or context-specific dynamics. Fascinating and insightful as they might be, profile statements run the risk of excessive generalization and stereotyping, or to quote John Blacking, "We cannot say that the Kwakiutl are more emotional than the Hopi because their style of dancing looks more ecstatic to our eyes" (1973: 33). To begin with, the manifestations of ecstasy cannot be explained merely as reflections of other realms of human

[5] In this light, Rouget's statement that "for *muṭrib* or *muṭriba*, are, in fact, applied to makers of popular music only, not to makers of learned music" (1985: 282) is incorrect as far as Egypt and the Levant regions are concerned, although the terms may apply as such in other parts of the Islamic world, for example in Iran and to some extent Iraq. As mentioned in Chapter 2, these terms may conjure the negative effects of professionalism, but can also denote musical specialization and technical sophistication, and can serve as titles of respect. See Racy 1986.

existence. For that matter, I find particularly problematic the idea of reducing artistic expressions to physical-environmental profiles or predicating musical sensibilities entirely upon social and political structures.

Explaining Arab ecstasy as the natural product of a desert ethos, or in a related sense, as an outcome of "a single level of consciousness" or an "endless linear ascent of emotional knowledge" (Asad 1954: 142, 144), would be incompatible with the character of ṭarab at least as we know it today. Although Arab folk communities, including desert dwellers, tend to have their own ecstatic traditions, the ṭarab experience per se has an orientation that is unmistakably urban. Closely linked to mysticism and centuries-old courtly traditions, ṭarab music appears distinctly non-desert-like, and arguably antithetical to the taste and temper of the region's historic nomads.[6] Nor should we assume that the connotations of ecstasy are exotic or for that matter erotic. Notwithstanding the Western romantic stereotypes and the Hollywood film portrayals, audiences of Aleppo, Damascus, Beirut, and Cairo do not habitually associate ṭarab music and musical instruments with camel caravans and Bedouin tents, or with dancing "harems" and reclining sultans.

Furthermore, the profiles themselves are sometimes defined in terms that are too arbitrary or too broad. In his comparative study, especially the chapter on "Music and Trance Among the Arabs," Rouget uses the term "Arab" as a cultural-historical entity that embraces various Near-Eastern traditions and performance contexts from the Middle Ages to the present. Thus, his profile covers a vast terrain of ethnic, devotional, and artistic orientations ranging from the Mevlevis of Turkey (essentially a non-Arab group) and possession cults of North Africa to Medieval Islamic court performances and modern Egyptian singers. *Music and Trance* relies quite heavily upon medieval scholars, for example al-Iṣfahānī and al-Ghazālī, whose ideas Rouget tends to project upon the broad "Arab" canvas and into the contemporary practice. Consequently, medieval trances, which frequently assume violent or bizarre manifestations, are treated as primary points of reference. Although acknowledging the existence of ṭarab symptoms that are almost invisible or totally internalized, the book essentially represents the ṭarab condition as being drastic and trance-like.[7]

6 The "non-folkish" or non-rural character of ṭarab has often been reflected in the ṭarab artists' complaint that the regional influx into the cities has diluted the ṭarab tradition in favor of more folk and popular genres. More recently, however, the ṭarab aesthetic has extended to various areas of the Near East and the Arabian Peninsula, especially after the 1970s with the expanded "pan-Arabization" or "Egyptianization" of various indigenous traditions.

7 Rouget actually states that ". . . *ṭarab* can . . . lead to the worst extremes of madness, even death, or, on the contrary, be reduced to a pure and simple musical emotion of which no sign, or almost none, is externally visible" (1985: 282). Yet, obviously using drastic conditions as the standard, he adds that "nowadays, however, especially in urban settings, trance as an expression of musical emotion, of *ṭarab*, is less customary than it was in the past. It still occurs, nevertheless, mainly in country districts" (Ibid).

Profile theories may establish direct causalities between the culture's ecstatic predilections and particularly conducive internal agencies. However, also to be considered are the various tensions, reversals, and contradictions that contribute to the individuality of various world profiles and define them as autonomous systems. This study has shown that various religious, social, and political institutions may or may not contribute to the development of a "hyperesthesiac" Arab society.[8] It is often the case that such institutions seek to check or attenuate ecstasy and to confine the display of musical emotions to socially sanctioned venues. Thus, ecstasy, which shapes culture, is in turn socialized by it. Indeed, Berque's notion of complementarity through disparity is quite pertinent. Accordingly, musical ecstasy thrives not despite but because of the existence of cultural forces that are antithetical to it. Although imbued with symbols that make it Arab, or "Oriental," the ecstatic realm can be construed as a sanctioned experiential alternative rather than a mere manifestation of a broader cultural pattern.

The nature of ecstasy

As an emotional state, ṭarab has certain observable characteristics. The ecstatic individual may appear drawn to the music, absorbed by the listening experience, and removed from the realm of ordinary consciousness. As shown in previous chapters, the music may prompt a variety of behaviors ranging from clapping and singing along to listening quietly and in some cases crying. Also to be included are the typical verbal exclamations and the variety of listening-related physical reactions.

Moreover, ṭarab has a quintessential auditory base. Broadly conceived, the ṭarab experience embraces a wide variety of components: visual, semantic, physiological, mental, and associative. Nevertheless, ṭarab can be defined as a state of consciousness whose core component is musical. Although in certain literary contexts the concept "ṭarab" refers to aesthetic transformation in general, for example as a result of listening to poetry, ṭarab ecstasy is commonly recognized as the emotional state evoked by ṭarab music. In its purest and most irreducible form, ṭarab is an aural experience. Its basic aurality is stressed by the leader of a ṭarab ensemble from Aleppo. Asked why his group has not "kept up with the times" by producing "video-clips" (music videos), Muḥammad Qaṣṣāṣ explains:

[8] Rouget (1985: 298) has used the term "hyperesthesia" in reference to high susceptibility to trance, particularly among the Arabs, adding that this worldwide phenomenon has been regressing in time.

> We are against the visual trend and against the so-called video-clip because music is an art that relies on the auditory rather than the visual sense. The use of modern technology has contributed to the blocking out of thc "auditory vision" – if we may use the expression. From this position, we insist that our performance be aural. Through cassette tapes, we hope soon to record the ensemble's works and to document the Arab heritage aurally. (quoted in Ṭaha 1995: 20)

At the same time, the concept of aurality, or "auditory vision," needs to be understood in broad terms, since ṭarab ecstasy appears quite encompassing both physically and psychologically. A product of creative listening rather than passive hearing, the experience tends to be visceral and for that reason the music is said to be "felt."

In this light, we may reassess the appropriateness of the term "altered state of consciousness," which Rouget criticizes as being generically noncommittal, favoring instead dichotomies that are more discrete or precise.[9] I share Rouget's dissatisfaction, but perhaps for a different reason. More specifically, I suspect that the concept of altered states of consciousness as we generally use it does not fully encompass such a multi-dimensional experience as ṭarab. In one sense, the term is attractive because it directs our attention to the subject's internal psychological process, and because it points toward subjective inwardness rather than merely depicting objectified outward manifestations. However, the aesthetic state generated by ṭarab music appears to extend beyond the strict bounds of psychological or sensory transformation. Although musical experiences do entail modification of consciousness, the transformativeness of ṭarab music needs to be seen holistically so as not to lose sight of the behavioral, auditory, and physiological dimensions of the ecstatic condition, and, just as significantly, not to underplay the primary juncture between the sensory and the aesthetic.

The ṭarab state is not always trance-like, and as a rule does not lead to total transition, or loss of consciousness. Generally, the experience is nontraumatic and is not accompanied by temporary amnesia. Although emotionally transformed, the modern ṭarab connoisseur is less likely to experience such extremes as fuzziness in the perception of ordinary cause–effect relationships,[10] or the blurring of natural expectancies, or the envisioning of certain physical objects as entities of great significance.[11] More typically perhaps, ṭarab ecstasy exists as a "borderline" state of consciousness.[12] During the ṭarab state, listeners tend to retain a general, albeit modified, awareness of the world around them, and quite significantly,

[9] More specifically, Rouget laments that "altered states of consciousness," which has been used by scholars in the United States, is a catchall, or "psychiatrically neutral concept" (1985: 16).

[10] Ludwig 1969: 15.

[11] Anonymous 1962: 351–354.

[12] Tart 1969: 2.

to remain fully cognizant of the musical stimulus that causes them to become ecstatic. Indeed, the concept of muḥāsabah, as a form of analytical listening known to inspire highly effective ṭarab performances, adds to the musical process a significant cerebral dimension.

Conceived in this way, the ṭarab experience seems to occupy an ambiguous position in Rouget's system of delineations. Inspired by French structuralism, Rouget attempts to demystify a tremendously diversified and complex mass of music-and-trance-related data. Accordingly, the material is represented in terms of a dense web of binary oppositions: trance–ecstasy, sacred–profane, possession–shamanism, musicant–musicated, self conducted–induced by others, active–passive, voluntary–involuntary, and so on. At least as encountered today, the ṭarab condition seldom manifests "the principal symptoms" of trance as outlined by Rouget: "trembling, shuddering, horripilation, swooning, falling to the ground, yawning, lethargy, convulsions, foaming at the mouth, protruding eyes . . ." (1985: 13), as well as the frequently noted signs of "hysteria" and "madness" (Ibid.: 12–17). Similarly, "ecstasy" (which according to Rouget's definition, unlike trance, never utilizes music and which exhibits such symptoms as immobility, silence, solitude, no crisis, and so on) essentially excludes the ṭarab experience, which is musically based but can also be quiet or contemplative. Although Rouget states that ecstasy and trance should be viewed as "the opposite poles of a continuum" (Ibid.: 11), his categories are generally strict and mutually exclusive. It may be that the experience of musical ecstasy is inherently averse to Procrustean stretching and trimming. Definitional compartmentalization can provide conceptual order and facilitate the production of theoretical constructs, but it may also sacrifice cross-generic fluidity. Some musical experiences may be efficacious precisely because they are ambivalent or fall within conceptual gray areas. In this study, I have learned to "live with" and at times appreciate the elusive boundaries that seem to exist, for example, between the involuntary and the willed, the mental and the physical, the emotional and the aesthetic, the sacred and the profane.

The ṭarab condition is basically transient, although like the mystical state it may be remembered or cherished. It is difficult to speak of the duration of ṭarab experiences because the lines that differentiate them from "ordinary" experiences are often quite fuzzy. If we define "ṭarab" loosely as musical engagement of some sort, the ecstatic feeling may span the length of entire performances. However, in a stricter sense (for example when salṭanah is clearly felt) the ecstatic condition tends to be much shorter or may not exist at all. More specifically, in a ḥaflah a listening connoisseur may experience heightened moments of ecstasy only sporadically, perhaps for a few minutes at a time. However, at an intimate musical gathering the ecstatic state may gradually build up, continue for some time, and come to a resolution. In this case, the ṭarab experience can be compared to the phenomenon of *duende*, namely the magical or highly inspirational state that flamenco performers and listeners sometimes experience. In a study by Miriam Phillips (1987) we read that in the *tablao*, or nightclub performance, which brings together a large number of spectators and tends to be more choreographed, the sense of duende usually occurs in separate episodes with limited degrees of intensity. However, at a *juerga*, or a more intimate gathering characterized by active audience participation and wine drinking, the sense of duende (which in this context tends to be received, rather than given, by the artists) comes to fruition and persists in an intensified form for an extended period of time.[13]

The ṭarab state also generates a certain level of perceptual transformation. For example, the listeners may feel that time has come to a standstill. Such frequently voiced expressions as "I could listen to this all night" and the occasional feeling that the evening has "split away from time" bear testimony to the notion that the ṭarab state can appear timeless. Particularly when intensely engaging, the performance tends to create its own mode of temporal awareness, as a sense of "virtual time" replaces the feeling of "practical time" (Langer 1953: 125). Certain physical reactions may also occur. Depending on the music and the individual, ṭarab manifestations may suggest loss of control, specifically in the case of the more extroverted audience members. At ḥaflah events, such members may suddenly lapse into and out of seemingly involuntary episodes of listening-related frenzy. By comparison, the diehard listener may become musically absorbed, or at times listen with a critical ear.

At the same time, the ṭarab state can be physically empowering. It may raise the participants' threshold of physical tolerance or as frequently demonstrated, boost the singers' level of endurance on the stage. Ecstatic transformation may also lead to a heightened sense of musicality. The state of salṭanah, in the form of tonal and modal fixation, elevates the performing artist momentarily to a higher plateau of musical creativity. In this respect, ṭarab is reminiscent of *ḥāl*, literally "state," or "mystical state," a term used by classical Iranian musicians to describe their extraordinary feeling of spiritual and musical empowerment. As explained by Morteza Varzi (1986/1988), a *kamanjeh* (upright-fiddle) player, music teacher, and thinker, Iranian classical music is revered as a divine expression. The ḥāl state is seen as ". . . the spiritual mood of the audience and performer"(Ibid.: 4); we are told that "in a state of *ḥāl*, the musician does things which are not necessarily planned, but just 'come out' because he is not himself" (Ibid.: 4–5). Despite their broad similarities, the Arab and the Iranian modalities of musical empowerment exhibit some notable differences. As generally described by Varzi and observed in many Iranian classical musical performances, the ḥāl

13 Phillips 1987: 47–50.

state appears characteristically contemplative, introspective, and mystical. By comparison, the Arab counterpart seems elative, extroverted, and more worldly oriented. In some ways, the Iranian ḥāl is closer to Rouget's notion of "ecstasy," if that notion were to incorporate a primary musical component.[14]

Moreover, the ṭarab state, like its mystical counterpart, is conceptually elusive. As indicated at the beginning of this book, the ecstasies of the musicians and listeners are largely experiential and difficult to articulate. Becoming musically ecstatic may produce a feeling of rejuvenation or generate a cathartic effect or serve as an antidote to the stress of daily life. Nevertheless, the experience cannot be easily verbalized. Comparably, the Spanish poet and dramatist García Lorca speaks of *duende* as "a power and not a construct, . . . a struggle and not a concept" (1955: 154). Although ṭarab songs embrace a certain realm of "meaning" through the use of highly stylized amorous texts, the ecstatic sensation as such tends to be neutral or abstract and thus defies direct semantic explication. The ineffability of the ṭarab state is illustrated by the prevalent use of metaphors that explain how the music is "felt," as in such expressions as: "filling the head," "making you feel invincible," and "forcing you to say: Ah!"

Finally, the ṭarab condition carries no specific noetic intentions. Unlike the mystical state, which James and others have depicted as a potential path toward higher knowledge or divine intuition, ṭarab ecstasy appears conceptually versatile and ideologically flexible. It can be hypersuggestive, thus lending itself to various interpretations: political, amorous, religious, and so on. For that matter, the inherently efficacious but essentially neutral character of the ṭarab state may explain the make-up of mystical wajd, which Rouget aptly defines as ṭarab emotion to which an ideological component has been added. And more broadly, the efficacy and suggestive versatility of ṭarab ecstasy contributes to the wide utility and remarkable adaptability of ṭarab as a musical aesthetic.

The ṭarab condition, which is programatically noncommittal, inherently nonnoetic, and flexibly suggestive, differs from what is usually defined as "sentiment." This latter term has been explained as "a disposition to act in a certain way toward another person or object" (Chaplin 1968: 483) or as "sensibility toward something" (Angeles 1981: 256) and has been connected with such familiar experiences as fear, anger, hate, joy, and sadness. Although ṭarab lyrics can express definable sentiments, for example those

[14] Mr. Varzi indicates that sometimes, Iranian classical musicians try to go into a meditative state, or "to be alone with the Divine," by turning the lights off before and during the performance. The lights may be turned back on during the *reng*, or concluding dance-piece (from a conversation with Mr. Varzi on December 3, 2000). This strikes an interesting contrast with the Arab model, specifically in the case of Ṣabāḥ Fakhrī. See Chapter 3, Note 27.

connected with love, separation, and reunion, it would be misleading to explain the ecstatic state itself in plain sentiment-related terms. Similarly, the affects of the individual melodic modes (although sometimes articulated in reference to sentiments, physical sensations, mental states, and images) are essentially experienced as abstract emotional "flavors," rather than explicit sentiment-like conditions.[15] Nor is ṭarab a specific emotion, or "a feeling and its distinctive thoughts, psychological and biological states, and range of propensities to act" (Goleman 1994: 289). The ecstatic condition has psychological and biological components, and may inspire certain thoughts and tendencies to act. However, such thoughts and tendencies are not always explicit or predictable, and their aesthetic-experiential base tends to elude emotional specificity.

Ṭarab ecstasy may be described as a feeling, but in a rather abstract sense. Swiss analytical psychologist Verena Kast has defined feeling as "an emotion that can be perceived and named, accompanied by images that can be communicated," or as something that "has definite causes and goals" (1991: 164). However, as used in this study, the term "feeling" is best interpreted as something resembling the ṭarab-based concept of *iḥsās*. This latter term stands for "feeling" (rather than "feelings" in the plural) and is not committed to any particular emotional or sentimental profile.

Nonetheless, standard Arabic dictionaries use specific emotional, as well as other experiential, conditions when explaining what ṭarab is. However, as a rule, these various conditions are intended to work collectively so as to produce new and highly suggestive representations of the ṭarab state. Thus, the definitions utilize what, for lack of a better term, I call *transformative blending*, the creation of new blends that are no longer identifiable in terms of their inner, mostly emotional, ingredients, or no longer emotional in the familiar sense.[16] Although they may individually allude to certain aspects of the ṭarab state, these individual conditions would jointly intimate what ṭarab "feels like." In the following discussion, seven such conditions, or ingredients, are highlighted.

First, we encounter an emotional conglomerate that operates internally on the principles of opposition and transformative blending. Dictionaries from various historical eras associate ṭarab with either joy or sadness, or sometimes with a combination of both. In this case, the two emotions

[15] Such modal affects were presented in various premodern treatises and usually linked to different cosmological and therapeutic realms. Today, Arab performers and composers tend to correlate the modes with a variety of human conditions (for example, Rāst, serious; Ḥijāz, nostalgic; Ṣabá, sad; Sīkāh-Huzām, heroic, and so on). Perhaps comparable to the ways we speak of red as "cheerful," blue as "peaceful," green as "relaxing," and so on, such correlations are not always consistent or well-articulated. For further information on maqām associations see Touma 1996: 43–45.

[16] Such blending has been recognized in Western musical and aesthetic discourse. See for example the descriptions in Budd 1985: 3.

represent opposite but interconnected poles, and as such can be said to belong to the same experiential complex. A juxtaposition of the two emotions appears, for example, in the definition of the medieval Ibn Manḍḥūr (d. 1311) who states that ṭarab is joy (*faraḥ*) and sadness (*ḥuzn*) (1955: 557). The later al-Zabīdī (d. 1790) states that ṭarab is the stirring of joy and of sadness as an opposite (AH 1306: 354). And the nineteenth century dictionary of Buṭrus al-Bustānī defines ṭarab as the experience of joy and sadness, "which are opposites" (1869: 1226).

Second, these sources highlight the theme of intensification. For example, in the definitions of Ibn Manḍḥūr, al-Jurjānī (d. 1413), al-Bustānī, and the twentieth-century Iraqi scholar Ḥusayn ʿAlī Maḥfūḍḥ (1977), we encounter the expression *shiddat*, "extreme-ness," or "intensity" applied to either joy or sadness. Here, quantification appears to contribute to the qualitative sense generated by the definition as a whole.

Third, reference is made to key physiological changes. Specifically introduced are the two phenomena of *khiffah*, "lightness" and *ḥarakah*, "movement," both of which indicating a temporary state of kinesthetic or bodily transformation. For example, Ibn Manḍḥūr speaks of "lightness that overcomes a person due to extreme joy or extreme sadness and worry," and may also be connected to "movement" (1955: 557). Al-Jurjānī defines ṭarab as "lightness that overcomes humans due to extreme sadness or joy" (1983: 141). Al-Zabīdī states that ṭarab "is lightness that overcomes you whether it makes you joyful or sad, as it predominates during conditions of extreme joy or sadness or gloom." He adds that according to some sources, ṭarab "is derived from movement," and occurs for example when chanting (*ḥidāʾ*) causes camels to be overwhelmed by ṭarab and to become "light" and fast in their walking (AH 1306: 354). And in the music dictionary of Ḥusayn ʿAlī Maḥfūḍḥ we read that ṭarab is both "lightness that overcomes you, thus causing you to be joyous or sad," and "lightness that results from extreme sadness or extreme joy" (1977: 203).

Fourth, various sources associate ṭarab with a drastic shift from one emotional state to another, specifically, a shift from "sadness" to "joy." Ibn Manḍḥūr writes: "It has been said that it is the setting in of joy and the going away of sadness" (1955: 557). The same definition is affirmed by al-Zabīdī, although he and several other authors stress that equating ṭarab merely with joy is a fallacy (AH 1306: 354).

Fifth, a further emotional ingredient is added, one that centers around the concept of *shawq*, literally "longing" or "yearning." This addition introduces a dimension of directionality or purpose as it embraces such notions as "love" and "remembrance." Ibn Manḍḥūr cites one authority who defines ṭarab as "longing and togetherness (*jamʿ*)" (1955: 557). A comparable description, with an illustrative poem, appears also in al-Zabīdī, who states that when camels are overcome by ṭarab through the ḥidāʾ of the camel drivers, they yearn for their homes (AH 1306: 354). Reference to the camels' movement and longing reappears in al-Bustānī's dictionary (1869: 1226).

Sixth, an aesthetic, or performative, element is included, namely, singing. Often used is the verb *ṭarraba*, "to create intensive ṭarab," from the abstract noun *taṭrīb*. For example, Ibn Manḍhūr observes that to say someone has produced taṭrīb in his singing means he has fragmented the text, stretched it musically (*rajjaʿa*), and sung it with ornaments (*zayyana*). He cites part of a poem illustrating the process in reference to bird singing (1955: 557). In the nineteenth century, al-Bustānī comments that "a man who produces taṭrīb is one who sings enchantingly (*taghanná*), who produces vocal elongations (*madda*), and who makes his singing beautiful (*ḥassana*)" (1869: 1226).[17] In various medieval and post-medieval dictionaries, the aesthetic component seems to lie primarily in *taḥsīn al-ṣawt*, "improving" or "beautifying the voice," thus placing a great emphasis upon singing. However, in modern dictionaries the aesthetic component is applied to the sound of instruments as well. For example, in Maḥfūḍh's dictionary we read that one of the definitions of ṭarab is *ʿazf*, namely "playing" on musical, or "ecstasy-producing" instruments (*ālāt muṭribah*) (1977: 203).[18]

Seventh, the definitions of ṭarab introduce the concept of *shajan*, which, as discussed earlier, can be explained as a combination of both sadness and elation, or as something similar to enchanting melancholy.[19] Also included is the effect of *shajū*, which likewise embraces seemingly opposite meanings and is evoked by the voice that captivates through its beauty or rather, overwhelms through its sweet pathos. Similarly, a voice is considered *shajī* if it imparts in us a feeling of enchanting melancholy. Along similar lines, a medieval text by Khurdādhbih (d. AH 211) indicates that according to one authority: "Song (*al-ghināʾ*) causes you to become ecstatic (*aṭrabaka*) thus making you dance, and causes you to cry thus making you enchantingly melancholic (*ashjāka*), and anything other than that is woe and gloom" (Khashabah ed. 1984: 44).[20]

To conclude, the ways of explaining the ṭarab experience have changed very little in the course of almost a millennium, although some modern departures are noteworthy. Such consistency may reflect certain literary

17 The exact meanings and applications of the terms *rajjaʿa* (noun, *tarjīʿ*) and *madda* (noun, *madd*) are not totally clear. An informative explication of these and other early usages appears in Nelson 1985: 24–27 and 79–81).

18 The word *ʿazf*, which is currently used to mean performing on an instrument (from the verb *ʿazafa*), goes back to ancient Arabia, and is related to *ʿazīf*, the ominous sound produced by the *jinn*, or demonic spirits (See Farmer 1929/1973: 8).

19 More specifically, refer back to Chapter 6, in particular Note 41.

20 The modern editor of this work states in a footnote that although in the manuscript the text appears as such, perhaps it makes more sense to have the causal relationship between crying and becoming melancholic reversed. As he puts it, "it is more difficult for humans to cry than to have *shajan* (or elative melancholy)" (Khashabah ed. 1984: 44).

inertia, as the various scholars have tended to repeat or "recycle" the texts of their predecessors. However, the articulations persevere in part because they hint at the ṭarab state through suitably transformative means. The merger of both familiar and extraordinary human conditions evokes the "feeling" of the defined phenomenon and grants the definitions a certain timeless appeal.

The generation of ecstasy

Attesting to the complex nature of the ṭarab experience, these local sources imply that the modalities of creating ecstasy are not always neatly ordered or streamlined. With this in mind, one may assess the applicability of standard theories that explain possession trances or altered states of consciousness in general. In particular, one may question the notion that such transitional states result from some form of boundary crossing, through either sensory overload or sensory deprivation. As already shown, ṭarab allows a certain role for sensory manipulation. Arabic definitions of ṭarab allude to such extremes as intense joy and sadness, and such overwhelming experiences as lightness, movement, and obsessive longing.

Manipulation occurs through the use of various physical and mental "boosters." Examples include performance-related visual effects, lighting, consumption of food, and in certain cases drug use, as well as the added self-inducement that may result from singing along, dancing, swaying, cheering, and so on. Such an association between heightened stimulation and musical transformation is found in numerous other traditions. It is illustrated, for example, by the use of ḥashīsh in connection with rembetika music in early twentieth-century Greece, specifically in an underworld that centered around the so called *café-aman* and favored improvisatory genres such as the instrumental *taximi* and the vocal *amanes* and the use of the *bouzouki*, a type of long-necked fretted lute.[21] Similarly, in her study of wedding songs among Prespa Albanians, Jane Sugarman (1997) demonstrates that the men's singing is intimately linked to the creation of *muabet*, or friendly camaraderie, and to social drinking. The consumption of *raki*, a fruit brandy, and the sharing of appetizers contribute to the overall feeling of *qeif* or "elation."[22]

The role played by physiological, visual, and mental stimuli is complex and appears to vary considerably depending upon the individual, the context

[21] See Holst 1975 and Morris 1981: 79–90.

[22] Sugarman 1997, especially 148–154, and 278–280. The word *muabet* comes from the Turkish *muhabbet*, originally Arabic *maḥabbat* (or *maḥabbah*), "affection." The word *qeif* derives from the Turkish *keyif*, or Arabic *kayf*, "elation."

of music making, and the music being performed. Generally, the music and the various adjunct stimuli both complement and influence one another. For example, intoxicating substances may create states in which the participants are able to "let go" and to become more connected to the music. Ḥashīsh in particular may intensify the musical sensations themselves and grant them a certain aura or profundity. On the other hand, the musical stimulus may create a suitable mindset, or perhaps an acceptable pretext for drinking, smoking, feasting, and so on. In this capacity, the music plays a socializing role. More directly, music "modulates" the other stimuli, making them more special or more elative. However, the symbiotic relationship between music and these various stimuli entails a delicate functional equilibrium. For example, musical ecstasy, said to empower performers and enable them to withstand a higher threshold of drug tolerance, is likely to diminish or wither away as a result of excessive drug intake, or stimulation overload.

Just as important, the ṭarab state is capable of full fruition without significant sensory manipulation. Particularly in listening-oriented settings, many of the typical enhancers can be dispensed with. Although influenced by the performance context (and in earlier epochs considered prone to external cosmological interventions) the music can generate its own brand of stimulation. In this respect, it can operate independently as an experience that is inherently transformative.

Meanwhile, the relationship between the ecstasy makers and their audience tends to vary, depending largely upon the performance genre. To this point, Rouget's Arab trancing-models can be applied, but with certain qualifiers.[23] Rouget's musician–trancee dichotomy is noticeable in the typical ṭarab event. His classical-samāʿ model, which is derived from medieval Sufi sources and applied to Arab "profane," or "emotional trance," fits the basic pattern of ṭarab evocation. The audience is supposedly passive, being "musicated" by musicians who presumably induce "trance" within the listeners without going into trance themselves. In this fashion, music leads to trance, which may in turn inspire the listeners to dance.

More appropriately, however, the samāʿ model fits the listening-oriented ṭarab events. Basically, it applies to the sammīʿah who, although they do not usually dance, focus their full attention upon the musical message generated by the performers. In the ṭarab culture, the ecstatic experience develops significantly through active listening, through the creative musician–audience feedback that energizes the performance. Therefore, the idea of passivity, which James and others have associated with the mystical state, applies only loosely. Indeed, passive listening in the strict sense is neither appreciated nor considered conducive to ecstatic transformation.

[23] These various models are discussed in detail in Rouget's chapter "Music and Trance among the Arabs" (1985: 255–312).

Furthermore, music makers do experience the ṭarab effect themselves, albeit in their own quiet, focused, and creatively directed ways. True, the professional performers are largely "musicators" whose emotional reactions are relatively restrained. The performing mode does require a certain degree of mental control, whereas the listening posture provides suitable grounds for emotional release. Nevertheless, the music makers' feeling of salṭanah (as a concentrated form of ecstasy typically linked to the melodic modes) constitutes the basis for their most inspired performances. As this study has shown, the relationship between ecstasy and music is cyclical: ecstasy generates music, which in turn generates ecstasy, as each embodies the essence of the other.

By the same token, the classical-samāʿ model is less representative of the extroverted or agitational mode of relating to ṭarab music. Some of Rouget's other models, specifically the Sufi *dhikr* and to a lesser extent the Mevlevi *samāʿ*, seem more applicable. In these models, we encounter highly participatory ceremonies in which dancing leads to trancing, whereby the participants prompt their own trances. As suggested earlier, the ecstasy of the non-sammīʿah, although instigated by the performance proper, results in some degree from autostimulation in the form of singing, dancing, clapping, and so on. Rouget's *fakirist* model, notably the use of rhythmic and textual symbols to trigger the trance, strikes an interesting resemblance to the ṭarab musicians' use of "signal pieces" to produce immediate ecstatic frenzy among the impassioned listeners.

Essentially, confining the performer–listener relationship to strictly delineated transformative models has its shortcomings. Often, the various modalities of ecstatic evocation overlap or operate simultaneously. For example, at a dhikr ceremony the dervishes who breathe rhythmically, dance, and reiterate certain verbal formulas may also listen ecstatically to the munshid's concurrent chanting. Thus, they would be both self-entranced and entranced by others. Similarly, in secular performances the passive and active modes of developing ecstasy, far from being mutually exclusive, are often difficult to separate or differentiate from one another.

Ṭarab as music

As a medium of ṭarab ecstasy, music may be viewed both as a cultural expression and as a distinct aesthetic system. Like the sensations it evokes, ṭarab music has been recognized as a prime conveyor of the "Oriental" ethos, as an expression that "defines us as Easterners." It is possible to find points of resemblance between the music's overall structure and the ways in which performers work together or relate to one another professionally. As shown earlier, aspects of individuality, compatibility, and leadership that typified the work relations among members of the early twentieth century takht ensemble tended to resemble the ways in which the music itself was internally patterned.[24] On a finer experiential level, however, social–musical homologies appear highly interpretive since music and society are essentially different as well as interdependent. More specifically, among the four main realms of the ṭarab complex, the specific social milieu referred to earlier as "ṭarab culture" lends itself most readily to structural comparisons with other venues of Arab social life. Yet such comparisons become more elusive or merely symbolic as we proceed toward the performative process and ultimately into the musical-ecstatic core. Such elusiveness speaks in general terms of music's autonomy as an expressive domain and specifically of ṭarab music's distinctness as an emotional experience. Emotionally speaking, the music of ṭarab tends to operate on four closely related levels: idiom, musical vocabulary, compositional design, and interpretation.

Idiom

An encompassing concept, idiom can be defined as the overall style or simply, the substance that makes the music what it is. In the Arab Near-East, ṭarab has constituted a widely shared musical idiom, thus confirming Rouget's observation that trance musics in general represent the current or familiar musical practices of the cultures they belong to. At the same time, it can be argued that narrowly defined, ṭarab music manifests special emotive proclivity, a culturally recognized tendency toward ecstatic evocation. By and large, the ṭarab idiom exhibits recognizable traits. In some respects, an outgrowth of the pre-World-War-I takht practice, the music can exist in solo, ensemble, instrumental, and vocal formats. It is predominantly vocal and gives distinct prominence to the solo voice. Ensemble performance tends to highlight individuality as well as group coordination. Moreover, the ṭarab idiom makes extensive use of love poetry. Highly stylized, the sung poems reinforce or add a potent ingredient to the overall ṭarab experience. However, in order to generate ecstasy, ṭarab music does not have to be vocal or text-based. Purely instrumental music is common. Melodic and metric modes are used, although a significant portion of the music is nonmetric. The music also tends to be abstract or non-programmatic, a trait best illustrated by the solo instrumental improvisation.

Clearly, theories that restrict the operation of ṭarab ecstasy to verbal-semantic stimulation are at best inadequate. The notion that among Arabs

[24] See Racy 1988.

textual meaning is a fundamental requirement for musical evocation (a notion that is taken for granted and reiterated throughout Rouget's discussions on Arab trances) appears to stem from a cursory treatment of key Sufi treatises, above all the one by Abū Ḥāmid al-Ghazālī (1058–1111).[25] A more critical reading of al-Ghazālī's original Arabic text, specifically the chapter titled, *Kitāb Ādāb al-Samāᶜ wa-al-Wajd*, roughly, "The Book of the Manners of Listening and Ecstasy", leads to a different and more reasonable interpretation. As the title indicates, the work is polemical and prescriptive, as it specifies which musics are appropriate for the Sufi samāᶜ. Al-Ghazālī, who does not advocate the wholesale banning (*taḥrīm*) of music, identifies those categories whose ecstatic effect is conducive to spiritual transcendence. A Muslim theologian and jurist as well as a mystic, al-Ghazālī is conscious of a legacy of religious conservatism that condemns the salient forms of secular entertainment and the use of certain instruments. But he also realizes that certain types of music are to be excluded not for their lack of ecstatic power, but on the contrary, because their evocative efficacies, as well as their sensuous, and hence "immoral," connotations, are overwhelming.

In fact, al-Ghazālī provides us with a list of what constitutes lawful material (*mubāḥ*) for spiritual listening. To begin with, he cites sayings from the authoritative book, *al-Ḥadīth* to confirm the spiritual value of the aesthetically pleasing voice. He also advocates the use of what he calls *alḥān mawzūnah*, which can be explained as rhythmically patterned melodies or tunes, those that are based on metered or poetically structured texts, or perhaps simply as metric sung-poetry. Al-Ghazālī also argues for the use of comprehensible texts (*kalām mafhūm*) that direct the heart unequivocally toward the Divine. In addition, he stresses that the mystical performance must activate within us the love (*ᶜishq*) of God.

Al-Ghazālī further clarifies his position by illustrating the types of usages that are either morally objectionable or ecstatically inappropriate. For example, he provides several reasons why the Qur'ān, although so powerful as to cause listeners to cry, is not well-suited for the generation of mystical ecstasy. His reasons are consistent with his position on what is or is not acceptable as samāᶜ material. First, the Qur'anic verses, particularly when instructing on matters of social conduct, laws of inheritance, death, and so on, may not correspond to the emotional states of the listeners at the time of wajd. Second, the listeners' familiarity with the verses makes Qur'anic chanting unsuited for the arousal of ecstasy since "there is pleasure in everything new" (n.d.: 263). Third, Qur'anic verses, unlike poetry, are devoid of

[25] Examples of Rouget's statements to this effect are: "It is clear that for Arabs music possesses the emotional power with which we are concerned here only insofar as it is associated with words, which is to say with meaning" (1985: 299); and "for an Arab music has the power of inducing trance only because it is a vehicle for words, and because these words are charged with meaning" (Ibid.: 300).

metric structure, and therefore are impracticable for exerting the required influence upon the soul. Accordingly, "a beautiful measured voice differs from a beautiful unmeasured voice" (Ibid.: 264). Fourth, measured poetry is rendered effective through the use of musical modes (*ṭuruq* and *dastānāt*) and through the musical manipulations of the texts, for example lengthening short syllables and shortening long ones, as well as allowing for pauses in the middle of the words and splitting certain word structures. Al-Ghazālī tells us that such interventions are not permissible or appreciated if used in connection with the divinely revealed Qurʾanic prose. Significantly, he adds that these effects would be ecstatically powerful if rendered non-textually, for example on instruments, but in that case they become undesirably meaningless, or devoid of clear spiritual sense. Fifth, measured tunes, unlike Qurʾanic chanting, are enhanced by rhythmic beats, which are produced on percussion instruments, "as weak wajd cannot be uplifted except through powerful means" (Ibid.: 264). Sixth, in ordinary singing, or *ghināʾ*, listeners have the prerogative of avoiding texts they do not desire to listen to or of requesting texts that suit their emotional states at the time of listening. Taking such liberties may serve the purpose of wajd, but would be unconscionable in the case of the Qurʾān. Al-Ghazālī adds a seventh, primarily theological, consideration that he associates with a particular school of thought: because the Qurʾān is God's words, rather than a created object, its divine nature is above the emotional or ecstatic substance of created things.

From these discussions it is clear that al-Ghazālī is fully aware of the ecstatic power of music as music. Although he considers "measured" and "meaningful" categories as the ones befitting the mystical experience, his polemics tacitly recognize the potency, as well as the spiritual inappropriateness, of music that is unmeasured or nonsemantic. A careful reading of al-Ghazālī's Ādāb clearly shows that he recognizes the inherent ecstatic powers of music in general. He takes note of the efficacy inherent in such aesthetic auditory stimuli as: the pleasing vocal timbre, metric accents, percussive reinforcement, the melodic modes, correct melodic intervals, the sounds of various types of string and wind instruments, and the artful manipulation of song texts.

For al-Ghazālī, nonmystical music generates nonmystical, and therefore undesirable, ecstasy. Having no teleological purpose or lacking spiritual meaning, such music leads to unmistakable, albeit directionless, ecstatic sensations. As al-Ghazālī explains, such sensations are akin to sexual desire felt by someone who grows up in total seclusion and has never known about or experienced sexual intercourse. Thus, knowledge about the object of mystical yearning is a prerequisite for the attainment of mystical transcendence. As he explains what is lawful or spiritually conducive, al-Ghazālī at least tacitly acknowledges the potency of music as a category of experience. Thus, a large array of secular and sacred practices are inappropriate for the

Sufi samāʿ not because they are ecstatically ineffective, but rather because their contents or ecstatic orientations are not suited for the inducement of wajd. Rouget's implicit negation of the ecstatic value of nontexted Arab music seems to stem from construing al-Ghazālī's prescriptive constructs as descriptive statements, which Rouget applies to all Arab music, secular as well as sacred.

Obviously, ṭarab is more than meter and semantics. This is illustrated by the numerous musical genres that are nonmeasured and whose verbal content is sparse and highly stylized. Whereas excessive wordiness may detract from the ecstatic finesse of the music, textual minimalism and stylization tend to prevent the verbal material from encumbering the strictly musical component. In a sense, they allow the singing to be more musical. In performance, the semantic component becomes particularly diffuse through taṭrīb, in the form of long melismatic interjections, word stretching, and textual fragmentation. A comparable effect results from the practice of ṭasarruf. Ultimately, the absence of meter is best represented by the improvisatory practice, which is central to a wide variety of Sufi traditions and also basic to the art of Qurʾanic chanting.

Finally, the assumption that music cannot evoke ecstasy without some explicit ideology negates music's ability to operate emotionally on a more abstract level. This study has already addressed ṭarab music's tendency toward abstraction and lyricism. It has also shown that Arab secular music in its instrumental, or nontexted form, far from being aimless or amorphous, is capable of conveying its own aesthetic message, its own emotional directionality.

Musical vocabulary

At a more detailed level, ṭarab music can be studied in terms of individual musical ingredients or "building blocks" (Nettl 1974: 13) that are ecstatically imbued. Examples of such building blocks are the widely favored timbres, ornaments, metric patterns, stylized textual fillers, melismas, and cadential patterns. The maqāmāt can also be studied as larger building blocks. Ṭarab connoisseurs speak of the magic inherent in each of the modes, in essence portraying them as self-contained spheres of potential affect. As indicated earlier, these modes also owe some of their efficacies to particular modal components, for example the "neutral" microtones, which are thought to embody a great deal of ecstasy and to contribute significantly to the distinctive flavor of Arab music. Textual ingredients are also to be included, namely the various amorous expressions and depictions that the lyricists employ.

Compositional design

At the level of compositional design, full ecstatic fruition stems from the manner in which the individual ecstatic ingredients are assembled. Ṭarab feeling occurs when the building blocks work in musically coherent ways, or serve as signifiers within a meaningful musical-ecstatic syntax. Using structural linguistics as a model, John Blacking has explained that, like verbal units, musical structures become intelligible when the order of musical tones follows an established musical grammar. Confusion may occur if the "deep structure" is disregarded (1973: 23). Differently stated, ṭarab compositions operate as gestalts within which individual musical components realize their full potentials as affective tools.

In practical terms, the composers or improvisers consciously or intuitively determine the proper placements, degrees of prominence, and inner details of various compositional ingredients: melodic, textural, metric, structural, and so on.[26] At this level also, modal creations are achieved through such processes as: 1) the development of a tonal center or centers through such devices as droning and tonal reiteration; 2) the creation of appropriate progressional (melodic) tracks; 3) the execution of correct melodic intervals, for example, the various diatonic and neutral steps and leaps and the minute microtonal readjustments that affect various scaler degrees; 4) the proper use of phrasing, pausing, and cadencing, particularly in solo improvisations; and 5) the introduction of effective modulations to other modes. Naturally, variety is also expected. Successful musical works usually call for creative, thematic, modal, and structural diversions. Such compositional features lend referential meaning to other more familiar components. They also make the overall musical work less stereotypical or less static and ultimately, more engaging both mentally and emotionally.

Compositionally speaking, the modal improviser or composer tends to operate on two levels of musical consciousness. At the first level, he appeals to common modal sense. Largely subliminal, such sense exists not so much in terms of concretely perceived structures, but rather in the form of potential modal configurations, tonal affinities, intervallic tendencies, and motivic options. Essentially, it corresponds to a cognitive musical grammar that the musicians and their initiated listeners would have already internalized through prior musical enculturation. Furthermore, the shared modal sense encompasses certain margins of digression, or acceptable thresholds of modal ambivalence. Accordingly, a taqāsīm performance, for example,

[26] Compositionally speaking, Rouget's observation that trance musics usually exhibit a gradual increase in tempo and loudness has some applicability to ṭarab music. These two features are perhaps most noticeable across long performance stretches or in nightclub, especially dance related, routines. They are certainly more observable in Sufi dhikr performances.

works in part because the performer follows, and in many cases manipulates, the culture's subliminal, or at times theorized, reservoir of musical-emotive directives.

At the second level, the modal artist operates within a more immediate realm of modal consciousness, more precisely, an instantaneously generated track of musical possibilities. Here, he works within a more concrete modal framework (a specific pitch level, a certain melodic mode, a tonic, an opening phrase or phrases, and so on) that he himself or a fellow musician has set in motion. In this context, the improviser, for example, attempts to make linear sense vis-à-vis the musical framework that has just been established. Conscious of the compositional potentials provided by the already established track, he may fulfill, flesh out, or work around such potentials as he brings the entire performance to a full completion.

The two levels of compositional consciousness are organically linked. When a singer, for instance, improvises a mawwāl after a dūlāb or following an introductory taqsīm on the qānūn, his improvisation would be guided by both the conventional modal sense and the specific set of melodic tendencies already initiated by the introductory material. An ecstatically charged device such as the dūlāb both activates the artist's and the listener's shared modal instincts and offers likely scenarios for actual, internally coherent musical renditions. However, quite often the modal improviser who toys with the musical expectancies implied by each of the two realms described above resembles a painter who creates a painting on the spot before a group of spectators. As the artist begins by outlining the trunk of a tree, the spectators who are naturally cognizant of trees may anticipate, if only approximately, how the painting will proceed. In turn, the painter may fulfill such anticipation, albeit in his own specific ways, or may even deliberately "tease" the spectators by producing a different but perfectly sensible rendition of a full tree image. Comparably, a skilled taqāsīm performer may satisfy or digress from the obvious projections of those who are both familiar with the musical genre and conscious of the specifics of his actual performance. He may also allow the listeners' minds to "fill in" as he deliberately skips certain obvious notes or alludes to them through mutually understandable musical innuendoes. Thus, the effective improviser attempts to achieve a successful balance between common sense and uncommon sensibility.

Meanwhile, the lyricists produce effective textual compositions through the artful integration of emotionally loaded expressions, enchanting sound and sense combinations, and transformative amorous narratives. The manner in which such compositions work ecstatically entails a process of cognitive transposition. When sung, the love poems cause separate but highly compatible genres of experience, namely the poetical-amorous and the musical-aesthetic, to collapse into one homogenized conceptual pool. Through metaphoric suggestion, or sometimes direct reference, the distinctions between such phenomena as intoxication and ecstasy, the love affair and the musical experience, the garden party and the ḥaflah, are blurred. Similarly affected are the conceptual barriers that separate the poet, the lover, the musician, and the listener, who instead are all recast into one generalized category of emotionally transformed players. Also underplayed is the difference between feeling as a by-product of the amorous condition and feeling as a function of aesthetic transformation. In effect, the two emotional realms are rendered extensions of one another. With this accomplished, the listener is enabled to feel the poetical ambiance musically as well as to sense the musical substance poetically. In other words, by internalizing the newly formed conceptual–emotional amalgam, the motivated ṭarab seeker becomes better prepared to translate the lyrical message into musical ecstasy.

Interpretation

Beyond mere compositional design, ecstatic evocation stems from the ways in which the music is contextually presented and experienced. At this level, we speak in terms of both the stylistic "fine tuning," which, inspired by various performance related factors, makes a musical rendition particularly efficacious. We also consider the phenomenological "filtering" which, owing to various contextual and personal dynamics, shapes the overall musical experience. At the level of musical interpretation, ecstasy's musical base, which can be equated with salṭanah as a musical quality, seems particularly elusive and difficult to represent in concrete analytical terms. At the same time, the interpretational musical dimension, although in some ways an extension or a refinement of the preceeding three levels, tends to enjoy a qualitative edge, or perhaps a certain mystical aura.

Performance-related factors that inspire compositional fine tuning are numerous. They include the physical setting, the cultural and artistic backgrounds of the participants, and the physical and emotional preparedness of the musicians (for example whether or not they have salṭanah). Such dynamics may grant additional efficacy to music that is structurally correct or that is inherently ecstatic. Conversely, such dynamics may impede the ecstatic potentials of a musical composition and make it less engaging.

Musically speaking, an affective interpretation or improvisation tends to combine ingenuity with succinctness, for instance, in the application of tonal emphasis, linear motion, intonational detail, phrasing and pausing, cadencing, ornamentation, and accentuation. Also achieved is a delicate balance between such extreme poles as overstating–understating, reiteration–digression, and convention–originality. Furthermore, the inspired interpreter may masterfully utilize, or manipulate, the two levels of modal consciousness described earlier, namely the collectively shared musical sense and the performance-specific musical tendencies.

In collective interpretations, musical ecstasy is felt particularly when individual performers produce simultaneous divergences in rhythmic detail while remaining within the basic accentual or metric framework of the musical composition. A similar effect may result from the soloist's deliberate and well calculated deviations from an accompanying beat pattern, or sometimes an ostinato. These features can be compared to the collective rhythmic variances and the breaking away from strict metronomic time in jazz music, phenomena that Charles Keil refers to as "participatory discrepancies," or as being "in synch but out of phase" (1995: 8).[27] Similarly, J.A. Prögler indicates that a desirable aesthetic effect "occurs when the musicians are a bit out of time, or out of phase with one another" (1995: 21). Part of a musical subsyntax, such discrepancies are said to represent the "play" that brings out the music's powerful magic, its "groove," "swing," and "feel."

Ultimately, the emotional impact of ṭarab renditions is subject to the listeners' own interpretations, which in turn reflect their temporary moods, as well as their levels of musical initiation. The ecstatic message is what the musical participants feel, or as musical psychologist Carl E. Seashore explained some sixty years ago:

> Hearing of music is subject to vast limitations; among these are the limitations of musical talent or aptitude, musical information, musical skills, general intelligence, temperament, and countless other factors. On the other hand, the listeners may put a great deal more into the music than was originally intended or is actually present in the musical form, as, for example, the vivacious responses to primitive tom-toms or to present-day ragtime. Fundamental to this issue is the fact that there is not a one-to-one relationship between music as performed and music as experienced. (Seashore 1938/67: 381–382)

Music as feeling

Despite such filtering, ṭarab music remains the core of the ecstatic experience. For that reason, Rouget calls it "pure message" (1985: 315). More specifically, the musical substance operates ecstatically in the sense that its message is perceived ecstatically by those who are musically trained to perceive it as such. Through a certain "mutual tuning relationship" (Schutz 1977: 115) the ecstatic condition that haunts the ṭarab composer or performer

[27] Keil mentions that he derived this last expression from one of Stephen Feld's works in which the phrase "in-synchrony while out-of-phase" denoted an aspect of stylistic expressivity, which Feld referred to as "lift-up-over sounding" (Feld 1988: 82–83).

Lebanese singer Wadīʿ al-Ṣāfī in performance during the 1950s.
Photo courtesy of Dār al-Ṣayyād.

is conveyed in the musical product itself, and ultimately is felt by the properly attuned listener. Along similar lines, the artist himself or herself is said to be ecstatic, or: "He has salṭanah," "She has feeling," "He has soul," "Umm Kulthūm can fill the head," and so on. Then, comparable attributes are applied to the very music that such an artist creates: "The music has salṭanah," "The music is full of ṭarab," "It fills the head." In performance, such ecstatic transpositions are extended to the listener as well, who becomes maṭrūb, or "ecstatic," who feels the music, and whose "head is filled."

Thus, when we speak of music as being inherently "ecstatic," we are implicitly describing an organic process through which ecstatic sensations are musically conceived, codified, and transmitted. We are alluding to a broader context in which listeners process the music in ecstatically meaningful ways. In this encompassing sense, the music can be said to evoke, to impress, and to affect. To these expressions we can certainly add Rouget's musically focused, although linguistically peculiar, verb "to musicate," which I think captures the gist of what ṭarab music does.

The musical substance produces ecstasy through the collaborative work of its various components. Generally speaking, Leonard Meyer's dynamics of suspense and release find certain application in ṭarab music's structure, within which patterns of statement, digression, and resolution are quite prevalent. Furthermore, Meyer's treatment of "emotion" and "meaning" essentially as nonreferential or abstract phenomena is consistent with the ways in which this work has dealt with these and other related concepts. However, the "hydraulic" notion that arousal occurs when musical expectations are momentarily suppressed or suspended, or when moments of anxiety or ambiguity are temporarily introduced does not fully explain how the ecstatic emotion is generated in ṭarab music. In the first place, the above model is more concerned with the musical product and its perceptual base than with the contextual or symbolic forces that shape the musical experience. Also, as others have noted, the surprise factor alone does not tell us why we often indulge in recreating or listening to musical works that we already know quite well.[28] We may similarly wish to know what happens when we perform or improvise our own music alone for our own pleasure. By itself, the principle of suspense and release does not account for the ecstatic impact of reiteration, for example of a metric pattern or a religious verbal formula in the dhikr ritual. The same may be said of the various forms of intensification, including the gradual tempo increase we frequently encounter in trance rituals. Moreover, that principle does not adequately show how salṭanah, or modal ecstasy works – specifically, the emotional impact of such cumulative effects as drones, tonicity, and intervallic design.

The dynamics of ṭarab evocation also call into question the direct correlation between emotional provocation and the frustration of musical expectations whose fulfillment is somewhat anticipated. The hypothesis is that ". . . affect or emotion-felt is aroused when an expectation – a tendency to respond – activated by the musical stimulus situation, is temporarily inhibited or permanently blocked" (Meyer 1956: 31). Accordingly, the temporary conditions of anxiety or ambiguity thus generated would be felt as a type of affect, or heightened emotional arousal that is meaningfully released when such conditions are ultimately resolved. In this case, we may

[28] See for example Budd 1985: 173–174.

ask if emotional arousal does not also stem from the musical resolution itself, or as Malcolm Budd explains: ". . . it would be a misrepresentation of musical experience to construe the emotional release experienced when tension is resolved as the release from, rather than the release of, emotion: the discharge of tension is experienced with emotion" (1985: 161). As the study of ṭarab indicates, ecstatic arousal may stem from the resolutions, as well as from the digressions or ambiguities. Indeed, the listeners' emotional responses, including their verbal gestures, are most vividly displayed during or immediately after the execution of highly conclusive cadential patterns.[29]

Feeling as music

One of the main conclusions of this study is that ecstatic evocation is not confined to a single structural principle or grand design, but rather realized through a variety of affective tools and maneuvers. For one thing, musical artistry utilizes both the cumulative effects of individual auditory stimuli and the emotional "agitation" that results from dynamic musical procedures, or figuratively speaking, from both the therapeutic massage and the shock treatment. A combination of musical elements and microprocesses, the agents of ṭarab include the following: specific timbres; resonant sound effects; suitable tessituras; certain ornaments; soloistic designs; drones; heterophony; appropriate use of melodic intervals, including neutral steps and finer microtonal readjustments; proper progressional flow within modal structures; certain modal consistency; timely and well-executed modulations; effective cadences; stylistic intensification, for example proceeding from soloistic to ensemble genres; cumulative effect, for instance through extended listening; delayed resolutions, including brief digressions just before a final cadence; rhythmic flexibility, especially in improvisatory genres; rhythmic intricacy, particularly in the case of cadences; heterorhythm; metric regularity; phased metric buildup; reiterative elements, such as refrains; proper rendering of melodic fillers, for example by instruments between vocal phrases; verbal economy and the use of vocalizations; proper enunciation; the use of texts that are lyrical and stylized; emphasis on words and expressions that are sonically appealing, as well as emotionally evocative; the utilization of texts that are transformatively suggestive; and others.

In context, these elements are used in a variety of shades and intensities.

[29] In view of this, Habib Touma's notion that the qaflah "puts the listener in a state of tension, for he does not know what is going to happen" (1976: 35), does not fully explain the role of the qaflah as an emotive device.

They are chosen selectively and are often blended with other strictly-speaking non-ṭarab musical elements. Ultimately, the practical applications are guided by the artists' creative instincts and by the social and physical dynamics surrounding the individual musical events. The compositional renditions may, for example, reflect the various modalities of listening among the audience members. Conceived somewhat arbitrarily, the two extremes of focused listening (for example of the sammīʿah) and ordinary listening (for example of the general public), tend to correspond to the following contrastive musical tendencies respectively:

- the inclusion of purely instrumental music vs. preference for singing;
- frequent occurrence of solo performing vs. emphasis on ensemble music;
- interest in improvisation vs. predominence of precomposition;
- the inclusion of nonmetric genres vs. prevalence of metric music;
- frequent appearance of salṭanah vs. often performing without salṭanah;
- attention to modal consistency vs. modal inconsistency;
- appreciation for music's subtle features vs. excitation through metric drive, raised volume, and percussiveness;
- verbal sparsity vs. verbal density;
- flexible and novel interpretations vs. songs that everybody knows;
- pieces from the older (qadīm) repertoire vs. recent popular compositions;
- through-composed structures vs. predominance of strophic songs;
- abstract amorous lyrics vs. textual realism through factual references;
- the introduction of unusual maqāmāt and modulations vs. adherence to the more familiar modes;
- the inclusion of complex, or more "intellectual" īqāʿāt vs. emphasis on short dance meters;
- special interest in the qaflāt, particularly the subtle but effective ones vs. responsiveness to the more "flashy" cadences;
- pieces for listening vs. pieces for dancing;
- gradual and organically structured progressions from one genre to another vs. variety shows;
- focus on the music vs. reliance upon various extra-musical stimuli, food, drinking, and visual effects;
- pieces that require judicious listening vs. excitational, or "signal," pieces;

- material that the artists feel inspired to perform vs. pieces that the audience members request;
- and so on.

Needless to say, a vast number of gradations can exist between such extremes. Furthermore, the various patterns are not always predictable or clear cut. Depending upon their momentary musical moods and the particular listening circumstances, the same individuals may alternate between musical and behavioral orientations that are remarkably different.

Ṭarab evocation certainly goes beyond the implementation of standard musical "recipes." Its modus operandi are complex and largely intuitive, keeping in mind that the musical idiom allows for considerable freedom and flexibility, as well as embraces various implicit and explicit rules. Indeed, affective music-making relies a great deal upon the talent and sensitivity of the individual artists. In this light, we can understand the challenges and rewards of performing and listening to ṭarab music and sense the differing levels of competence among the various ṭarab practitioners. We may accordingly appreciate the genius of ʿAbduh al-Ḥāmūlī, Umm Kulthūm, Riyāḍ al-Sunbāṭī, Ṣabāḥ Fakhrī, Wadīʿ al-Ṣāfī, and many others whose mastery of the music has made them veritable cultural icons.

A global perspective

These various findings may not all be unique to ṭarab music. For one thing, the material investigated has close historical and stylistic ties to the modally based musical legacies of neighboring North Africa, Turkey, and Iran. Also, in less direct ways it can be related to the musical practices of more distant areas, for example in Asia and Europe. Similarly, we may wonder if ecstatic transformation as such is not shared by musical cultures worldwide. Clearly such phenomena as "the flow of music," (Csikszentmihalyi 1990: 108–113) and "the dissolution of one's personal self into the fabric of tone and timbre" (Becker 1983: 75), can be applied to a wide array of musical traditions, whether West African drumming, Viennese opera, or Javanese gamelan. It is clear, however, that ṭarab music's internal design and the ways in which that design translates emotionally in the minds of trained ṭarab listeners and practitioners grant the music both individuality and local relevance. This prompts us to ask, as Clifford Geertz does, whether the locus of interest for students of human culture lies simply in those phenomena that seem universally obvious and predictably consistent or in the diverse manifestations that in their totality appear distinctly human. We may similarly realize that the two realms cannot but imply one another.[30]

[30] Geertz 1973: 41–43.

With this in mind, we can speak of ṭarab music's humanness in terms of its specialness.

Likewise, the individuality of a musical culture cannot be fully understood without reference to that culture's relationship to the rest of the musical world. Since the Middle Ages, the Arab Near-East has influenced numerous musical traditions in Europe, Africa, and Asia and in turn assimilated a vast number of musical ingredients, particularly from the modern West. In the twentieth century, a period characterized by growing Western consciousness, ṭarab emerged as an urban musical mainstream, a pan-cultural idiom that came to represent the indigenous musical character of the region. Its status as such gave it tremendous vitality but also made it vulnerable. Arab modernists whose views favored the West and its cultural institutions expressed ambivalence, and at times outright hostility toward the local music and its ecstatic connotations. In some cases, the traditional genres and the related mannerisms of performing and listening were stigmatized as products of an outdated and less progressive social order.

Popularized through the mass media, ṭarab music also became a prime arena for East–West negotiations, or more specifically, a matrix for modernist musical experimentation. In Egypt, Sayyid Darwīsh's theatrical and folkloristic compositions and Muḥammad ʿAbd al-Wahhāb's eclecticism, manifested for example in the grafting of "Arabized" melodic motifs from Beethoven, Rossini, Rimsky-Korsakov, and others into traditionally based compositional structures, are among the prominent illustrations. Further, in the late 1960s, Cairo witnessed the rise of a large, typically government-sponsored, type of ensemble that presented traditional Arab music in formal and highly standardized renditions. Widely emulated, the emerging ensemble-type featured a mixed chorus of some twenty or more men and women accompanied by a similarly sizable group of conventional Arab instruments. The new format essentially eliminated solo in favor of monophonic choral singing and did away with all improvisation, thus presenting the various pieces as fixed compositions. Western notation was used for conducting and the instrumental accompaniment. The performances took place in concert halls under the baton of the conductor, who controlled the tempo and dynamics throughout the musical performance. Printed programs were distributed and faithfully followed. Also, as Salwa El-Shawan notes, applause had to take place only after the pieces had ended, and audience responses voiced during the performance proper were strictly forbidden.[31]

[31] See El-Shawan 1984: 276–281. In this context, of interest is Sayyid Makkāwī's admonition that "in order to be saved from distortion (*taḥrīf*), the old heritage must not be sung chorally" (from the 1994 interview).

Meanwhile, increasingly transformed and internally varied, the musical mainstream had to vie with more recent and more novel-sounding musical expressions. One example was a Lebanese urban popular style which, pioneered in the late 1950s by the Raḥbānī Brothers and associated with the celebrated female vocalist Fayrūz, derived elements from the local folk repertoire, Western music, and traditional Arab music. Similarly, in the last few decades the urban musical domain witnessed the growing influence of a variety of regionally based styles, notably those coming from the Arabian Peninsula, including the Arab Gulf states.

Today, Arab music in general displays a combination of traditional, modern, and postmodern traits. To begin with, the musical experience is becoming increasingly mediated. Satellite broadcasting and electronic communication are widening the scope of contact between the Arab world and other neighboring popular cultures, particularly in the West. The familiar geographical and political delineations appear more blurred while the various urban and rural areas seem to be merging into one large continuum. Moreover, while the familiar modernist rhetoric continues to predominate particularly within official circles, the worldviews of a vast number of young music makers and consumers are becoming well-attuned to the so-called global pop culture. Also, since the mid-1980s, the urban musical arena has been dominated by a new broadly based style that borrows from the prevalent Arab folk-dance music and the recent popular musics of the West, including the United States. Giving prominence to electronic instruments and favoring constant rhythmic drive, the current popular mainstream incorporates a major audio-visual component, namely the widely disseminated and often elaborately produced music video, or "video-clip."

In the early twenty-first century, the culture and artistry of ṭarab would appear to have lost a great deal of vitality. Some say that ṭarab has declined since the deaths of its major proponents, Umm Kulthūm, al-Sunbāṭī, al-Aṭrash, and others. Certainly, this is the impression one gets when visiting some of the Arab world's fast changing cities today. As the director of an Arab music ensemble explains, the musical heritage is striving to find a place for itself amidst two powerful and largely unsympathetic domains: the conservatory-based Western classical music, which is government supported; and the new popular music, which is sustained by a large market economy.[32]

However, ṭarab endures in one form or another. It appears to do so through a dual pattern of adapting to current social and technological realities on the one hand, and keeping a rather discreet profile on the other. Accessible to ṭarab afficionados through the various media networks, the music tends to occupy a less conspicuous niche, the type of peripheral space

[32] From a conversation in September 1999.

usually filled by the world's more specialized musics. Its new position appears to give it a certain protection against the systemic patterns of westernization that had dominated the broader mainstream style. Moreover, the very essence of the musical expression, ideally represented by the improvised modal recitation, remains firmly anchored in the Islamic devotional practice and is guarded by the practice-related doctrines. It has been said that the art of Qur'anic chanting and the various related expressions will continue to nourish and preserve the modal tradition, and even the entire Arab musical heritage.[33]

Ṭarab music is capturing the interest of many young listeners.[34] It also continues to engage serious performers and music aficionados in the Arab world and abroad. Public performances by such artists as Wadīʿ al-Ṣāfī and Ṣabāḥ Fakhrī attract large audiences of various nationalities and cultural backgrounds. As the ṭarab public becomes more globalized, reissues of twentieth-century recordings by major Arab artists Umm Kulthūm, Farīd al-Aṭrash, and others are listened to in Paris, New York, and Los Angeles, as well as in Tunis, Riyadh, and Cairo.[35] Fans also obtain their recordings and exchange ṭarab related information directly through the internet. Simultaneously, Arab instrumentalists are experimenting with their native idiom and exploring its ecstatic potentials in broader world contexts. Traditional Arab genres are being studied and performed by students in Europe and North America.[36] At a major music conservatory in the United States, instruction in Near Eastern and other world musics has been described as a sign of the

[33] It is frequently noted, for example, that the well-known Egyptian Jewish composer Dāwūd Ḥusnī (1870–1937) said: "As long as there is the Qur'ān, Arab music will always live" (quoted in Danielson 1997: 26). Also, the renowned violinist Sāmī al-Shawwā (1887–1965), a Christian, had reportedly "viewed the *tawāshīḥ* and religious *qaṣāʾid* as exemplars of traditional Egyptian music, part of the culture shared by all Egyptians" (Ibid.: 26). These reports are based on earlier sources, including Fu'ād 1976: 399. Similarly, Muḥammad ʿAbd al-Wahhāb explained that the Qur'ān is the Arab singers' fundamental source of inspiration, for example in terms of correct delivery, and the *khushūʿ*, or "profound reverence," which leads to iḥsās, or "feeling" (see "Muḥammad ʿAbd al-Wahhāb li-al-Ḥawādith: . . ." 1986: 75–76).

[34] In a 1997 study based on interviews with 200 young male and female listeners from Lebanon, Saudi Arabia, Egypt, Morocco, and Syria, Frédéric Maʿtūq, a Lebanese sociologist, described the following trends: the open boundaries between the Arab youth and popular Western culture; common preferences for certain regional Arab musics; the wide popularity of lyrics in Lebanese and Egyptian colloquial Arabic; and significantly, the continued popularity of some ṭarab singers, even those who are now deceased. See Maʿtūq 1997.

[35] Today, recordings by major ṭarab artists can be purchased at major record stores in the West as well as in the Arab world. Furthermore, in recent years, reissues of old Egyptian 78-rpm records, some from pre-World-War-I years, have been offered on a CD series by Club du Disque Arabe in France with the general title "Les Archives de la Musique Arabe." The material is selected and documented by Frédéric Lagrange. Renditions of early takht-music have also been offered by Nidaa Abou Mrad (a Lebanese violinist) and his ensemble, usually recorded under the general title "Musique de la Nahda; Renaissance Arabe du XXe Siècle."

[36] I have directed an ensemble of traditional Arab instruments at the University of California at Los Angeles regularly since 1978.

institution's courage "to imagine itself as a part of a future culture in which Beethoven might actually thrive as one voice among many."[37] Similarly, at a time when retaining a sense of one's own individuality is found desirable in the face of overriding worldwide cultural and artistic homogenization, indigenous music is being reclaimed and in some cases systematically promoted through government-sponsored tours, conservatory student and staff performances, and special radio and television programs.

From one perspective, the music of ṭarab seems curtailed and marginalized. From another, it appears well-rooted, timeless, and increasingly internationalized. Together, these perspectives remind us of music's vulnerability and resilience as a human expression. Obviously, the future of ṭarab will depend on how the coming generations will experience and value its message.

[37] From personal correspondence with Robert R. Labaree in reference to the New England Conservatory of Music. A performer and instructor himself, Dr. Labaree directs the Conservatory's Summer Intercultural Institute, which offers these various courses. I am grateful to him for allowing me to include the quote above.

Glossary

This list consists of terms that are typical of the ṭarab milieu. The definitions mainly reflect the ways in which the terms are applied by the musicians and the listeners.

ādāb (singular, *adab*): codified rules of conduct pertaining to members of various professions, including musicians.

āhāt (singular, *āh*): vocalizations on the syllable "āh" by the soloist with responses by the chorus within the dawr.

ālāt al-ṭarab: musical instruments, especially ṭarab instruments.

arāḍī (from *arḍ*, or ground): the low register or low notes, for example, of a vocal composition.

arḍiyyah (literally, ground or base): low-pitched ostinato pattern, for example, in the Sufi dhikr performance.

'azf: a formal term that means playing on an instrument.

'āzif: performer on an instrument, or instrumentalist.

bashraf (from the Ottoman-Turkish *peşrev*): a precomposed instrumental genre that is metric and follows a rondo-like structure.

basṭ: a state of elation or mood of merriment.

brova: a rehearsal or preparatory musical session.

buzuq: a long-necked, fretted lute with metal strings.

dawr: a mostly precomposed vocal genre that uses colloquial Arabic text, prevalent in Egypt primarily during the late nineteenth and early twentieth centuries.

dhikr (literally, remembrance or reiteration): a term for the Sufi ritual, also more specifically for the practice of repeating certain religious verbal phrases.

dūlāb: a short, precomposed, instrumental prelude traditionally used for establishing the mood, or "feeling" of the *maqām*.

dūzān: the way an instrument is tuned or the process of tuning, also referred to as *taṣlīḥ* (fixing) or *taḍḥbīṭ* (adjusting).

fann (literally, art): *ṭarab* music in general, especially as a professional domain.

fannān (from *fann*, or art): a man who pursues ṭarab artistry, usually as a profession.

fannānah (from *fann*, or art): a woman who pursues ṭarab artistry, usually as a profession.

fāṣil: a medley of pieces that normally share the same maqam and consist of *muwashshaḥāt* and other genres. It is generally associated with Syrian music.

firqah: the relatively large urban ensemble typical of modern ṭarab music.

ḥaflah (literally, festive gathering): a large, usually public, musical event.

hank: a passage that appears within the *dawr* and consists of solo–chorus alternations.

hāwī: amateur, also known as *ghāwī*, both literally meaning, "infatuated" or "passionately in love."

iḥsās (also, *ḥiss*): feeling, or the ability to sense the music and perform it ecstatically, or with feeling.

insijām (roughly, harmoniousness): being in a musically agreeable, or ecstatic state.

īqāʿ (plural, *īqāʿāt*): metric mode or pattern, also referred to as *wazn* (plural, *azwān*) and *ḍarb* (plural, *ḍurūb*).

jalsah: a small informal gathering in which music may take place.

jawāb (literally, answer): a note an octave higher.

jawābāt (singular, *jawāb*): the high notes of a modal scale or composition, or on a musical instrument.

jaww: atmosphere, ambiance, or desirable mood for performing.

kabarēh (or cabaret): nightclub.

khānāt (singular, *khānah*): the variable sections that intervene between the *taslīm* repeats within a *bashraf* or *samāʿī*; also applies to the digressive musical section of a *muwashshaḥ*.

kalām (literally, speech): ṭarab lyrics, or texts, sometimes also called *nuṣūṣ*, singular, *naṣṣ*.

kamanjah (also known as *kamān*): in today's speech, the Western violin, which is used as a ṭarab instrument.

kayf: a mood of elation conducive to making ṭarab music or to becoming entertained by the music, also the elative state that the music produces.

laḥn: tune or melody.

lawn (literally, color): musical style or "flavor," also referring to a stylistically distinct segment within an eclectic piece of music.

layālī: vocalizations on the syllables *yā layl* and *yā ʿayn*, as a rule leading into a *mawwāl*.

lāzimah (plural, *lawāzim*): a short instrumental interlude or filler between vocal phrases.

maqām (plural, *maqāmāt*): melodic mode.

mawwāl: a vocal improvisation that uses a colloquial poetical text and is typically preceded by a *layālī* section.

mazāj (literally, disposition, or temperament): the mood of the performer or listener, also the emotional state that inspires a musician to perform well.

muḥāsabah: listening carefully and judiciously.

mundamij: being emotionally self-absorbed or drawn to the music.

munsajim: being in an ecstatically harmonious or musically agreeable state.

mūnūlūj (or monologue): a through-composed (nonstrophic) vocal genre of irregular structure and expressive lyrical content particularly popular in Egypt in the 1930s.

muṭrib: a male, typically professional, singer of ṭarab.

muṭribah: a female, typically professional, singer of ṭarab.

muwashshaḥ: a precomposed, metric vocal genre.

nafas (literally, breath): ability to feel ṭarab music and to perform it well, for example, in the expression *nafas Sharqī*, or "Eastern breath."

nashāz: bad intonation or being out of tune.

naghmah (plural, *anghām*): tune or melodic mode.

nāy: a type of reed-flute.

qudūd (singular, *qadd*): strophic songs that use colloquial Arabic texts and are associated with Aleppo, Syria.

qadīm (literally, old): earlier ṭarab music, usually from the late nineteenth and early twentieth centuries.

qaflah: a cadential pattern ending a musical phrase and usually followed by a pause.

qānūn: a type of plucked zither.

qarār (literally, repose, or conclusion): tonic, or final note.

qarārāt (plural of *qarār*): the low notes of a modal scale or composition, or on a musical instrument.

qaṣīdah (literally, poem): an often improvised vocal genre, both Sufi and secular, based on a poem in classical Arabic.

riqq: a small tambourine.

rubʿ (literally, quarter; plural, *arbāʿ*): the quarter-tone increment within the theoretical scale; also loosely refers to the basic microtonal steps, namely those flattened or sharpened by approximately a quarter-tone each.

rūḥ (literally, soul, or spirit): locally based ability to feel ṭarab music or to perform it affectively, as in the expression *rūḥ Sharqiyyah*, or "Eastern soul."

sahrah: an evening gathering during which music may be performed.

salṭanah a creative ecstatic state typically experienced by performers, and usually linked to the melodic modes.

samaʿ (literally, hearing): usually meaning to listen to music attentively.

samāʿ (literally, listening): in Sufi tradition, listening to spiritual music, also the musical performance itself or in a broader sense, the ritual performance as a whole.

samāʿī (from the Ottoman-Turkish *saz semai*): a precomposed instrumental genre that has a rondo-like structure and follows a specific ten-beat pattern, except for the last *khānah* before the final *taslīm*.

sammīʿ (plural, *sammīʿah*): a person who listens to ṭarab music attentively and reacts to it in idiomatically appropriate ways.

shughl (literally, work): performing music, usually professionally, or as "work."

ṭabaqah: pitch level, or tessitura.

ṭablah: an Arab goblet-shaped hand-drum.

taḥmīlah: a metric instrumental genre incorporating solo improvisations that alternate with refrain-like ensemble responses.

tajallī (roughly, revelation): a state of inspirational transformation typically felt by the performers.

takht (literally, platform): a small instrumental ensemble prevalent in the late nineteenth and early twentieth centuries. The term may also include the singer and the chorus.

talbīs (literally, to dress up or custom fit): the percussionist's deliberate repositioning of the beat so as to accommodate a metric idiosyncrasy within a composition, or to reestablish the metric track when a leading artist accidentally goes off beat.

taqāsīm: (plural of *taqsīm*): instrumental improvisation as a genre. The singular, *taqsīm* may similarly refer to the improvisatory genre or to a single improvisatory rendition, which is also known as *taqsīmah*.

ṭaqṭūqah: light strophic song in colloquial Arabic.

ṭarab: the traditional urban music, especially the *qādīm*, or older more ecstatically oriented repertoire; also the ecstatic feeling that the music produces.

tarannumāt (or *tarannum*): specific words and word combinations added to song lyrics, particularly in the *muwashshaḥāt*.

tarjamah (literally, translation): instrumental accompaniment that "echoes" or paraphrases a leading musical passage.

taṣarruf: the taking of certain liberties when interpreting precomposed musical works.

taṣdīr: making well-calculated and ecstatically effective departures from the beat pattern.

taslīm: the refrain-like passage within a *bashraf* or *samāʿī*.

taṣwīr (literally, drawing): transposition from one pitch level to another.

taṭrīb: engendering powerful ṭarab feeling, especially through the use of vocalizations and the stretching out of syllables.

tawrīq (from *waraq*, or leaf): accompanying in subtle ways, or merely providing ornate fillers.

tawshīḥ: a Sufi vocal genre usually of flexible metric quality and with alternations between florid vocal solos and choral responses.

turāth (literally, heritage): the traditional musical legacy, especially the *qadīm* repertoire.

ʿūd: a non-fretted short-necked lute.

ughniyah (literally, song): the generic term for song, especially in post-World-War-II decades.

ʿurab (singular, *ʿurbah*): roughly, very small intervallic increments or microtonal inflections; also the tuning levers on the *qānūn*.

ustādh: a common title of respect used for addressing knowledgeable musicians, music teachers, and learned men in general.

waḥdah (literally, unit or one): a generic word for "beat pattern" or more specifically, a single-down-beat meter of a certain length.

waḥdajī: a musician with an excellent sense of rhythm.

waṣlah: a traditional medley with generic components that share the same melodic mode, typical of late-nineteenth- and early-twentieth-century Cairo.

References

ʿAbd al-Majīd, Aḥmad. 1970. *Li-Kull Ughniyah Qiṣṣah*. Cairo: Maktabat al-Anjlū al-Miṣriyyah.

Abu-Lughod, Lila. 1986. *Veiled Sentiments: Honor and Poetry in a Bedouin Society*. Berkeley: University of California Press.

ʿAjjān, Maḥmūd. 1990. *Turathunā al-Mūsīqī*. Damascus: Ṭalās li-al-Dirāsāt wa-al-Tarjamah wa-al-Nashr.

Andrews, Walter G. 1985. *Poetry's Voice, Society's Song: Ottoman Lyric Poetry*. Seattle: University of Washington Press.

Angeles, Peter A. 1981. *Dictionary of Philosophy*. New York: Barnes & Noble Books.

Anīs, Ibrāhīm. n.d. *Mūsīqá al-Shiʿr*. Cairo: Dār al-Fikrah li-al-Ṭabʿ wa-al-Nashr.

Anonymous. 1969. "The Effects of Marijuana on Consciousness." In *Altered States of Consciousness*, ed. by Charles Tart, 343–364. Garden City, NY: Doubleday & Company Inc.

Archer, William Kay. 1964. "On Arabitude and Some Aspects of Its Position in Musical Influence: A Preliminary Conspectus," (unpublished paper to appear in the *Proceedings of the Conference on Arabic Music and its Relations with Eastern and Western Forms of Music*.). Baghdad: Ministry of Culture and National Guidance.

Asad, Muhammad. 1954. *The Road to Mecca*. New York: Simon and Schuster.

ʿĀshūr, Aḥmad. collector, AH. 1340. *Sulṭān al-Aghānī wa-al-Ṭarab*. Cairo: Muḥammad Abū al-Dhahab al-Kutubī.

ʿAṭiyyay, Muḥammad ʿAlī, collector, n.d. *Maghānī al-Jins al-Laṭīf*. Cairo: al-Maktabah al-Miṣriyyah.

Azzam, Nabil Salim. 1990. "Muḥammad ʿAbd al-Wahhāb in Modern Egyptian Music." Ph.D. diss., University of California, Los Angeles.

al-Baʿalbakī, Rūḥī. 1992. *al-Mawrid: Qāmūs ʿArabī-Inkilīzī*. Beirut: Dār al-ʿIlm li-al-Malāyīn.

Baer, Gabriel. 1964. *Egyptian Guilds in Modern Times*. Jerusalem: The Israel Oriental Society.

al-Baqlī, Muḥammad Qandīl, collector, 1984. *Al-Ṭarab fī al-ʿAṣr al-Mamlūkī: al-Ghināʾ, al-Raqṣ, al-Mūsīqá*. Cairo: al-Hayʾah al-Miṣriyyah al-ʿĀmmah li-al-Kitāb.

Bauman, Richard. 1986. *Story, Performance, and Event: Contextual Studies of Oral Narratives*. Cambridge: Cambridge University Press.

Becker, Judith. 1983. "'Aesthetics' in Late 20th Century Scholarship." *The World of Music* 25(3): 65–77.

Bell, Catherine. 1977. *Ritual: Perspectives and Dimensions*. New York: Oxford University Press.

Berque, Jacques. 1964. *The Arabs: Their History and Future*. London: Faber and Faber.

Besmer, Fremont E. 1983. *Horses, Musicians, & Gods: The Hausa Cult of Possession-Trance.* Zaria, Nigeria: Ahmadu Bello University Press.
Bin Dhurayl, ʿAdnān. 1969. *al- Mūsīqá fī Sūriyyah.* Damascus: Maṭābiʿ Alif Bāʾ.
Bin al-Khaṭīb, Muḥammad. 1980. "Maḥmūd Ṣubḥ Kamā ʿAraftuhu: Aw Kamā Yajib an Yuʿraf." In *Maḥmūd Ṣubḥ: Ḥayātuhu wa Mūsīqāh*, by Muḥammad Maḥmūd Ṣubḥ. 70–73. Cairo: al-Hayʾah al-Miṣriyyah li-al-Kitāb.
Blacking, John. 1968. "Percussion and Transition." *Man* 3(2): 313–314.
——. 1973. *How Musical Is Man?* Seattle: University of Washington Press.
——. 1980. "The Context of Venda Possession Music: Reflections on the Effectiveness of Symbols." *Yearbook for Traditional Music* 17: 64–87.
Bourdieu, Pierre. 1990. *The Logic of Practice.* Stanford, CA: Stanford University Press.
Bourguignon, Erika. 1976. *Possession.* San Francisco: Chandler & Sharp Publishers, Inc.
Budd, Malcolm. 1985. *Music and the Emotions: The Philosophical Theories.* London: Routledge & Kegan Paul.
al-Būlāqī, Maḥmūd, collector, 1927. *al-Mughannī al-Miṣrī.* Cairo: Maṭbaʿat al-Shabāb.
al-Bustānī, Buṭrus. 1869. *Kitāb Qaṭr al-Muḥīṭ.* Beirut: Maktabat Lubnān.
Buṭrus, Fikrī. 1967. *Al-Mawsūʿah al-Fanniyyah li-Aʿlām al-Mūsīqá wa-al-Ghināʾ al-ʿArabī*, Vol. 1. Alexandria, Egypt: n.p.
Cachia, Pierre. 1973. "A 19th Century Arab's Observations on European Music." *Ethnomusicology* 17(1): 4–51.
Carlson, Marvin. 1996. *Performance: A Critical Introduction.* London: Routledge.
Chaplin, J.P. 1968. *Dictionary of Psychology,* Revised Edition. New York: Dell Publishing Co.
Crapanzano, Vincent. 1973. *The Hamdsha: A Study in Moroccan Ethnopsychiatry.* Berkeley: University of California Press.
Csikszentmihalyi, Mihaly. 1990. *Flow: The Psychology of Optimal Experience.* New York: Harper & Row.
Danielson, Virginia. 1991a. "Artists and Entrepreneurs: Female Singers in Cairo during the 1920s." In *Women in Middle Eastern History: Shifting Boundaries in Sex and Gender*, ed. by Nikki R. Keddie and Beth Baron, 292–309. New Haven, CT: Yale University Press.
——. 1991b. "Shaping Tradition in Arabic Song: The Career and Repertory of Umm Kulthūm." Ph.D. diss., University of Illinois.
——. 1997. *The Voice of Egypt: Umm Kulthūm, Arabic Song, and Egyptian Society in the Twentieth Century.* Chicago: The University of Chicago Press.
al-Darwīsh, Nadīm, collector. 1955. *Min Kunūzinā: al-Muwashshaḥāt al-Andalusiyyah.* Aleppo, Syria: Maṭbaʿat al-Sharq.
Davies, Stephen. 1994. *Musical Meaning and Expression.* Ithaca, NY: Cornell University Press.
DjeDje, Jacqueline Cogdell. 1984. "Song Type and Performance Style in Hausa and Dagomba Possession (Bori) Music." *Black Perspective in Music* 12(2): 167–182.
Doniach, N.S., ed. 1982. *The Concise Oxford English-Arabic Dictionary.* Oxford: Oxford University Press.
During, Jean. 1988. *Musique et Extase: l'Audition Mystique dans la Tradition Soufie.* Paris: Albin Michel.
Ebers, Georg Moritz. 1879. *Egypt: Descriptive, Historical, and Picturesque*, Vol. 2. New York: Cassell.

Elkholy, Samha. 1978. *The Tradition of Improvisation in Arab Music*. Giza, Egypt: Imprimerie Rizk.

El-Shawan Castelo-Branco, Salwa. 1984. "Traditional Arab Music Ensembles in Egypt Since 1967: The Continuity of Tradition within a Contemporary Framework." *Ethnomusicology* 28(2): 271–288.

——. 1987. "Some Aspects of the Cassette Industry in Egypt." *The World of Music* 29(2): 32–45.

Erlmann, Veit. 1982. "Trance and Music in the Hausa Bòorii Spirit Possession Cult in Niger." *Ethnomusicology* 26(1): 49–58.

Ernst, Carl W. 1985. *Words of Ecstasy in Sufism*. Albany, NY: State University of New York Press.

Fahmī, Amīn. n.d. *Shaykh al-Mulaḥḥinīn: Zakariyyā Aḥmad*. Cairo: Dār al-Khashshāb li-al-Ṭabʿ wa-al-Tajlīd.

Farmer, Henry George. 1929/1973. *A History of Arabian Music to the XIIIth Century*. London: Luzac & Co. Ltd.

——. 1943. *Saʿadyah Gaon on the Influence of Music*. London: Arthur Probsthain.

Feld, Steven. 1988. "Aesthetics as Iconicity of Style, or 'Lift-up-over Sounding:' Getting into the Kaluli Groove." *Yearbook for Traditional Music* 20: 74–113.

Fernea, Elizabeth W. and Basima Q. Bezirgan. 1976. *Middle Eastern Muslim Women Speak*. Austin: University of Texas Press.

Friedrich, Paul. 1979. *Language, Context, and Imagination: Essays by Paul Friedrich, Selected and Introduced by Anwar S. Dil*. Stanford, CA: Stanford University Press.

——. 1986. *The Language Parallax; Linguistic Relativism and Poetic Indeterminacy*. Austin: University of Texas Press.

Fuʾād, Niʿmāt Aḥmad. 1973. *Aḥmad Rāmī: Qiṣṣat Shāʿir wa-Ughniyah*. Cairo: Dār al-Maʿārif bi-Miṣr.

——. 1976. *Umm Kulthūm: Wa ʿAṣrun min al-Fann*. Cairo: al-Hayʾah al-Miṣriyyah al-ʿĀmmah li-al-Kitāb.

Furguson, John. 1976. "Ecstasy." In *Encyclopaedia of Mysticism and the Mystery Religions*, by John Furguson, 51. London: Thames and Hudson.

García Lorca, Federico. 1955. *Poet in New York*. New York: Grove Press.

Geertz, Clifford. 1973. *The Interpretation of Cultures*. New York: Basic Books, Inc.

——. 1985. *Local Knowledge*. New York: Basic Books Inc.

al-Ghazālī, Abū Ḥāmid. n.d. *Iḥyāʾ ʿUlūm al-Dīn*, Vol. 2. Damascus: Maktabat ʿAbd al-Wakīl al-Durūbī.

Ghose, Sisirkumar. 1982. "Mysticism." In *The New Encyclopedia Britannica* Vol. 12. 786–793. Chicago: Encyclopedia Britannica, Inc.

Gibb, H.A.R. and J.H. Kramers, editors. 1974. "Shaṭḥ." In *Shorter Encyclopedia of Islam*, 533. Leiden: E.J. Brill.

Giffen, Lois A. 1971. *Theory of Profane Love among the Arabs: The Development of the Genre*. New York: New York University Press.

Gilsenan, Michael. 1973. *Saint and Sufi in Modern Egypt: An Essay in the Sociology of Religion*. Oxford: Clarendon Press.

Godwin, Joscelyn, ed. 1987. *Music, Mysticism and Magic: A Sourcebook*. New York: Arkana.

Goleman, Daniel. 1995. *Emotional Intelligence*. New York: Bantam Books.

Goodman, Felicitas D. 1988. *Ecstasy, Ritual, and Alternative Reality*. Bloomington: Indiana University Press.

Ḥāfiḍh, Muḥammad Maḥmud Sāmī. 1971. *Tārīkh al-Mūsīqá wa-al-Ghinā' al-'Arabī*. Cairo: Maktabat al-Anjlū al-Miṣriyyah.
Ḥammād, Muḥammad 'Alī. 1970. *Sayyid Darwīsh: Ḥayāt wa Nagham*. Cairo: al-Hay'ah al-Miṣriyyah al-'Āmmah li al-Ta'līf wa-al-Nashr.
Herndon, Marcia and Norma McLeod. 1979. *Music as Culture*. Norwood, PA: Norwood Editions.
al-Ḥilū, Salīm. 1961. *al-Mūsīqá al-Naḍhariyyah*. Beirut: Dār Maktabat al-Ḥayāt.
——. 1965. *al-Muwashshaḥāt al-Andalusiyyah: Nash'atuhā wa Taṭawwuruhā*. Beirut: Dār Maktabat al-Ḥayāt.
Holst, Gail. 1975. *Road to Rembetika; Music of a Greek Sub-Culture; Songs of Love, Sorrow & Hashish*. Athens: Denise Harvey & Company.
Hourani, Albert. 1991. *A History of the Arab Peoples*. Cambridge, MA: The Belknap Press of Harvard University Press.
Ḥusayn, 'Alī Ṣāfī. 1964. *Al-Adab al-Ṣūfī fī Miṣr, fī al-Qarn al-Sābi' al-Hijrī*. Cairo: Dār al-Ma'ārif bi-Miṣr.
Huxley, Aldous. 1954. *The Doors of Perception*. New York: Harper and Row.
Ibn Manḍhūr. 1955. *Lisān al-'Arab*, Vol. 5. Beirut: Dār Ṣādir.
James, William. 1902/1929. *The Varieties of Religious Experiences: A Study in Human Nature*. New York: The Modern Library.
Jones, L. JaFran. 1987. "A Sociohistorical Perspective on Tunisian Women as Professional Musicians." In *Women and Music in Cross-Cultural Perspective*, ed. by Ellen Koskoff, 69–83. Urbana: University of Illinois Press.
Jourdain, Robert. 1997. *Music, the Brain, and Ecstasy*. New York: Avon Books, Inc.
al-Jundī, Adham. 1954. *A'lām al-Adab wa-al-Fann*. Damascus: Maṭba'at Majallat Ṣawt Sūriyyah.
al-Jundī, Aḥmad. 1984. *Ruwwād al-Nagham al-'Arabī*. Damascus: Ṭalās li-al-Dirāsāt wa-al-Tarjamah wa-al-Nashr.
al-Jurjānī, al-Sharīf 'Alī bin Muḥammad. 1983. *Kitāb al-Ta'rīfāt*. Beirut: Dār al-Kutub al-'Ilmiyyah.
Kāmil, Maḥmūd. 1971. *'Abduh al-Ḥāmūlī: Za'īm al-Ṭarab wa-al-Ghinā', 1841–1901*. Cairo: Muḥammad al-Amīn.
Kast, Verena. 1991. *Joy, Inspiration, and Hope*. College Station: Texas A & M Universtiy Press.
Keil, Charles. 1995. "The Theory of Participatory Discrepancies: A Progress Report." *Ethnomusicology* 39(1): 1–19.
Kepferer, Bruce. 1983. *A Celebration of Demons: Exorcism and the Aesthetics of Healing in Sri Lanka*. Bloomington: Indiana University Press.
Khalifa, Ahmad M. 1975. "Traditional Patterns of Hashish Use in Egypt." In *Cannabis and Culture*, ed. by Vera Rubin, 195–205. The Hague: Mouton & Co.
Khan, Sufi Inayat. 1988. *Music*. Claremont, CA: Hunter House Inc.
Khashabah, Ghaṭṭās 'Abd al-Malik, ed. 1984. *Kitāb al-Malāhī wa Asmā'ihā, Ta'līf al-Mufaḍḍal Bin Salmah al-Naḥawī – Mūjaz fī al-Lahū wa-al-Malāhī min Riwāyat Ibn Khurdādhbih*. Cairo: al-Hay'ah al-Miṣriyyah al-'Āmmah li-al-Kitāb.
al-Khula'ī, Kāmil. ca. 1904. *Kitāb al-Mūsīqá al-Sharqī* (AH 1322). Cairo: Maṭba'at al-Taqaddum.
Kitāb Mu'tamar al-Mūsīqá al-'Arabiyyah. 1933. Cairo: al-Maṭba'ah al-Amīriyyah.
Kivy, Peter. 1989. *Sound Sentiment: An Essay on the Musical Emotions*. Philadelphia: Temple University Press.
Koskoff, Ellen. 1987. "An Introduction to Women, Music, and Culture." In *Women*

and Music in Cross Cultural Perspective, ed. by Ellen Koskoff, 1–23. Urbana, IL: University of Illinois Press.

Kramers, J.H. 1987. "Sulṭān." In *E.J. Brill's First Encyclopaedia of Islam 1913–1936*, Vol. 7, ed. by M. Th. Houtsma et al., 543–545.

Lagrange, Frédéric. 1996. *Musiques d'Égypte*. Paris: Cité de la Musique/Actes Sud.

Lane, Edward W. 1860/1973. *An Account of The Manners and Customs of the Modern Egyptians*. New York: Dover Publications, Inc.

——. 1863/1984. *Arabic–English Lexicon*, Vol. 1 and Vol. 2. Cambridge, England: The Islamic Texts Society.

Langer, Susanne K. 1942/1979. *Philosophy in a New Key*, 3rd edition. Cambridge, MA: Harvard University Press.

——. 1953. *Feeling and Form: A Theory of Art*. New York: Charles Scribner's Sons.

Laughlin, Charles D. et al. 1979. "Introduction." In *The Spectrum of Ritual: A Biogenetic Structural Analysis*, ed. by Eugene G. d'Aquili et al. 1–116. New York: Columbia University Press.

"The Legacy of Muhammad Asad." In *Threshold: A Journal of Sufism*. n.d. 18–19. Brattleboro, VT: Threshold Books.

Lévi-Strauss, Claude. 1979. "The Effectiveness of Symbols." In *Reader in Comparative Religion: An Anthropological Approach*, 4th edition, ed. by William A. Lessa and Evon Z. Vogt, 318–327. New York: Harper and Row.

Lewis, I.M. 1971/1989. *Ecstatic Religion: A Study of Shamanism and Spirit Possession*, 2nd edition. London: Routledge.

Lex, Barbara. 1979. "The Neurobiology of Ritual Trance." In *The Spectrum of Ritual: A Biogenetic Structural Analysis*, ed. by Eugene G. d'Aquili et al. 117–151. New York: Columbia University Press.

Lomax, Alan. 1968. *Folk Song Style and Culture*. New Brunswick, New Jersey: Transaction Books.

Ludwig, Arnold M. 1969. "Altered States of Consciousness." In *Altered States of Consciousness*, ed. by Charles Tart, 11–24. Garden City, NY: Doubleday & Co., Inc.

al-Maghrabī, Saʿd. 1963. *Ḍhāhirat Taʿāṭī al-Ḥashīsh: Dirāsah Nafsiyyah Ijtimāʿiyyah*. Cairo: Dār al-Maʿārif bi-Miṣr.

Maḥfūḍh, Fuʾād. 1963. *Taʿlīm Ālat al-ʿŪd, 3*. Damascus: Maṭbaʿat al-Thabāt.

——. 1964. *Taʿlīm Ālat al-ʿŪd, 4*. Damascus: Maṭbaʿat al-Thabāt.

Maḥfūḍh, Ḥusayn ʿAlī. 1977. *Qāmus al-Mūsīqá al-ʿArabiyyah*. Baghdad: Dār al-Ḥurriyyah li-al-Ṭibāʿah.

Mansī, Aḥmad Abū al-Khiḍr. 1965/1966. *Al-Aghānī wa-al-Mūsīqá al-Sharqiyyah: Bayna al-Qadīm wa-al-Jadīd*. Cairo: Dār al-ʿArab li-al-Bustānī.

Marcus, Scott L. 1992. "Modulation in Arab Music: Documenting Oral Concepts, Performance Rules and Strategies." *Ethnomusicology* 36(2): 171–195.

al-Maṣrī, Khalīl and Maḥmūd Kāmil, collectors, n.d. *Kawkab al-Sharq Umm Kulthūm: al-Nuṣūṣ al-Kāmilah li-Jamīʿ al-Aghānī*. Cairo: al-Lajnah al-Mūsīqiyyah al-ʿUlyā.

Maʿtūq, Frédéric. 1997. "al-Shabāb al-ʿArabī wa-al-Mūsīqá wa-al-Ghināʾ." *Al-Ḥayāt* (12688): 20; (12689): 20; (12690); (12691): 20.

al-Maṭwī, Muḥammad al-Hādī. 1989. *Aḥmad Fāris al-Shidyāq 1801–1887*, Vol. 2. Beirut: Dār al-Gharb al-Islamī.

Meyer, Leonard B. 1956. *Emotion and Meaning in Music*. Chicago: University of Chicago Press.

Milson, Menahem, ed. 1975. *A Sufi Rule for Novices: Kitāb Adāb al-Murīdīn of Abū al-Najīb al-Suhrawardī*. Cambridge, MA: Harvard University Press.

Mīnah, Ḥannā. 1978. *al-Shams fī Yawm Ghā'im*. Damascus: Dār al-Ādāb.

Miṭrān, Khalīl. 1938. "Awwal ʿAhdī bi -ʿAbduh al-Ḥāmūlī." In *al-Mūsīqá al-Sharqiyyah*, Vol. 2. ed. by Qisṭandī Rizq, 133–135. Cairo: al-Maṭbaʿah al-Aṣriyyah.

Moore, Sally F. and Barbara G. Myerhoff, eds. 1977. *Secular Ritual*. Amsterdam: Van Gorcum and Comp.

Morris, Roderick Conway. 1981. "Greek Café Music." *Recorded Sound: Journal of the British Institute of Recorded Sound* 80: 79–90.

"Muḥammad ʿAbd al-Wahhāb li-al-Ḥawādith: al-Fann al-ʿArabī bazagha min . . . al-Masjid." 1986. *al-Ḥawādith*. (1558), 12 September: 75–77.

Munawwar, Hiyām. 1989. "Shakhṣiyyāt: Riyāḍ al-Bandak Yuḥaqqiq Maʿjizat al-ʿUmr." *Fann* (12) October: 70–73.

Myerhoff, Barbara G. 1975. "Peyote and Huichol Worldview: The Structure of a Mystic Vision." In *Cannabis and Culture*, ed. by Vera Rubin, 417–438. The Hague: Mouton Publishers.

al-Najmī, Kamāl. 1970. *Muṭribūn wa-Mustamiʿūn*. Cairo: Dār al-Hilāl.

——. 1972. *Siḥr al-Ghināʾ al-ʿArabī*. Cairo: Dār al-Hilāl.

Nasr, Seyyed Hossein. 1987. *Islamic Art and Spirituality*. Albany, NY: State University of New York Press.

Needham, Rodney. 1967/1979. "Percussion and Transition." In *Reader in Comparative Religion*: 4th Edition, ed. by William A. Lessa and Evon Z. Vogt, 311–317. New York: Harper & Row.

Neher, Andrew. 1962. "A Physiological Explanation of Unusual Behavior in Ceremonies Involving Drums." *Human Biology* 4: 151–160.

Nelson, Kristina. 1982. "Reciter and Listener: Some Factors Shaping the Mujawwad Style of Qurʾanic Reciting." *Ethnomusicology* 26(1): 41–47.

——. 1985. *The Art of Reciting the Qurʾān*. Austin: University of Texas Press.

Nettl, Bruno. 1974. "Thoughts on Improvisation: A Comparative Approach." *The Musical Quarterly* 60(1): 1–19.

Nettl, Bruno and Ronald Riddle. 1973. "Taqsim Nahawand: A Study of Sixteen Performances by Jihad Racy." *Yearbook of the International Folk Music Council* 5: 11–50.

Newcomb, Anthony. 1984. "Sound and Feeling." *Critical Inquiry* 10(4): 614–642.

Nicholson, Reynold A. 1921. *Studies in Islamic Mysiticism*. Cambridge: Cambridge University Press.

Nieuwkerk, Karin van. 1995. *A Trade Like Any Other?: Female Singers and Dancers in Egypt*. Austin: University of Texas Press.

Nketia, J.H. Kwabena. 1981. "The Juncture of the Social and the Musical: The Methodology of Cultural Analysis." *The World of Music* 23(2): 27–35.

Nurbakhsh, Javad. 1978. *In the Tavern of Ruin: Seven Essays on Sufism*. New York: Khaniqahi-Nimatullahi Publications.

Phillips, Miriam. 1987. "Where the Spirit Roams: Toward an Understanding of 'Duende' in Two Flamenco Dance Contexts." *UCLA Journal of Dance Ethnology* 11: 45–63.

Prögler, J.A. 1995. "Searching for Swing: Participatory Discrepancies in the Jazz Rhythm Section." *Ethnomusicology* 39(1): 21–54.

Qūjamān, Y. 1978. *Al-Mūsīqá al-Fanniyyah al-Muʿāṣirah fī al-ʿIrāq*. London: ACT Arabic Translation.

Racy, Ali Jihad. 1976. "Record Industry and Egyptian Traditional Music: 1904–1932." *Ethnomusicology* 20(1): 23–48.
——. 1977. "Musical Change and Commercial Recording in Egypt, 1904–1932." Ph.D. diss., University of Illinois.
——. 1980. "Waṣlah Ghināʾiyyah." *Ethnomusicology* 24(3): 603–607.
——. 1981. "Music in Contemporary Cairo: A Comparative Overview." *Asian Music* 13(1): 4–26.
——. 1983a. "Music in Nineteenth-Century Egypt: An Historical Sketch." *Selected Reports in Ethnomusicology* 4: 157–179.
——. 1983b. "The Waṣlah: A Compound-Form Principle in Egyptian Music." *Arab Studies Quarterly* 5(4): 396–403.
——. 1986. "Words and Music in Beirut: a Study of Attitudes." *Ethnomusicology* 30(3): 413–427.
——. 1988. "Sound and Society: The Takht Music of Early Twentieth-Century Cairo." *Selected Reports in Ethnomusicology; Issues in the Conceptualization of Music* 7: 139–170.
——. 1991a. "Historical Worldviews of Early Ethnomusicologists: An East–West Encounter in Cairo, 1932." In *Ethnomusicology and Modern Music History*, ed. by Stephen Blum et al., 68–91. Urbana, IL: University of Illinois Press.
——. 1991b. "Creativity and Ambience: An Ecstatic Feedback Model from Arab Music." *The World of Music* 33(3): 7–28.
Rice, Timothy. 1994. *May It Fill Your Soul: Experiencing Bulgarian Music*. Chicago: University of Chicago Press.
Rifʿat, Muḥammad, ed. n.d. *Mudhakkarāt Muḥammad ʿAbd al-Wahhāb*. Beirut: Dār al-Thaqāfah.
Rizq, Qisṭandī. ca. 1936. *Al-Mūsīqá al-Sharqiyyah wa-al-Ghināʾ al-ʿArabī*, Vol. 1. Cairo: al-Maṭbaʿah al-ʿAṣriyyah.
——. ca. 1938. *Al-Mūsīqá al-Sharqiyyah wa-al-Ghināʾ al-ʿArabī*, Vol. 2. Cairo: al-Maṭbaʿah al-ʿAṣriyyah.
Rosaldo, Renato I. 1984. "Grief and a Headhunter's Rage: On the Cultural Force of Emotions." In *Text, Play, and Story: The Construction and Reconstruction of Self and Society*, ed. by Edward M. Bruner, 178–195. Washington DC: The American Ethnological Society.
Rouget, Gilbert. 1985. *Music and Trance: A Theory of the Relations between Music and Possession*. Chicago: University of Chicago Press.
al-Ṣabbāgh, Tawfīq. 1950. *al-Dalīl al-Mūsīqī al-ʿĀmm: Fī Aṭrab al-Anghām*. Aleppo, Syria: Maṭbaʿat al-Iḥsān.
Saḥḥāb, Ilyās. 1980. *Difāʿan ʿan al-Ughniyah al-ʿArabiyyah*. Beirut: al-Muʾassasah al-ʿArabiyyah li-al-Dirāsāt wa-al-Nashr.
Saḥḥāb, Victor. 1987. *al-Sabʿah al-Kibār: Fī al-Mūsīqá al-ʿArabiyyah al-Muʿāṣirah*. Beirut: Dār al-ʿIlm li-al-Malāyīn.
Said, Edward. 1978. *Orientalism*. New York: Pantheon.
al-Saʿīd, Labīb. 1970a. *al-Adhān wa-al-Muʾadhdhinūn: Baḥth Fiqhī, Tārīkhī, Ijtimāʿī*. Cairo: al-Hayʾah al-Miṣriyyah al-ʿĀmmah li-al-Taʾlīf wa-al-Nashr.
——. 1970b. *al-Taghannī bi-al-Qurʾān: Baḥth Fiqhī, Tārīkhī*. Cairo: al-Hayʾah al-Miṣriyyah al-ʿĀmmah li-al-Taʾlīf wa-al-Nashr.
Salvador-Daniel, Francesco. 1976 (1915). *The Music and Musical Instruments of the Arab*, ed. by Henry George Farmer. Portland, Maine: Longwood Press.
Sawa, George. 1981. "The Survival of Some Aspects of Medieval Arabic Per-

formance Practice." *Ethnomusicology* 25(1): 73–86.
——. 1989. *Music Performance Practice in the Early ʿAbbasid Era, 132–320 AH/750–932 AD*. Toronto: Pontifical Institute of Medieval Studies.
Schechner, Richard. 1976. "From Ritual to Theatre and Back." In *Ritual, Play, and Performance: Readings in the Social Sciences/Theatre*, ed. by Richard Schechner and Mady Schuman, 196–222. New York: Seabury Press.
Schimmel, Annemarie. 1975. *Mystical Dimensions of Islam*. Chapel Hill, NC: University of North Carolina Press.
Schutz, Alfred. 1977. "Making Music Together: A Study in Social Relationship." In *Symbolic Anthropology: A Reader in the Study of Symbols and Meanings*, ed. by Janet L. Dolgin, et al. 106–119. New York: Columbia University Press.
Schuyler, Philip D. 1979. "Music Education in Morocco: Three Models." *The World of Music* 21(3): 19–31.
Scruton, Roger. 1974. *Art and Imagination: A Study in the Philosophy of Mind*. London: Methuen & Co. Ltd.
Seashore, Carl E. 1938/1967. *Psychology of Music*. New York: Dover Publications, Inc.
Seeger, Charles. 1961. "Semantic, Logical, and Political Considerations Bearing upon Research in Ethnomusicology." *Ethnomusicology* 5(2): 77–80.
Shafīq, Ibrāhīm. n.d. *Turāthunā al-Mūsīqī: Min al-Adwār wa-al-Muwashshaḥāt* 1. Cairo: al-Lajnah al-Mūsīqiyyah al-ʿUlyā.
——. 1963. *Turāthunā al-Mūsīqī: Min al-Adwār wa-al-Muwashshaḥāt* 3. Cairo: al-Lajnah al-Mūsīqiyyah al-ʿUlyā.
Shafīq, Ibrāhīm and Maḥmūd Kāmil. n.d. *Muḥammad ʿUthmān: al-Muṭrib, al-Mulaḥḥin*. Cairo: M.M. al-Amīn li-al-Tabʿ wa-al-Nashr.
al-Sharīf, Ṣamīm. 1988. *Al-Sunbāṭī wa Jīl al-ʿAmāliqah*. Damascus: Ṭalās li al-Dirāsāt wa-al-Tarjamah wa-al-Nashr.
Sharma, Arvind. 1978. "Ecstasy." In *The Encyclopedia of Religion*, Vol. 5. ed. by Mircea Eliade, 11–17. New York: Macmillan.
al-Shidyāq, Aḥmad Fāris. 1966. *al-Sāq ʿalá al-Sāq: Fī mā huwa al-Faryāq*. Beirut: Dār Maktabat al-Ḥayāt.
Shihāb al-Dīn, Muḥammad. ca. 1840/ca. 1892. *Safīnat al-Mulk wa Nafīsat al-Fulk*. Cairo: Maṭbaʿat al-Jāmiʿah.
Shiloah, Amnon. 1979. *The Theory of Music in Arabic Writings (ca. 900–1900): Descriptive Catalogue of Manuscripts in Libraries of Europe and the U.S.A.* München, Germany: G. Henle Verlag.
——. 1995. *Music in the World of Islam: A Socio-Cultural Study*. Detroit: Wayne State University Press.
Shūshah, Muḥammad al-Sayyid, n.d. *Ruwwād wa Rāʾidāt al-Sīnamā al-Miṣriyyah*. Cairo: Maṭābiʿ Muʾassasat Rūz al-Yūsuf.
Storr, Anthony. 1992. *Music and the Mind*. New York: Ballantine Books.
Sugarman, Jane C. 1997. *Engendering Song: Singing & Subjectivity at Prespa Albanian Weddings*. Chicago: University of Chicago Press.
Ṭaha, Saḥar. 1995. "Muḥammad Qaṣṣāṣ: al-Taghrīb Tashwīh li-al-Turāth wa-al-Mūsīqá li-al-Simāʿ la li-al-Baṣar." *al-Ḥayāt* (11897): 20.
Tame, David. 1984. *The Secret Power of Music*. Rochester, VT: Destiny Books.
Tart, Charles. 1969. "Introduction." In *Altered States of Consciousness*, ed. by Charles Tart, 1–6. Garden City, NY: Doubleday & Company Inc.
al-Ṭawīl, Muḥammad. n.d. *Mūsīqār min Sunbāṭ*. Cairo: Dār al-Maʿārif.

Touma, Habib Hassan. 1976. "Relations Between Aesthetics and Improvisation in Arab Music." *The World of Music* 18(2): 33–36.
——. 1996. *The Music of the Arabs*. Portland, Oregon: Amadeu Press.
Turner, Victor. 1969. *The Ritual Process: Structure and Anti-Structure*. Ithaca, NY: Cornell University Press.
——. 1977. "Variations on a Theme of Liminality." In *Secular Ritual*, ed. by Sally F. Moore and Barbara G. Myerhoff, 36–52. Amsterdam: Van Gorcum, and Co.
——. 1985. "Symbols in African Ritual." In *Magic, Witchcraft, and Religion: An Anthropological Study of the Supernatural*, ed. by Arthur C. Lehmann and James E. Myers, 55–63. Mountain View, CA: Mayfield Publishing Company.
Underhill, Evelyn. 1955/1974. *Mysticism: A Study in the Nature and Development of Man's Spiritual Consciousness*. New York: New America Library.
Van Gennep, Arnold. 1960. *The Rites of Passage*. Chicago: University of Chicago Press.
Varzi, Morteza. 1986/1988. Performer–Audience Relationships in the *Bazm*. In *Cultural Parameters of Iranian Musical Expression*, eds. Margaret Caton and Neil Siegel, 1–9 Redondo Beach, California: The Institute of Persian Performing Arts.
Villoteau, M. 1826. *Description de l'Égypt: De l'État Actuel de l'Art Musicale en Égypt,* Vol. 14, 2nd edition. Paris: Imprimerie de C.L.F. Panckoucke.
Vive L'Amour. n.d. New York: Egyptian Film Company.
Von Hammer, Joseph, ed. 1846/1968. *Narratives of Travels in Europe, Asia, and Africa in the Seventeenth Century, by Evliyá Efendí* Vol. 1. New York: Johnson Reprints.
Wāṣif, Mīlād. 1956. *Qiṣṣat al-Mawwāl: Dirāsah Tārikhiyyah, Adabiyyah, Ijtimāʿiyyah*. Cairo: al-Muʾassasah al-Miṣriyyah al-ʿĀmmah.
Waugh, Earle H. 1989. *The Munshidin of Egypt: Their World and their Song*. Columbia, SC: University of South Carolina Press.
Webster's Third New International Dictionary of the English Language, Vol. 3. 1966. Chicago: Encyclopaedia Britannica, Inc.
Winkelman, Michael. 1986. "Trance States: A Theoretical Model and Cross-Cultural Analysis." *Ethos* 14(2): 174–203.
al-Zabīdī, Muḥammad Murtaḍá. AH 1306. *Tāj al-ʿArūs: Min Jawāhir al-Qāmūs*, Vol. 1. Cairo: al-Maṭbaʿah al-Khayriyyah.
Zakī, Muḥammad. 1986. *Al-Mukhaddirāt wa-al-Mujtamaʿ: Dirāsah Maydāniyyah* . . . ʿAyn Shams, Egypt: Jāmiʿat ʿAyn Shams.

Index

Other books in the series

1 Parvin Paidar
Women and the Political Process in Twentieth-Century Iran
0 521 47340 3 hardback
0 521 59572 X paperback

2 Israel Gershoni and James Jankowski
Redefining the Egyptian Nation, 1930–1945
0 521 47535 X

3 Annelies Moors
Women, Property and Islam: Palestinian Experiences, 1920–1990
0 521 47497 3 hardback
0 521 48355 7 paperback

4 Paul Kingston
Britain and the Politics of Modernization in the Middle East, 1945–1958
0 521 56346 1

5 Daniel Brown
Rethinking Tradition in Modern Islamic Thought
0 521 57077 8 hardback
0 521 65394 0 paperback

6 Nathan J. Brown
The Rule of Law in the Arab World: Courts in Egypt and the Gulf
0 521 59026 4

7 Richard Tapper
Frontier Nomads of Iran: The Political and Social History of the Shahsevan
0 521 583365

8 Khaled Fahmy
All the Pasha's Men: Mehmed Ali, His Army and the Making of Modern Egypt
0 521 56007 1

9 Sheila Carapico
Civil Society in Yemen: The Political Economy of Activism in Modern Arabia
0 521 59098 1

10 Meir Litvak
Shi'aini Scholars in Nineteenth-Century Iraq: The Ulama *of Najaf and Karbala*
0 521 62356 1

11 Jacob Metzer
The Divided Economy of Mandatory Palestine
0 521 46550 8

12 Eugene L. Rogan
Frontiers of the State in the Late Ottoman Empire: Transjordan, 1850–1921
0 521 66312 1

13 Eliz Sanasarian
Religious Minorities in Iran
0 521 77073 4

14 Nadje Al-Ali
Secularism, Gender and the State in the Middle East: The Egyptian Women's Movement
0 521 78022 5 hardback
0 521 78504 9 paperback

15 Eugene L. Rogan and Avi Shlaim (eds)
Rewriting the Palestine War
1948 and the History of the Arab-Israeli Conflict
0 521 79139 1 hardback
0 521 79476 5 paperback

16 Gershon Shafir and Yoav Peled
Being Israeli
The Dynamics of Multiple Citizenship
0 521 79224 X hardback
0 521 79672 5 paperback

CPSIA information can be obtained
at www.ICGtesting.com
Printed in the USA
LVHW101608140123
737185LV00001B/62

9 780521 316859